The
Imprinted
Brain

of related interest

Can the World Afford Autistic Spectrum Disorder?
Nonverbal Communication, Asperger Syndrome and the Interbrain
Digby Tantam
ISBN 978 1 84310 694 4

The Complete Guide to Asperger's Syndrome
Tony Attwood
ISBN 978 1 84310 669 2 paperback
ISBN 978 1 84310 495 7 hardback

Dietary Interventions in Autism Spectrum Disorders
Why They Work When They Do, Why They Don't When They Don't
Kenneth J. Aitken
ISBN 978 1 84310 939 6

The Imprinted Brain

HOW GENES SET
THE BALANCE
BETWEEN AUTISM
AND PSYCHOSIS

Christopher Badcock

Jessica Kingsley Publishers
London and Philadelphia

First published in 2009
by Jessica Kingsley Publishers
116 Pentonville Road
London N1 9JB, UK
and
400 Market Street, Suite 400
Philadelphia, PA 19106, USA

www.jkp.com

Library of Congress Cataloging in Publication Data
A CIP catalog record for this book is available from the Library of Congress

British Library Cataloguing in Publication Data
A CIP catalogue record for this book is available from the British Library

ISBN 978 1 84905 023 4

Printed and bound in the United States by
Thomson-Shore, 7300 Joy Road, Dexter, MI 48130

Contents

Preface

The history of science is not always what it ought to be. By rights, Galileo should have had Foucault's pendulum to prove that the Earth turns, and Darwin—not Mendel—should have discovered genetics. Instead of introducing an arbitrary term to avoid it, Einstein should have boldly predicted the expanding universe, and so on. No one knows what the future will say of our times, but if history were the way it should be rather than the way it is, some may look back and think that the late Bill Hamilton—had he lived—should have been the author of this book. As I explain in the main text, Hamilton was the originator of the so-called *selfish gene* view of modern Darwinism which Richard Dawkins famously popularized in the book of that title. The critical findings described here only emerged after Hamilton's untimely death in 2000, and no one knows how differently things would have worked out had he lived. At the very least, Hamilton's own acknowledged autistic tendencies (see pp. 34–35) and his ground-breaking insights into genetic and mental conflict would surely have made the theory outlined here of enormous interest to him, and—who knows?—he might even have been the first to formulate it, so naturally does it follow from the lead he gave. But history, alas, is not always as it should be, and men of genius such as Hamilton do not always live to reap the harvest that should have been theirs. Nevertheless, he was the one who laid the foundations on which his heirs have built and remains the person to whom I owe a fundamental debt of gratitude in writing this book.

However, the greatest debt of gratitude I owe is to my colleague and co-author, Bernard Crespi, Killam Research Fellow in the Department of Biosciences at Simon Fraser University in Vancouver. At a time when I was temporarily incapacitated, he took up the idea that imprinting might underlie autism and paranoia and both generalized it to include psychosis in general and did much to secure its factual foundations. Without his help, I would have proceeded much more slowly and uncertainly, and probably missed many important insights altogether—particularly where genetics and brain science are concerned. I am particularly indebted to him for parts of Chapters 5 and 6, and for the originals on which the diagrams in Chapters 6 and 7 are based. Where original research has been done by Professor Crespi, I cite his or our joint publications which provide the detailed references; where I cite the original sources myself, the work was done by me independently or in parallel with him.

Additionally I must thank Ahmad Abu-Akel, Ken Aitken, Chris Ashwin, Abdallah Badahdah, Simon Baron-Cohen, Kingsley Browne, Benedict Carey, Martin Conway, Charles Crawford, Diana Fleischman, Temple Grandin, Francesca Happé, Ayla and Nick Humphrey, Satoshi Kanazawa, Ben Kaplan, Nicola Knight, Patrick McNamara, Alex and Marian Monto, Charlotte Moore, Randolph Nesse, Daniel Povinelli, Bill Shropshire, John Skoyles, Sarita Soni, Thomas Suddendorf, Teresa Tavassoli, Paul and Gilles Tréhin, Alfonso Troisi, Gus Uht, Tony Vladusich, and Andy Wells. I must also thank Lily Morgan of Jessica Kingsley Publishers and an anonymous reviewer for their kind assistance and sound advice on the manuscript.

Introduction

What causes conditions such as autism and schizophrenia? We have long known that they run in families and therefore must have a genetic dimension, but until now no one has ever been able to specify exactly what it is or discover the critical genes. The same is true of the known environmental, non-genetic factors: it has not been possible to bring them together under one theory, and certainly not to relate them to any genetic mechanism. Indeed, where autism is concerned, leading authorities have recently gone on record to declare that the time has come to give up the search for a single explanation.[1]

This book sets out a new approach to mental development and disorder based on recently discovered genetic effects involving not just the inheritance of genes, but their expression. The imprinted brain theory is unique in relating these novel aspects of gene expression to brain development, symptoms, behaviour, and physical side-effects in a way that reveals a new view of the mind, both normal and disturbed. The genetic mechanism in question (so-called imprinting) links together previously unconnected syndromes and suggests that many—and perhaps most—of the symptoms of mental illness can be understood in terms of it. An added bonus is that the theory may be able to explain not only the genetics of mental illness but also some environmental causes of disorders like autism and schizophrenia, such as poisons, poverty, or pathogens. Furthermore, the fact that diet is now known to affect gene expression means that the theory might even ultimately be able to cast light on the controversial dietary dimension to autism.[2]

The fundamental genetic insight from which the theory derives is the recent discovery that genes from the mother and from the father are in conflict over the size of their child. Those from the mother favour restraint in growth because she has to gestate and give birth to the baby. But the father's genes demand more of her resources, which are from his point of view the biological equivalent of a free lunch for his offspring. The result has been graphically portrayed as a tug-of-war, and the new theory suggests that a win for the father can sometimes produce children with autistic tendencies, whereas a win for the mother can occasionally result in children being born with an enhanced vulnerability to psychotic disorders in later life. A balanced, no-win situation results in normal development, and is by far the most likely outcome. However, early environmental insults, such as starvation of the mother during pregnancy, can produce essentially the same result because they can both affect gene expression and mimic these genetic effects. Starvation during pregnancy has been shown to alter the expression of key growth-determining genes and could also be seen as mimicking the resource-reducing effect of maternal genes, perhaps explaining why it significantly increases the likelihood of psychotic illness in the children born in such circumstances. Increased birth-weight, on the other hand, might also explain part of the apparent epidemic of milder forms of autism in modern societies, where standards of living have reached unprecedented levels.

However, these novel genetic effects and the environmental factors that sometimes work with them are only part of the story. Where understanding the mind and mental development is concerned, recent research into autism has been revolutionary, and forms the second leg on which the new theory stands. The reason that autism has begun to reveal so much about the mind and mental development is that autistics have been shown to lack—or at least often to be significantly deficient in—certain key cognitive skills which make up normal mental functioning. Whenever such deficits are discovered in science, dramatic advances often result because the deficit-condition indicates the critical factors for normal development. Visual agnosia and optic ataxia provide telling examples.

Visual agnosia describes a bizarre affliction in which, following brain damage, a person can competently grasp and manipulate objects, but cannot name or recognize them until they can feel them by hand. So, if confronted with a yellow fruit, a person with visual agnosia may remark that the object is definitely yellow, but be unable to say if it is a lemon or a banana until they pick it up and feel its shape. However, optic ataxia describes a parallel disorder in which a person can correctly recognize and name seen objects, but cannot grasp or manipulate them competently, despite having nothing whatsoever wrong with their hands or motor co-ordination independent of sight. These syndromes, along with a great deal of other evidence, reveal that human beings have two distinct but complementary visual systems, each with its own pathway in the brain. Normally we are never aware of them because they work together seamlessly, but in these two rare disorders the failure of one reveals the existence of the other in a way that would otherwise be difficult to discern.[3]

In a similar kind of way, autistic deficits in key cognitive skills have revealed the basis of normal development and given us a unique and unexpected insight into the mind. Specific cognitive skills often missing or deficient in autism reveal how the normal mind works and explain both the social and cognitive difficulties of autistics. Thanks to these insights, the new theory proposes that the spectrum of autistic disorders is mirrored by a psychotic one, and that where autistics show deficits in mental development, psychotics show pathological overgrowth: cancers of the mind, so to speak. And just like visual agnosia and optic ataxia, the contrasting deficits of autism and psychosis reveal two parallel cognitive systems that normally blend more or less perfectly, but expose their fundamental differences when one or the other disorder supervenes.

I hope that this book will appeal to a wide readership, though there is one type of reader in particular to whom I know this book will appeal, and that is to all those with an interest in or concern with autism. My story begins with the discovery and naming of autism, and insights from research into autism spectrum disorders provided the key ideas which inspire the theory I shall be setting out. As readers will then I hope see for themselves, autism is the key which unlocks the secrets of the mind!

New theories usually need new terminology, and so in the first two chapters I introduce the twin basic concepts I use in relation to the mind and cognition, and explain why they are preferable to alternatives. The next two chapters are devoted to psychosis, and primarily to the extraordinary Schreber case: the most discussed in the entire psychiatric literature. Why yet another discussion? First, because Schreber's own account illustrates so many important features of paranoid schizophrenia at first hand, and without any intervening interpretation. But more importantly as far as this book is concerned, his symptoms stand in striking contrast to those of autism, and take on a new meaning once they are seen in this context. No one has ever looked at Schreber—or at any other psychotic—in exactly this way before. And although, as I point out, there have been a few who have groped towards the solution I offer here, no one has ever before propounded the simple insight that psychoses such as this are the mirror-image of autism. However, some images in mirrors have to be seen to be believed—particularly where they reverse mentality rather than left and right—and this is why I devote two entire chapters to portraying this one. Without illustration, the basic idea might seem far-fetched, but begins to look very different if examined in the light of what psychotics such as Schreber actually report.

Nevertheless, the striking antithetical symmetry of autism and psychosis would remain just an appearance unless some plausible mechanism could be found to explain it. Chapters 5 and 6 are devoted to revealing what this mechanism is and to showing how imprinted genes routinely produce syndromes with such reversed symptoms. Chapter 5 concentrates on imprinting as the first genetic factor explaining mental disorders such as autism and psychosis, and Chapter 6 adds sex as a second. Readers will find that Schreber makes yet another appearance here, and that the new theory casts an intriguing new light not only on paranoia, but on homosexuality as well.

In my concluding chapter I discuss the implications of the new theory for helping us to understand genius and the madness that is often associated with it. I also consider some literary and cultural insights to which the new ideas give rise, and raise a previously unsuspected possibility thrown up by the view of mental development proposed here. This is that there could be so-called savantism on the psychotic side of the spectrum just as there is on the autistic one, and conclude by considering psychoanalysis as a telling case in point. As I suggest in my final remarks, the imprinted brain theory could offer a new conceptual foundation for modern psychiatry and psychotherapy comparable to that which psychoanalysis promised but failed to deliver.

At the time of writing, the genes implicated in autism and psychosis remained largely unknown. However, the theory set out here makes clear predictions about what kind of genes they should be, how those genes should be expressed, and what kind of effects they should be found to have on development, the brain, and behaviour. Scientific theories ought to be testable, and a precise prediction which is later confirmed is always more persuasive than a retrospective re-interpretation, so this in itself is a good reason for writing this book. As readers will see, it clearly sets out what future researchers should find and as such provides a map to a new conceptual continent, with empirical landmarks and factual features clearly indicated. Nevertheless, and as I shall point out later, there is already much tantalizing evidence confirming the theory, some of it from physical side-effects of the critical genes. Indeed, the strongest single link between genetics and a mental disorder known at the time of writing seems made to order for the imprinted brain theory (that between duplication of maternal chromosome 15 and psychosis explained on pp. 164–165). And as I hope to show, the new way of looking at things makes striking new sense of a lot of what is currently known about the mind and mental illness.

New theories, however well founded on fact or otherwise, inevitably reflect on existing knowledge and ideas, and, even if flawed in themselves, can sometimes cast important new light on longer established ones. Here again the imprinted brain theory has much to offer, and certainly reflects on some well-worn controversies. An example might be nature/nurture, where it suggests that nurture is only an effective factor in psychiatric illnesses such as schizophrenia and autism where it mimics natural, genetic effects: nurture via nature, you might say, by contrast to the conventional wisdom of nature via nurture.

But when all is said and done, and whatever the final outcome, one thing is clear. Nature, not conventional wisdom, will have the last word! Given the rapid progress now being made in neuroscience and genetics, we should not have to wait long for her verdict.

Chapter 1

Autism and Its Compensations

Once, autism was thought to be a condition with few if any positive aspects, but today a more balanced view has emerged. In this chapter I aim to show that autism is not simply a combination of deficits as was once supposed, but is associated with some remarkable sensory and cognitive compensations. As we shall see, research into autism suggests that human beings have evolved two parallel ways of thinking. One, which you might call *people-thinking, mentalistic cognition*—or more simply *mentalism*—is wholly concerned with understanding human beings, their minds, motives, and emotions; the other, which by contrast you could call *things-thinking* or *mechanistic cognition* is concerned with understanding and interacting with the physical, non-human universe of inert objects. It is to the latter that we owe our technological, scientific, and material mastery of the world, and we shall see that although autistics symptomatically have deficits in mentalistic people-thinking, they are often superior where basic sensory sensitivity is concerned, and can sometimes show extraordinary abilities in mechanistic things-thinking. Furthermore, this way of looking at autism suggests that the exact opposite cognitive configuration—superior mentalistic skills with deficits in basic senses and in mechanistic cognition—could also exist. Later I shall argue that it indeed does in psychotic disorders such as schizophrenia and that what passes for normality is nothing but a more or less stable balance of both tendencies. The fundamental insight is that autism is part of a much bigger picture which includes both psychosis and sanity, and lies at the heart of human genius, as I shall argue in my conclusion.

But this is to anticipate. First, let me set the scene with a brief historical summary of what we have come to know about autism.

Autism, schizophrenia, and Asperger's syndrome

The word *autism* was originally coined by one of the founding fathers of modern psychiatry, Eugen Bleuler (1857–1939), to describe a style of thinking found in schizophrenia (itself another Bleuler coinage).[1] He derived it from the Greek αυτοσ (autos) meaning "self," and defined it as "detachment from reality, together with the relative and absolute predominance of the inner life."[2] In 1936 the paediatrician, Hans Asperger (1906–1980), gave a lecture at the Vienna University Hospital in which he described the characteristics of "autistic psychopaths," and in 1938 and 1944 published details of more such cases.[3,4] Meanwhile, in 1943 the psychiatrist, Leo Kanner (1896–1981), also published an account of 11 children at Johns Hopkins University Hospital in Baltimore who were suffering from what he called "early infantile autism." He concluded that "Profound aloneness dominates all behaviour" in the autistic child, adding that "We must, then, assume that these children have come into the world with innate inability to form the usual, biologically provided affective contact with people, just as other children come into the world with innate physical or intellectual handicaps."[5a]

It is not known whether Asperger's discovery influenced Kanner or even if he knew of its existence. In any event, Asperger remained largely unknown to the English-speaking world until the 1980s[6] and his name was not so much as mentioned in one of the most well-informed and wide-ranging reviews of the autism literature published in the 1960s.[7] Recently an account of six cases diagnosed in 1926 as various types of "schizoid personality disorder" has been translated from the original German. Some of these subjects were also described as "autistic" by its author and bear striking similarities to the type of high-functioning autism now associated with Asperger.[8,9] However, even earlier accounts certainly exist.[7a,10] Indeed, there is evidence of a five-year-old autistic boy having been admitted to Bedlam in 1799. The case was described in a textbook of 1809 by John Haslam, the Apothecary of Bethlehem Hospital, and this may well be the earliest description of autism in the psychiatric literature.[11] Nevertheless, authors such as Jane Austen (1775–1817) and Sir Arthur Conan Doyle (1859–1930) appear to have had an implicit awareness of features of autism and to have been able to portray autistic characters in their fictional works quite independently of science and psychiatry[12] (for more on Conan Doyle, see pp. 196–198).

Today autism and schizophrenia are thought to be separate disorders, and Bleuler himself later substituted *dereistic* for *autistic* as a description of schizophrenic thought that was less likely to be misunderstood.[13] However, a major theme of this book will be to argue that there is indeed an important link between them. Later I shall suggest that autism and psychoses such as schizophrenia could be seen as extremes on a single line of development—with normality balanced precariously in between. Just as both over-sensitivity and under-sensitivity to light or sound will cause visual or hearing short-comings, so we shall see that both over- and under-sensitivity to your own and other people's minds can cause the contrasting mental deficits seen in autism and psychosis. If this is so, you might wonder to what extent the early association of the two disorders in psychiatry was an anticipation of what is now beginning to look like a profound connection ultimately explicable in terms of genetic findings that are only now coming to light.

Autism is a disorder that usually first becomes apparent in childhood, mainly as a result of failure to develop normally. A consensus panel of the American Academy of Neurology recommends that a child with any of the following symptoms should be evaluated for possible autism: no babbling, gesturing, pointing, or waving good-bye by 12 months; no single words by 16 months; no two words spoken together spontaneously by 24 months; and any loss of language or social skills at any time.[14] As the last item suggests, children can develop normally

Typical symptoms and signs of autism

- deficits in non-verbal communication such as eye-contact, facial expression, and body language

- self-absorption, egocentricity, and lack of awareness of and insensitivity to others, with difficulty in establishing relationships, friendships, or peer-relations

- delay, or total lack of language competence, with communication deficits or peculiarities in speech, gesture, and conversation

- repetitive and/or stereotyped movements (such as hand-flapping), with distress over change and insistence on routine, or a compulsion to carry out rituals

- fragmented sensory perception with inability to generalize, and pre-occupation with parts rather than wholes

- abnormal pre-occupation with or intensity of interest in one subject or activity, perhaps with isolated areas of expertise and/or exceptional rote memory alongside more general cognitive impairment

Additional features often found associated with autism

- mental retardation (found in about 75% of cases)

- unusual beauty, often looking younger than they are, with a characteristic "autistic look" described by Kanner as "beatific serenity"

- odd or unusual gait

- difficulties with hand-writing

- insensitivity to pain, often combined with indifference to cold (and sometimes lack of fear of heights and an amazing ability to survive falls)

- synaesthesia (mixing of perceptual categories) with confusion between different senses
- problems with depth-perception, "white-out" effects and other visual deficits, particularly in relation to moving objects, strange places, or novel situations
- unusual sensitivity to smell, sound, or other sensory perceptions, sometimes with sensations of "sensory overload"
- allergic or phobic reactions to specific foods, smells, or sensory perceptions, with resulting fastidious food preferences and avoidances
- bowel disorders
- sleep disorders
- epilepsy (25–35% of cases)
- intolerance of itchy and/or tight clothing
- chronic anxiety, often with excessive startle and fear reactions
- fear of crowds and strangers, and dislike of socializing
- panic reactions at being touched or hugged by people
- a liking for being wedged in small, enclosing spaces, or tightly squeezed into corners
- a fascination for spinning objects
- enthralment with machines, mechanisms, and gadgets of all kinds

up to a certain point, and then regress; while others can appear to have early delays in these respects that are later fully compensated and leave no lasting deficits.[15] Typical symptoms and signs of autism are set out in the box above along with a number of other features often mentioned in connection with autism although not found in all cases (for a more exhaustive discussion see [16].)

An important aspect of diagnosis in autism is the extreme variability of the symptoms. Autistic children within the same family can have strikingly different autistic traits,[17] and authorities point out that "None of the criteria exactly describes every individual with autism. Autism presents in a myriad of ways; every individual with autism is different and unique, and has features that would lead a person superficially examining them to say that this person can't have autism."[18a]

Another factor that has bedevilled diagnosis is confusion of autism with schizophrenia and other mental disorders, despite the fact that almost from the beginning some writers could see that they were antithetically different in many respects.[7] What we would now call autism was often given labels such as "schizoid personality disorder" or even "childhood schizophrenia" in the past, and more recently there was also a tendency to diagnose children as autistic but to substitute "schizophrenic," "psychotic," "borderline," or some similar diagnosis for the same symptoms when they grew up. Indeed, I shall argue in a later chapter that even today it is easy to confuse autism with psychotic disorders, and that although the symptoms might seem very similar, closer examination shows them to have completely different causes. Nevertheless, mis-diagnosis—principally of autistics as suffering from various forms of psychotic illness but also psychotics mis-diagnosed as autistics—has been a major factor in confusing autism with psychosis. This has certainly been true in forensic psychiatry where, despite the high numbers of autistics in secure prison hospitals,[18b] autism has tended to be regarded as a much less convincing plea of mitigation in the courts than has schizophrenia. A case in point is that of Theodore J. Kaczynski, otherwise known as the Unabomber, who has recently been diagnosed as a high-functioning autistic, but who was prevailed upon to plead insane on account of schizophrenia at his trial by his lawyers. Kaczynski's autism and associated social isolation resulted in a highly atypical career of lone terrorism which occasioned the longest and most expensive manhunt in the twentieth century, and was only brought to an end when he attempted to communicate his ideas by publishing *The Unabomber Manifesto*.[19] The result is that a classic case of autism has gone down in legal history as one of schizophrenia, and there is no way of telling how many other similar cases there may be.

Despite the fact that Kanner specifically remarked in his original report that "Even though most of these children were at one time or another looked upon as feebleminded, they are all unquestionably endowed with good *cognitive potentialities*,"[5b] Kanner's name has become associated with a more severe degree of disability. One reason may be that 8 out of 23 cases of autism reported by him in 1946 featured *mutism*: in other words, serious language deficits amounting to an inability to speak.[20] By way of contrast, Asperger's original cases were described as having well-developed speech and even "talking like grown-ups" in early childhood. What is now known as *Asperger's syndrome* shares many of the same central deficits and the restricted, repetitive patterns of behaviour, interest, and activity seen in classical autism, but is distinguished by the absence of delays or deficits in language and of obvious signs of cognitive impairment in childhood. Today about half of all children diagnosed with Asperger's syndrome have relatively advanced verbal skills and are sometimes described as *verbalizers*.[21a] Indeed, a leading clinician comments that from his experience he considers that children and adults with Asperger's syndrome just have a different, and not necessarily defective, way of thinking.[22] Alternatively, Asperger's syndrome is sometimes described as *high-functioning autism*[23]—and this was the actual autistic diagnosis of the Unabomber, mentioned just now.

Estimates of the relative proportion of high- to low-functioning autism vary, but a recent study in the UK concluded that 55 per cent of people with an autistic disorder are low-functioning, and 45 per cent are high-functioning.[24] However, in early childhood the distinction is not always clear-cut. According to the same clinician I have just cited:

At one point in a child's early development, autism is the correct diagnosis, but a distinct subgroup of children with autism can show a remarkable improvement in language, play and motivation to socialize with their peers between the ages of four and six years. The developmental trajectory of such children has changed and their profile of abilities in the primary or elementary school years is consistent with the characteristics of Asperger's syndrome.[21b]

For reasons such as this, there is now a tendency to think of classical, Kanner autism and Asperger's syndrome as the principal examples of *autism spectrum disorder*, or ASD for short (others include Rett syndrome, disintegrative disorder, and pervasive developmental disorder not otherwise specified).*

In the very first case of autism he described, Kanner recounts how the child in question was asked to subtract 4 from 10, and replied: "I'll draw a hexagon!"[5c] Of course, this is the wrong answer, but a hexagon is a six-sided figure, and even being able to make this connection so quickly and spontaneously hints at an unconventional geometric rather than arithmetic way of thinking that might be seen in some ways as more intelligent—and certainly more creative in certain respects—than the "correct" answer. Nor was this an isolated or untypical finding. As early as 1960, American writers on autism were pointing out that the autistic child is "not mentally retarded in the ordinary sense of the word, but rather is a child with an inadequate form of mentation which manifests itself in the inability to handle symbolic forms and assume an abstract attitude."[25] Today some leading authorities are arguing that the perceived association between autism and mental retardation is not based on the fact that they usually have common causes but is more likely to be because the presence of both greatly increases the probability of a clinical diagnosis.[26] Indeed, according to the latest research, intelligence in autistics has generally been under-estimated, and they are not as impaired in fluid intelligence as many theories predict. On the contrary, autistic intelligence is revealed by the most complex single test of general intelligence in the literature: Raven's

---

* For a fictitious, but remarkable insight into the world of a child with Asperger's syndrome see Mark Haddon's novel, *The Curious Incident of the Dog in the Night-time*. However, perhaps the most striking of all depictions of high-functioning autism in literature is found in Albert Camus' classic novel, *L'Étranger*, published in 1942.

Progressive Matrices.[27] Such findings have been interpreted to suggest that Asperger's syndrome in fact involves superior abstract reasoning ability or higher general fluid intelligence.[28]

For reasons which will be discussed in the next chapter, autistic people tend to perform poorly on subtests of intelligence that demand a high degree of communicative competence and/or social intelligence. An example would be comprehension tests, which require an ability to interpret the often implicit meanings, intentions, and understandings conveyed in a passage of writing. However, even where comprehension is concerned, there is a notable exception. A recent study compared autistics with normal subjects on tests of comprehension that involved sentences which demanded both verbal and visualization skills such as *The number eight when rotated 90 degrees looks like a pair of eye-glasses.* As the researchers point out, in sentences such as this the linguistic content must be processed to determine what is to be imagined, and then the mental image must be evaluated and related to the verbal meaning. Normal subjects only used mental visualization when necessary, but autistics were found to use it even when it was not, and the researchers comment that they were probably "thinking in pictures" much of the time. Indeed, the study suggested that as a result autistics might be better at visualizing linguistic information than normal people are.[29]

Autistics are also superior to normal when it comes to copying impossible figures,[30] and the same is true of more straightforward visualizing ability. High-functioning autistics often have a remarkable eye for detail, and notice things that might escape the attention of others. That such impressions are not without an objective basis was recently demonstrated when the vision of a group of people with ASD was compared with that of non-autistic controls. Astonishingly, all 15 of the ASD subjects tested had superior eyesight, which was 2.79 times better than average (giving a score of 20:7, meaning that they could see details from 20 feet that an average person could only see at 7 feet). As the researchers remark, this approximately two-to-three-fold superiority in vision is comparable to that of birds of prey, and their results suggest that increased visual acuity applies to individuals across the autistic spectrum, making this yet another respect in which autistics outperform the normal population.[31]

Indeed, there is now evidence that autistics may have heightened sensitivities in most senses. For example, despite sometimes giving the impression of being deaf, people with ASD often have superior hearing, as a number of studies have confirmed where discrimination of pitch is concerned.[32,33] A study which explored sensitivity to touch found that people with ASD had a lower threshold for tactile stimulations than normal controls.[34] Another which investigated both touch and hearing in 20 adults with and 20 without ASD matched for sex, age and IQ found that the autistic subjects were hyper-sensitive in both hearing and touch. The two sensitivities appeared to be correlated, suggesting a shared underlying factor (and perhaps explaining autistic symptoms such as intolerance for loud noises and itchy clothing, dislike of being touched, or difficulties with distinguishing individual voices in noisy environments).[35] Another experiment compared 17 ASD subjects with 17 normal controls in a standard test of sensitivity to smell. The autistic group proved able to detect the test odour at a mean distance of 24.1 cm compared to 14.4 cm in the case of the controls. The study also found a quantitative relationship between level of enhanced sensory processing and the number of autistic traits, with greater severity of autistic behaviour related to higher sensory perception. However, there was no correlation between sensory thresholds and age or level of cognitive functioning, suggesting that hyper-sensitivity to smell might be a core feature in ASD.[36] Some parents of autistic children credit them with extra-sensory perception, and these findings suggest that there may indeed be a major core of truth in the claim—at least in so far as those children's sensory sensitivities do in fact go beyond the normal range.[37]

As long ago as the mid-1960s, Rimland remarked that "Judging from his excellent ability to reproduce nursery rhymes and melodies, his memory for spatial relations and his motor performance and finger dexterity, the child with infantile autism has a clear and precise focus on the physical, if not the psychological, aspects of reality."[7b] Summarizing a wide range of studies, a recent review concludes that "The level of performance of persons with autism on tasks of spatial orientation, phonological discrimination, word perception, and simple geometrical patterns, is typically higher than their general level of development."[38] Indeed, if extraordinary facility with doing things such as jigsaw puzzles is included, the majority of people with autism would be classed as showing some specific talent.[39]

Again, the compulsive concentration on a single subject so typical of ASD need not always be counter-productive, as an autistic writer observes:

> While most clinicians with expertise in Asperger's syndrome would likely say that dwelling on certain subjects counts as negative, I must disagree. I have the trait of sticking to a project long enough to see it through to completion… Since I can think about subjects repeatedly for long periods of time without getting bored, my mind has greater access to deeper thinking about those subjects. I find that with repeated tenacious thoughts, things that were initially difficult to figure out do eventually get figured out.[40]

Savants and savantism

In his original paper on autism, Hans Asperger remarked that:

> To our own amazement, we have seen that autistic individuals, as long as they are intellectually intact, can almost always achieve professional success, usually in highly specialized academic professions, with a preference for abstract content. We found a large number of people whose mathematical ability determines their professions: mathematicians, technologists, industrial chemists, and high ranking civil servants… A good professional attitude involves single-mindedness as well as a decision to give up a large number of other interests… It seems that for success in science or art, a dash of autism is essential.

... Indeed we find numerous autistic individuals among distinguished scientists.[41]

Perhaps appropriately, Asperger himself has recently been put forward as an example of his own syndrome,[42] and autistic tendencies allied with outstanding skills and even genius have been detected in other famous scientists and mathematicians. Examples are Sir Isaac Newton (1643–1727); Albert Einstein (1879–1955); Paul Dirac (1902–84);[43] Alan Turing (1912–54);[44] and Charles Richter (1900–85), the seismologist who gave his name to the Richter Scale of earthquake intensity.[45] Another is Michael Ventris (1922–56), the cryptographer who deciphered the ancient Mycenaean script known as *Linear B*.[46] Others who have been retrospectively diagnosed as somewhere on the autistic spectrum include the poet, artist, sculptor, and architect Michelangelo Buonarroti (1475–1564); the philosopher Ludwig Wittgenstein (1889–1951); and the Indian mathematician, Srinivasa Ramanujan (1887–1920).[47,48] Writers and poets include Hans Christian Andersen (1805–75); Herman Melville (1819–91); Jonathan Swift (1667–1745); William Butler Yeats (1865–1939); and Lewis Carroll (Charles Dodgson, 1832–98), the author of *Alice in Wonderland*.[18] Politicians and statesmen too have been added to the list of those suspected of having been Asperger's cases: specifically Thomas Jefferson (1743–1826);[49] Eamon de Valera (1882–1975); and perhaps most interestingly of all, Adolf Hitler (1889–1945).[48]

Recently Michael Fitzgerald published a book about what he terms *Asperger's savants*: that is, "persons with high functioning autism or Asperger's syndrome who produce works of genius."[18c] Despite the fact that, as Fitzgerald himself notes, persons with Asperger's syndrome are often "anti-theory" and have problems with abstraction, he includes the philosophers Spinoza (1632–77), Immanuel Kant (1724–1804), and A. J. Ayer (1910–89). Less surprising perhaps is his inclusion of several famous musicians, such as Wolfgang Amadeus Mozart (1756–91); Ludwig van Beethoven (1770–1827); Eric Satie (1866–1925); and Béla Bartók (1881–1945); and along with Van Gogh, the painters L. S. Lowry (1887–1976) and Andy Warhol (1928–87).[18]

Understandably perhaps in the light of the on-going debate about the exact diagnosis of autism and Asperger's syndrome, not all of these suggestions have been accepted by everyone. In particular, Oliver Sacks has questioned whether Wittgenstein, Einstein, and Newton were "significantly autistic," contrasting their cases with that of the chemist, Henry Cavendish (1731–1810), who he believes certainly was. Sacks thinks that, unlike most other "supposed autistic geniuses," he showed "near-total incomprehension of common human behaviours, social relationships, states of mind, and money, as well as an almost obsessed attention to detail—which led him to the great generalizations he was later to erect."[50]

But however that may be, the combination of outstanding skill or talent and autistic tendencies is not confined to a few, famous cases. According to some authorities, up to 10 per cent of autistics, but only 1 per cent with other developmental deficits, show some kind of so-called *savant skills*: in other words, remarkable cognitive and/or memory ability found among more prevalent disability.[51] Such talents are usually limited to music, art, maths and calendar calculation, mechanical and spatial skills, often featuring astonishing memorization feats; while the combination of blindness, autism, and musical genius is unusually frequent.[52] For example, a pair of identical twin savants described by Sacks possessed calendar-calculating skills over an 80,000 year range; could not do simple arithmetic, but would calculate lengthy prime numbers for fun; could instantly count and factorize the number of matches that fell out of a box; and could remember the weather and the important political events on every day of their adult lives while having little or no memory of more personal events.[53] Kim Peek, the inspiration for the film *Rain Man*, walks with a sideways gait, needs help buttoning his clothes and managing many of the practical chores of daily life, has great difficulty understanding abstraction, and has an overall IQ of 87. Yet he has an encyclopaedic knowledge of history, political leaders, roads and highways in the USA and Canada, professional sports, the space program, movies, actors and actresses, Shakespeare, the Bible, Mormon doctrine and history, calendar calculations, literature, telephone area codes, major Zip codes, television stations, classical music, along with the detailed content of 9000 individual books at the time of writing.[54,55] (For further examples of savantism, see the box on p. 29: Musical savants.)

So-called *acquired savant syndrome* can occasionally emerge after brain injury or disease in a previously normal person. For example, a nine-year-old, who was deaf-mute and paralysed by a gun-shot wound to the left hemisphere, developed outstanding mechanical skills after the injury.[51] Another remarkable case is that of Daniel Tammet. Diagnosed with Asperger's syndrome, Daniel developed an unusual combination of synaesthesia and savantism following a series of childhood epileptic seizures. *Synaesthesia* describes the mixing of senses so that in Daniel's case, for example, every number up to about 10,000 is seen as a uniquely coloured and textured shape, occasionally also associated with a specific emotional feeling. By means of manipulating numbers visualized in this way, Daniel can perform calculations with the speed and accuracy of a computer, and currently holds the British and European record for the rote recitation of the places of π from memory to 22,514 places—a feat achieved in just over five hours. His synaesthesia also extends to words, and following a challenge from a TV producer, Daniel learnt one of the world's most difficult and distinct languages, Icelandic, in one week sufficiently well to be successfully interviewed live in the language on Icelandic television—so much so that one of the Icelanders described Daniel's linguistic skill as "not human"![56]

But acquired savant syndrome need not only be acquired in childhood. Dementia in older people can sometimes release remarkable artistic skills while devastating normal functions.[57] Experimental evidence pointing to the same conclusion comes from a remarkable study in which 11 right-handed male volunteers underwent magnetic stimulation of part of their brains before being asked to reproduce images of animals and faces by drawing. The magnetism had the effect of temporarily inhibiting the left frontal temporal lobe, which is the same part of the brain where damage or degeneration is known to be associated with the spontaneous appearance of savant skills in previously normal people. Although some autistic savants excel in pictorial art, the output, be it drawing, painting, sculpture, or modelling, is usually realistic,

Musical savants

Tom Wiggins (1849–1908), known as "Blind Tom," was purchased as a child at a slave auction in Georgia in 1850 along with his mother. A contemporary described him as "idiotic for any other purpose," and capable of nothing but "gyrations and melodies." He did not speak and could barely walk by the age of five and "gave no other sign of intelligence" apart from an "everlasting thirst for music." But despite having been blind from birth, he taught himself to play the piano by the time he was four, and by the age of 11 he was performing before the president at the White House, and later went on a successful concert tour to Europe. His vocabulary ultimately amounted to less than 100 words, but although incapable of learning anything else, his musical repertoire eventually included over 5000 pieces, and he was said to be able to reproduce perfectly passages of unfamiliar music up to 15 minutes long. Indeed, a panel of 16 outstanding musicians of the day concluded that "in…every form of musical examination" Blind Tom "showed a capacity ranking him among the most wonderful phenomena in musical history."[1a]

In a controlled experiment, Hermelin and O'Connor compared the performance of a 19-year-old musical autistic savant who had an IQ of 61 and almost total absence of spontaneous speech with that of an accomplished musician. Both listened to two pieces of recorded music that they had not heard before (Grieg's "Melody," opus 47 no. 3, and part of Bartók's "Mikrokosmos"). The autistic savant gave an almost note-perfect rendering of all 64 bars of "Melody," playing 798 notes of which only 8 per cent were wrong. By contrast, the professional pianist attempted to play only 354 notes, but in this much abbreviated version there were a total of 80 per cent wrong notes. Hermelin adds that after 24 hours during which he had not heard the piece again, the savant gave a second near-perfect performance. However, in the case of the less conventional piece by Bartók, the savant again played more notes (277 against the control's 153), but got 63 per cent of them wrong as compared to only 14 per cent in the case of the professional musician.

Leslie Lemke is a modern equivalent of Blind Tom who was born blind and with cerebral palsy, and who taught himself to play the piano in much the same way as his famous predecessor. He gives regular concerts and reproduces music from memory with such machine-like precision that members of the audience are asked to write down their requests rather than shout them out (because otherwise Lemke will insist on playing each and every one in the order in which he heard them, no matter how long it takes!).[1b]

In another experiment, Lemke was asked to reproduce and improvise on the same two pieces and was compared with another professional musician. Having first played a few bars of Grieg's "Melody" note-perfectly, Lemke produced 215 bars of improvisation, which the researchers described as played with enormous enthusiasm and verve. The professional pianist played only 95 bars. Then, in a manner reminiscent of Beethoven's famous improvisations (and who, as we have already seen, has also been diagnosed an Asperger's savant), the savant replaced Grieg's rather thin musical texture with something much more dense, extravagant and flamboyant. In contrast to Lemke's embellishments of Grieg's sparse texture, the professional musician tended to retain it, and his improvisations were simple, reflective, and restrained. Where the Bartók was concerned, Hermelin recounts that "the two participants resembled each other much more closely than they had done in their improvisations on the piece by Grieg, although for the Bartók, too, Leslie also gave a much richer interpretation, mostly by putting in more chords." However, like the other savant mentioned above, Lemke reproduced the piece by Bartók much less impressively than he had the one by Grieg, which he got almost note-perfect by comparison with the Bartók, which he got 80 per cent wrong—and much worse than the professional musician, who got the Bartók 76 per cent correct.[2] Although Bartók has been posthumously diagnosed as an Asperger's savant,[3] his music nevertheless seems more difficult for autistic performers to reproduce, perhaps because of its more modern, informal style.

rather than abstract or conceptual.[58a] Indeed, this is often how savants' artistic skills are first recognized: even as children they show technical competence in representing things which goes far beyond that normal for their age. The frontal-lobe magnetic-inhibition study found that some subjects showed a dramatic change of style towards a more life-like way of drawing, with more attention to realistic details and less of a tendency to caricature—but only after genuine stimulation, not after control sessions when no magnetism was applied. Indeed, one subject said that after the stimulation he was more "alert" and "conscious of detail," and that the experimenters had "taught him how to draw dogs!"[59a] (See the box on p. 32: Savant artists.)

Another study of five patients all diagnosed with fronto-temporal dementia noted that the creativity of these subjects was visual but never verbal. Similarly, the paintings, photographs, and sculptures were realistic copies lacking an abstract or symbolic content. The painters remembered realistic landscapes, animals, or people, and seemed to recall images that were then mentally reconstructed as pictures without the mediation of language. Also, despite progressive cognitive and social impairment, they showed increasing interest in the fine detail of faces, objects, shapes, and sounds. The authors of this study also cite the case of a Polish painter who suffered a left-hemisphere stroke associated with aphasia (loss of speech) but lost only the ability to create the highly symbolic pictures that he had previously painted, while retaining an ability to paint realistically without a flaw.[57]

Brain-imaging shows left-brain abnormalities in savants along with changes to the *corpus callosum*, the thick bundle of nerve fibres that connects the two hemispheres—indeed, Kim Peek lacks this structure altogether. Language is localized more on the left half of the brain than the right in most people. It is in the left hemisphere that the main speech centres are found, but in children with autism language develops much more on the right side of the brain than it does in normal children.[60] Exactly the same is found in the pattern of activity involving the prefrontal and parietal regions of the brain, which are normally correlated on the left in normal subjects, but on the right in high-functioning autistics.[61] Typical savant skills such as artistic, musical, and mechanical

Savant artists

Temple Grandin remarks that autistic savants can make perspective drawings without being taught how: "They're drawing what they see, which is all the little changes in size and texture that tell you one object is closer up and another object is further away. Normal people can't see all those little changes without a lot of training and effort, because their brains process them unconsciously. So normal people are drawing what *they* 'see,' which is the finished object, after their brains have put it together. Normal people don't draw a dog, they draw a *concept* of a dog. Autistic people draw the dog."[1] An outstanding example of what Grandin has in mind is the so-called "Living Camera," Stephen Wiltshire, an autistic savant who drew a remarkably accurate aerial view of London at the age of 11 after a helicopter ride over the city. Another is Gilles Tréhin, who made the drawing of New York illustrated here at the age of 14 and has gone on to create an entire imaginary city, drawn in astonishing detail and with stunning realism.[2]

Like the artwork of autistics, cave paintings are amazingly life-like and show great attention to detail and a natural sense of perspective, sometimes along with an equally striking neglect of the context in which the image is drawn. (Autistics, like the cave artists, will on occasions draw or paint over existing images—and in the latter case, often did so in astonishingly inaccessible places within the caves.) Nick Humphrey remarks in comparing the drawings of Nadia, an autistic child, with those found in the caves at Chauvet that animals almost seem to have been "snapped" in active motion.[3] Indeed, in a further comment, Humphrey notes that certain drugs can induce comparable "autistic" visual perception and that Aldous Huxley reported that in his experience of taking mescalin the artist whose work came closest to the resulting visual experience was Vermeer[4]—a painter who is strongly suspected of having used mirrors or lenses to create his images.[5]

Lascaux is the best known example of Palaeolithic cave art, but Chauvet dates from at least ten thousand years earlier. The fact that such stunningly realistic works of art can suddenly appear without any precursors, re-appear ten thousand years later, then finally vanish and be replaced by more rudimentary and more caricatured "stick-man" representations is difficult to explain if cultural tradition is believed to be the operative factor. Furthermore, there is no way that such realism could have been drawn directly from life nor aided by any means of imaging when you recall that these works are found deep inside caves and were made by stone-age hunters. However, if autistic savants existed among Palaeolithic peoples, they certainly might have been able to produce such images directly from memory just as savant artists such as Gilles Tréhin or Stephen Wiltshire do today, explaining the striking similarity in style and execution to autistic art.[6]

abilities are also found more on the right side of the brain. Taken together, these observations suggest that savant syndrome may result from compensation in the right hemisphere of the brain for damage in the left. The five- to six-fold predominance of savant syndrome in males may be explained by the left hemisphere completing its development later than the right. This might make it more vulnerable to pre-natal influence from the male sex hormone, testosterone, which slows and impairs neuronal function. The result would be enlargement of the right hemisphere, perhaps with a shift towards the right hemisphere skills typical of savants.[52] Musical savantism often features perfect pitch (as it did in the case of Mozart, for example), and according to some estimates up to a third of autistics have this gift.[62] A particular region of the auditory cortex in the right hemisphere is much more specialized for representing detailed pitch information than its counterpart on the left side of the brain, and tones that are close together in pitch seem to be better resolved by neurons on the right.[63]

People people and things people

Another name you might add to the catalogue of Asperger's savants is that of the person many would regard as the Darwin of the twentieth century, William D. Hamilton (1936–2000), the originator of the so-called "selfish gene" view of evolution popularized in the famous book of that title by Richard Dawkins. Hamilton described himself as "almost idiot savant" and rated himself "fairly good at woodwork as at other handicrafts" to the extent of having carpentry as a "reserve life plan" in case his theory proved un-publishable.[64,65a] Like the Unabomber—who was also a skilled woodworker and whose bombs were astonishingly made in large part of wood—Hamilton experimented with explosives as a child, in his case losing parts of three fingers and gaining some pieces of shrapnel permanently lodged in his lungs. Also as a child, Hamilton recalled typical autistic behaviour such as "pointless routine actions," making "odd clicking sounds," and hours spent "bouncing a ball into a corner to watch it spin."[65b] In games with other children he "was usually the one out of step and the slowest to pick up the rules."[66a] As an adult, he described himself as possessing "notably a trait approaching to autism about what most regard as the higher attributes of our species," and went on to portray himself as "a person who... believes he understands the human species in many ways better than anyone and yet who manifestly doesn't understand in any practical way how the human world works—neither how he himself fits in and nor, it seems, the conventions."[65c]

Hamilton made a telling discrimination between what he called "people people" as opposed to "things people." He observed that "people people just need people to interact with, not necessarily the understanding of them: They tend to be conformist and are seldom more than superficially critical of any ethos of their time."[66b] But Hamilton himself was obviously one of the things people: "in us things people...there occurs some aberration of a natural sequence that has been evolved for the purpose of bonding person to person. In us this sequence has grown awry somehow and gained untypical intensity directed towards inhuman objects." Nevertheless, he could also see that there were compensations when he added, "Yet the same misdirection, which is so often disastrous socially...can be very helpful in the making of [a] scientist, an engineer, or the like. Thus it is probably not wholly maladaptive. I believe it is in essence an aberration of this kind that makes me a successful scientist."[66c]

Hamilton's family background also seems to have featured a number of things people: his father was a well-known engineer (co-designer of the Callender-Hamilton bridge) and was followed into engineering by one of Hamilton's brothers, while a geriatrician sister had things skills to the extent that she developed an improved pressure-mattress for the treatment of bed sores.[67] The relevance of this to Asperger's syndrome is that it is sometimes called "the engineer's disorder," and children with autism are described as relating to others "as though they were machines rather than people."[68]

Folk physics is an intuitive ability to grasp physical principles involved in mechanical systems and machines. Reverting to Hamilton's distinction, you might call it *things-thinking* as opposed to *people-thinking*, understood as a corresponding intuitive ability to understand other people's behaviour and mentality. When tests of such things-thinking were administered to them, Asperger's cases functioned significantly above their mental age by comparison with normal children despite the fact that on comparable tests of folk psychology or people-thinking the autistic children performed predictably worse. Although the experiment could not determine whether such so-called folk physics and folk psychology are independent of one another or just inversely related, it did demonstrate a significant superiority in the Asperger's children where such things-thinking was concerned. Indeed, the fascination with machines of all kinds that is so frequently found in autistics is almost certainly another manifestation of the same bias towards inanimate objects, as the researchers themselves point out.[69]

According to a survey of 919 families of children with autism or Asperger's syndrome which listed occupations of parents, fathers of children with ASD were twice as often employed in engineering as were fathers in any of four control groups of children with Tourette's or Down syndrome. The *Autism-Spectrum Quotient* or AQ Test consists of 50 questions covering social skill, attention switching, attention to detail, communication, and imagination. Fifty-eight adults with Asperger's syndrome, 174 randomly selected controls, 840 students at Cambridge University, and the 16 winners of the UK Mathematics Olympiad were each sent a questionnaire by post. Results showed that the majority of people with Asperger's syndrome scored above 32 (out of a maximum of 50). But interestingly, among the students at Cambridge University, those in the sciences and technology had a higher AQ score compared to those in the arts and humanities. Mathematicians scored the highest of all—around 20 out of 50—and were closely followed by engineers, computer scientists, and physicists. Among the scientists, biologists and medics scored the lowest, around 14 out of 50.[70]

These results strongly suggest that people-thinking is independent of IQ, executive function (planning, prioritizing, and postponing), and reasoning about the physical world. The researchers conclude that there seems to be a small but statistically significant link between autism and engineering.[71] Indeed, it is one that can be seen in a sample of

Asperger's original cases. A recent study of these found that in 37 instances where the father's profession was mentioned, the most common form of employment was a technical one and that the most frequently seen profession was "engineer" or "electrical engineer."[72]

Temple Grandin, one of the world's most distinguished and famous autistics, confesses that as a child she "was completely turned on by machines instead of people" and that even as an adult who regards herself as partly recovered from autism, she is still "turned on by machines, especially control mechanisms designed to interact with people."[73a] Grandin had a maternal grandfather who she describes as "a brilliant, shy engineer who invented the automatic pilot for airplanes," and is herself a noted and very successful engineer to the extent that she has designed a third of all cattle- and pig-handling equipment in the USA. She relates "better to scientists and engineers, who are less motivated by emotion" than other people,[73b] and explicitly attributes her engineering success to her predominantly visual mode of thinking: "Every design problem I've solved started with my ability to visualize and see the world in pictures… I visualize my designs being used in every possible situation, with different sizes and breeds of cattle and weather situations. Doing this enables me to correct mistakes prior to construction".[74] Drawing on her extensive knowledge of autism and autistics, Temple Grandin speculates that:

> There may be two kinds of thinking—visual and sequential. Society needs to recognize the value of people who think visually… Misinterpretation of psychological test results could label a brilliant visual thinker as below average intelligence. Einstein was a visual thinker who failed his high school language requirement and relied on visual methods of study.[73c]

She adds that "People with autism can develop skills in fields that they can really excel in… I've known people who are engaged in satisfying jobs as varied as elevator repair, bike repair, computer programming, graphic arts, architectural drafting, and laboratory pathology. Most of these jobs use the visualization talents that many people with autism have."[73d]

Mechanistic or systemizing?

Nevertheless, according to another view, the autistic brain is predominantly hard-wired for understanding and predicting the behaviour of events and objects by building *systems*. *Systemizing* is defined as the drive to analyse and explore a system, to extract underlying rules that govern the behaviour of a system; and to construct systems. The systemizer intuitively figures out how things work, or what the underlying rules controlling a system are. Systems can be as varied as a pond, a vehicle, a plant, a library catalogue, a musical composition, a cricket ball, or even an army unit. They all operate on inputs and deliver outputs, using "if-then" correlation rules.[46a]

As we have already seen, there is a clear link between ASD and engineering, and to my way of thinking *mechanistic* describes most of the examples produced to justify it much more aptly than does *systemizing*.[46] As such, *mechanistic cognition* would be another term for folk physics or things-thinking: in other words, a system of cognition specific to the physical world in the same way in which folk psychology or people-thinking is specific to the human world. Indeed, where making this distinction is concerned, no less an authority than Kanner himself used the words "mechanized" and "mechanization" to try to capture the impersonal, cold relationship between autistic children and their parents.[75,76]

Another virtue of *mechanistic* as a term for autistic thinking is that it is already current. People with rich experience of autistics comment that "Individuals with autism assign not an everyday but a more mechanistic significance to things."[77a] Certainly, the notorious insistence on punctilious repetition and regular routine by autistics of all kinds might be called "systematic," but *mechanistic* catches its mechanical, mindless character better in my view. The same is true of the rigidly repetitive way that autistics often carry out instructions without any apparent thought about their meaning. Of course this is systematic, but *mechanistic* is a much more apt term, and certainly captures the mechanical, robotic quality that is often attributed to such behaviour by others.

The virtue of *mechanistic* rather than *systematic* is even found in art—at least if the comments of artists with autistic proclivities are considered. The essentially mechanistic inspiration of Warhol's work comes out in Michael Fitzgerald's observation that "One reason for Warhol's success may have been that he represented the machine age. Romanticism was meaningless to him; the machine age was everything." He goes on to quote Warhol remarking, "The things I want to show you are mechanical," adding, "I would like to be a machine, wouldn't you?" Fitzgerald concludes that Warhol "had the autistic mechanical mind."[18d] He also quotes other authorities who point out that Warhol "loved all sorts of machines and gadgets, embracing new techniques and technologies, working with tape recorders, cassettes, Polaroid, Thermofax, but the heart of all this experimentation had at its central focus photography and silkscreen for making a painting." They add that "This was by extension his love for the machine because the screen process was very machinelike."[18e] Describing Lowry, Fitzgerald comments that this "chronicler of industrial reality," who looked on other humans as comical automatons, "habitually avoided any conversation that hinted at inner meaning in art, or one that looked as if it might lead to such conclusions." Indeed, "the Lowry automaton" as he was sometimes called was not above teasing his own friends in this respect, "in order to deflate pomposity or pretension."[18f]

Where autistic savants are concerned, abilities like calendar-calculation (one of the most common of all) certainly seem to involve a system. But authorities on savants point out that, although able to perform such calculations, savants typically cannot account for how they do it, or explain the system to anyone else. Indeed, authorities on savants conclude that "The savant is a concrete calculator, not an abstract mathematician," and call such concrete thinking "an almost universal symptom or trait" of the condition.[54a] Nor is it limited to savants: although some Asperger's cases are gifted mathematicians, a common problem for them at school is that, although they are good at getting the right answers to maths problems, they are often unable to explain how they arrived at them.[21c] But systemizing something implies both that you can apply it yourself *and* could explain the system to someone else. *Systemizing*, in other words, suggests insight in a way that *mechanizing* does not. You would not necessarily expect a mechanism that could work out the date of Easter to enable you to know how it did it, but you would expect a *system* to work out the date of Easter to be comprehensible to you. An Easter-predicting mechanism would be a kind of calendrical clock, and it is worth pointing out that, although a rare savant skill, stop-watch-like accuracy in estimating the passing of time is occasionally found: a skill which might be described as *systematic*, but which literally works like clock-work and is *mechanistic* to that extent.[51a]

Again, if you describe something as "systematic" you imply that it is coherently consistent and does not have parts that are discrepant with or independent of the whole—that would obviously be *unsystematic*. In other words, *systemizing* implies a top-down or *holistic* approach, which focuses on an integrated whole. In his book on autistic thinking, Peter Vermeulen points out that "the first axiom in systems theory" is "that the whole is more than the sum of its parts... Systems theory regards the world in terms of the mutual relatedness and dependency of phenomena. The characteristics of a system, an integrated whole, cannot be reduced to its constituent parts." By contrast, he adds that "individuals with autism live in a multi-universe: a world of unaccountable, incoherent details that are experienced as having only one meaning: the literal meaning. The world of people with autism is more like a world of different bits and pieces."[77b] At its worst, this leads to a highly disintegrated and chaotic view of life that is anything but systematic in its cognitive quality. Speaking of one particular autistic young woman, someone who knew her well described her as follows:

> Kate knows and understands a great deal but seems to have very limited ability to structure. To use her way of putting things, her life is a heap of odd-shaped stones. Anything she tries to construct soon falls down, whereas other people build

amazing structures, which often seem impenetrable and mean-ingless walls to her, hemming her in on every side. The more structured a subject, the less it means to her...[58b]

Temple Grandin characterizes autistic cognition as *hyper-specific* and claims that "autistic people don't see their ideas of things, they see the actual things themselves. We see the details that make up the world, while normal people blur all those details together into their general concept of the world." According to Temple Grandin, "The problem with normal people is they're too cerebral," or what she calls "*abstracti-fied*."[78] *Mechanistic* avoids the abstraction implied by *systemizing* because it suggests that the thing it describes is working on concrete, mechani-cal, cause-and-effect principles. As such, I shall use the term from now on in preference to *systemizing* to epitomize the bottom-up, visual-rath-er-than-verbal, concrete thinking style of autism.

Controlled scientific studies of autistic savants certainly suggest that their cognitive style is mechanistic, rather than systematic. Consider the autistic savant with a measured verbal IQ of only 89 but a vocabulary score equivalent to an IQ of 121 who can understand, talk, read, write, and translate from Danish, Dutch, Finnish, French, German, Greek, Hindi, Italian, Norwegian, Polish, Portuguese, Russian, Spanish, Swedish, Turkish, and Welsh. However, he translates word-by-word like "an automaton," with no concern for the meaning of whole sen-tences. When asked to take his time and look at the whole sentence first, he became distressed and said that he could not do it.[58c] You could call this "systematic," but *mechanistic* seems a much better description. Indeed, this is precisely the way in which computer translation tends to turn out: fine for translating individual words, but weak on render-ing the sense of the whole. Contrast this with the method used by Sigmund Freud (1856–1939) when translating: "Instead of laboriously transcribing from the foreign language, idioms and all, he would read a passage, close the book, and consider how a German writer would have clothed the same thoughts—a method not very common among translators."[79] Perhaps not, but as a method of translation it was just as systematic as the one above in its own way, but was distinctly less mechanistic in its top-down, empathic, and holistic approach.

In the experiment described earlier in which normal volunteers' frontal lobes were inhibited by magnetic means, the same subjects who had shown the most notable change in their drawing style also showed the greatest improvement in a proof-reading test. But here again the improvement in proof-reading skill was only found after actual stimulation of the subjects' frontal lobes, not after the placebo. As the experimenters comment, "These proof-reading results provide non-subjective evidence of the ability to switch on savant-like skill by turning off part of the brain in healthy individuals."[59] Proof-reading requires close attention to detail—the kind of bottom-up, word-by-word approach seen in the linguistic savant described just now. You could also call proof-reading "systematic," but *mechanistic* seems a much more apt term for something that nowadays computers can do for you while you type.

In the box on musical savants (pp. 29–30) I pointed out in passing that both Leslie Lemke and another musical savant reproduced a piece by Bartók much less impressively than they had one by Grieg. As I suggested there, an explanation may lie in the relatively looser structure and greater informality of modern music. Another autistic with a musical talent complained that even though some of his favourite music was from the Romantic era, he felt lost in a sea of non-harmonic tones and was unable to impose an analytic structure upon the music. He added that "The resultant muddiness in the demarcation of the structural borders along with the increased use of tones that are not part of a given chord make it more difficult for me to separate the foreground from the background in order to determine the harmony."[80] At the very least, this suggests that, not only in memory and language skills, but in music also, autistic savants may be relying on a machine-like, things-thinking ability to achieve their distinctive results that might be best described as *mechanistic*.

Finally, *mechanistic* has the virtue of being a term that covers the purely manual, technical, and practical abilities that are also sometimes found associated with ASD in a way that *systemizing* does not. An example would be the carpentry skills possessed by both Hamilton and the Unabomber—and even by Temple Grandin, who was one of the first girls in her school "to be allowed to take wood-shop," at least until she was forced "to return to the traditional cooking class" and become "a failure once again"![73e] Furthermore, there are cases of true savantism where such skills are concerned. The "Genius of Earlswood Asylum," James Henry Pullen (1835–1916), was perhaps the most notable and bears comparison with the musical and artistic savants discussed in the boxes. Although described as "deaf and dumb," diagnosed as congenitally mentally retarded, and institutionalized in an asylum from the age of 15, his exquisite carving, carpentry, and model-making skills made him a national celebrity. His masterpiece was a model of the steamship, *The Great Eastern:* a ten-foot long replica held together by over a million wooden pins and containing 5585 rivets which reproduced the original in stunning detail. At a time when people such as Pullen were diagnosed as *idiot savants*, the Prince Consort understandably "expressed the greatest surprise that one so gifted was still to be kept in the category of idiots, or ever had been one."[54b] Such manual skills are not always accorded the same respect as more abstract, intellectual ones, but at the very least Pullen proves that they can feature in a form of genuine savantism, and would certainly be part and parcel of what I would call *mechanistic cognition.*

Chapter 2

Deficits in Mind

In the first chapter we saw that ASD sometimes goes with enhanced vision in various senses: enhanced visual acuity, greater ability to visualize mentally, and the stunning natural perspective skills and photographic realism of autistic artists. However, such gifts can cut both ways. One possibility is that they enable you to focus so closely on details that you fail to see the wider picture. In this chapter, we need to redress the imbalance of the last by concentrating not on the compensations, but on this and other deficits of autism. As we shall see, what will emerge is a second, parallel kind of cognition to place alongside the mechanistic one which we considered in the last chapter. This is one which often seems deficient in some respects in people with autism: what you might call *people-thinking* or *mentalism*.

Not seeing the wood for the trees

Summarizing findings relating to autistic savants of different kinds such as the ones I mentioned in the first chapter, Beate Hermelin concludes that "Savant ability appears to take a route leading from the detail to the whole, thereby reversing our dominant tendency of information processing."[1] Temple Grandin calls this *specific-to-general* thinking, and comments:

Looking at a lot of specific details and then piecing them to-gether is how people with Asperger's think. All my thinking goes from specific details to forming a general principle. I have learned from interviewing many people that most go from gen-eral concept to specifics. Their thinking is "top down" and my thinking is "bottom up."[2]

For example, she adds that:

When I think about a dog, I see a series of pictures of specific dogs, such as my student's dog or the dog next door. There is no generalized verbal dog concept in my mind. I form my dog concept by looking for common features that all dogs and no cats have.[3]

Brain-imaging reveals that normal controls use a global, top-down ap-proach which involves the use of working memory to solve embedded-figure puzzles, which require the child to find hidden elements within a larger picture. Autistic children, by contrast, solve them in a more fragmented, bottom-up way using regions involved in object percep-tion alone.[4] Perhaps this explains why autistic children in general, and those diagnosed with Asperger's syndrome in particular, perform better and show greater versatility than normal children on such tests of spa-tial ability.[5] In the case of block-design puzzles, the child is required to assemble a figure from parts represented on separate blocks. Prior segmentation of the parts of the block-design puzzle massively im-proves the performance of non-autistic children, whether normal or learning-disabled. But it has little effect on the performance of able children with autism, who are extremely fast even with un-segmented designs.[6a]

A model of the mind inspired by computational neuroscience pro-poses that we recognize objects by matching top-down expectations based on learnt categories against bottom-up representations of sen-sory features. *Vigilance* determines the amount of similarity required to define a match between categories and specific features. If vigilance is high, a great deal of similarity between categories and features is required for recognition to occur, whereas the converse is true if vigilance is low. It has been proposed that in ASD vigilance is abnormally high, which would explain why autistics are inordinately influenced by bottom-up features. High vigilance leads to the formation of highly specific, concrete categories and prevents the learning of general, abstract ones. Indeed, it may also explain why autistics often fail to recognize objects, such as faces, due to trivial variations in sensory features, such as changes in hair style. However, high vigilance ensures that autistic individuals very seldom mistakenly recognize an object as belonging to a category to which it does not belong.[7,8]

High vigilance, and a specific-to-general, bottom-up rather than top-down cognitive style, certainly seem to fit nicely with the recently proposed *under-connectivity theory* of ASD. Brain-imaging shows that in autistics the language network is less synchronized, and Broca's area (which serves an integrating function in language ability) is much less active. However, Wernicke's area, the other important speech centre that concentrates more on the processing of individual words, is more active in autistic brains (perhaps explaining the word-by-word translation method of the autistic language savant mentioned in the previous chapter). Again, the sentence-visualization study I mentioned earlier which found that autistics do indeed think in pictures also supported the conclusion that this comes about in part thanks to reduced connectivity within the brain. These findings suggest that the neural basis of disordered language in autism entails a lower degree of information integration and synchronization across the large-scale cortical network for language processing. Indeed, such a lack of integration within the brain might explain why some people with ASD have normal or even superior skills in some areas, while many other types of thinking are disordered. It could be that the brain adapts to the diminished inter-area communication in autism by developing more independent, free-standing abilities in certain brain centres. This might sometimes translate into the superior but isolated abilities typical of autistic savants.[9,10]

Although there is also good evidence of denser connections than normal at a local level, another recent study points out that in the brains of autistics, high local connectivity may develop in tandem with low long-range connectivity,[11] much as it does to a lesser degree in the normal male.[12] Certainly, the remarkable synaesthetic savantism of Daniel Tammet described in the previous chapter would fit this suggestion (despite being a very unusual condition). Synaesthesia has been seen as a result of overlapping and cross-talk between neighbouring brain areas—a theory which also seems to explain foot-fetishism (because the foot neighbours the genitals in the cortex: local over-connectivity indeed!).[13,14] It is certainly possible that communication between different centres within the brains of autistics retards global processing in much the same way that a large number of users logged onto a computer network tend to slow it down. Excesses in local connections along with deficits in overall brain integration might explain why autistics sometimes show faster processing in certain cognitive functions but not others.

Another way of describing the not-seeing-the-wood-for-the-trees deficit in ASD is to propose that autistics exhibit greater *field-independence* defined as a lack of influence of context in both visual perception and other perceptual tasks. So for example, breaking up the blocks in the block-design test mentioned just now could be seen as making the parts more independent of any context, and therefore easier for normal children to re-assemble correctly. However, if autistic children are much more field-independent to the extent that they are much less affected by any existing arrangement of the blocks, the finding that prior segmentation has little effect on them is explained.

Field-dependence has also been called *central-coherence*, and *strong* and *weak central-coherence* map closely onto the terms *field-dependence* and *field-independence*.[6b] An example is provided by the Ebbinghaus illusion. In reality, both central black spots are exactly the same size, but they seem different because of the size contrast of the surrounding figures. Francesca Happé found that autistics are less prone to this illusion, presumably because their greater field-independence makes them go from specific to general and consequently be less likely to be fooled by the surrounding circles. According to a model proposed by Happé, central-coherence/field-dependence (or the lack of it) can be found in

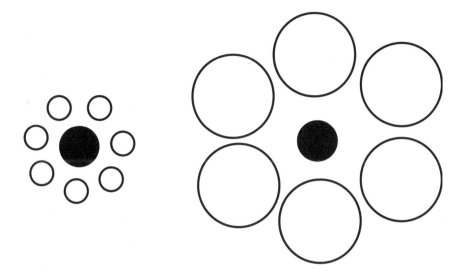

The Ebbinghaus illusion

visual, verbal, auditory, and other domains, and varies from strong to weak in the normal population, with autistics showing a similar range, but biased towards the less centrally-coherent/more field-independent extreme. She also suggests that normal people-thinking relies on field-dependence and in particular on the ability to place things in their context and relate them to their proper background.[15]

Central-coherence is certainly critical where normal understanding of speech is concerned because words owe their meaning to the way in which they are embedded within larger units such as phrases, sentences, or longer units of discourse. Again, field-dependence is particularly clearly seen in the way in which a listener discriminates words which have the same sound but different meanings by means of their verbal context, such as *there*, *their*, or *they're*. But autistics will typically read sentences such as: "He took a bow from his violin case" with exactly the same pronunciation of *bow* as in "He took a bow and everybody clapped"; or will speak of "a big tear in her dress" in exactly the same way as if it were a "big tear in her eye."[16] Indeed, machines make exactly the same mistake, as I discovered when I had my computer read this paragraph to me!

According to other authorities, "Field-dependent people are easily swayed by others' opinion and tend to take on the prevailing views of their group; field-independent people are unaffected by current crazes and don't care so much about other people's opinion. People with a high degree of social detachment tend to be good at spotting embedded figures."[6c] However, the implication is that field-independent people may also show serious deficits where caring about other people's opinions is concerned. Certainly, children who score high on field-independence in cognitive tests also score low on social competence. For example, in 1276 three-to-five-year-olds, those who were more field-independent showed more non-social play. Happé concludes that "individuals with weak central-coherence and detail-focused processing are less successful in putting together the information necessary for sensitive social inference."[15] The not-seeing-the-wood-for-the-trees problem, in other words, could have serious consequences for social adjustment and for normal interaction with other people. Indeed, that in itself might explain much about the social deficits and psychological problems of people with ASD.

But does it explain all of them? One of Kanner's tests for autism was to prick the child with a pin. If the child responded just to the pin or the hand that held it, it was a sign of autism, but not if the child responded to the person who had pricked them.[17] Is not-seeing-the-person-for-the-pin a failure of central-coherence attributable to field-independence? Or is it some other inability to relate to people, and to their minds and intentions?

Mind-blindness

A review of diagnosis and description of ASD leaves little doubt that "autistic children have *a primary inability to perceive others as people* and to conceive what they communicate."[18a] Reverting to Hamilton's *people people* and *things people* distinction (see p. 35), you might say that children with ASD have a deficit in *people-thinking*, even if not in *things-thinking*. Many would say that it is the possession of a mind that makes a person different from a thing, and consequently you might interpret autistics' deficits in people-thinking as an inability to relate to other people's minds, or, more graphically, as *mind-blindness*.[19] For example, one young autistic man complained that he couldn't "mind-read." He explained that other people seem to have a special sense by which they can read other people's thoughts and anticipate their responses and feelings. He knew this because they managed to avoid upsetting people whereas he was always "putting his foot in it": not realizing that he was doing or saying the wrong thing until after the other person became angry and upset.[20] But this problem is not linked in any way to deficits in intelligence, education, or opportunity. The philosopher A. J. Ayer for example, who as we saw in the last chapter has been posthumously diagnosed with an autistic disorder, once remarked that none of his philosophical pre-occupations had given him "as much trouble as the problem of our knowledge of other minds."[21]

A critical assessment of such deficits is the so-called *false belief* or *Sally-Anne test*. In the simplest version, a child is shown a tube of sweets and asked what they think is inside. Of course, the child replies, "sweets!" But the tube is opened to reveal a pencil. The child is then asked what another person, who has not yet been shown the tube and its unexpected contents, will think is inside it. Alternatively, a child is shown two dolls, Sally and Anne, each of which has a toy box. The child sees that Sally has a toy in her box, but Anne does not. Now the child is asked to imagine that Sally leaves the room, and while she is absent, Anne takes Sally's toy out of Sally's box and puts it into her own box, and shuts it again. Now Sally returns. The crucial question is: where does Sally think her toy is now? The majority of four-year-old children can appreciate Sally's false belief that her toy is still in her box despite the fact that they personally know that it is not, but autistic children even considerably older typically reply that Sally now thinks that her toy is in Anne's box. Exactly the same happens with the tube of sweets: most four-year-olds realize that someone not shown the pencil inside would think it contained sweets, but autistic children typically fail to understand this. Such reactions are taken to indicate that those who fail such tests are answering on the basis of their own knowledge, and seem unable to appreciate others' ignorance because they lack the ability to understand another person's different state of mind.[22,23]

This finding becomes even more remarkable when contrasted with a parallel test of perspective-taking on a changed scene, the so-called *false photo test*. In this test, a child is shown an arrangement of objects that is then photographed with a Polaroid camera. While the image is developing, the child sees one object moved to a new position and is then asked where the moved object will appear when the photographed image emerges.[24] Repeated experiments show that children with ASD perform as well as—and sometimes better than—age-matched normal controls, and similar results are obtained if a false map or diagram is substituted for the false photograph.[25]

So why are autistics so poor at tests of false belief? It cannot just be a question of not-seeing-the-wood-for-the-trees because, if so, why would a moved object be missed in the Sally-Anne scenario but correctly identified in the false photo test? Surely, if weak central-coherence or field-independence were the problem, it would affect both equally. And if it is a question of high vigilance, why does it get the right answer in one case but the wrong one in the other? It may be that Sally-Anne scenarios demand not just a contextual, top-down view of the situation, but an ability to put yourself in Sally's shoes and understand the situation from her point of view. Yet if autistics are good at seeing real scenes from another point of view as revealed by the false photo test, why can't they do it where mental view-points are concerned? If they are so good at visualizing, why can't they visualize Sally's state of mind, or that of a child who hasn't seen that a pencil is inside the tube of sweets? Could it be that the point of view in question in the false belief test is an abstract one, whereas that in the false photo test is a real one?

According to Premack and Woodruff, *theory of mind* describes the ability to infer that other people experience mental states like our own. They claim that such a capacity may properly be viewed as a theory because mental states are not directly observable, and can be used to make predictions about the behaviour of others. They claim, in other words, that it is an ability to make an abstract representation of other people's states of mind.[26] Experiments with the Sally-Anne test described above suggest that normal children acquire a theory of mind between the ages of three and five, but that autistic children are notably lacking in this respect. Studies show that autistic children do not differ from others in their ability to understand the functions of an internal organ such as the heart. Nor are they deficient in their knowledge about the location of organs such as liver or brain. However, whereas other children are able to understand that the brain has purely mental functions, autistic children tend to associate it only with behavioural ones, so that it appears that specifically mental, unobservable events are beyond their comprehension.[27]

Today a great deal of evidence of many kinds has accumulated in support of the view that theory of mind deficits characterize autism.[6,28] Furthermore, the latest research has even begun to reveal the brain structures that might be involved. In a recent experiment using brain-imaging, ten autistic and the same number of normal subjects viewed animations of two moving triangles on a screen in three different conditions: moving randomly, moving in a goal-directed fashion (chasing, fighting), and moving interactively with implied intentions (coaxing, tricking). The last condition frequently elicited descriptions in terms of mental states that viewers attributed to the triangles. The autism group gave fewer and less accurate descriptions of these latter animations, but equally accurate descriptions of the other animations compared with controls. While viewing animations that elicited mentalizing, in contrast to randomly moving shapes, the normal group showed increased activation in parts of the brain previously identified with theory of mind functions. The autism group showed less activation than the normal group in all these regions. As the researchers comment: "The claim that individuals with autism spectrum disorders, regardless of general intelligence, have an impairment in the attribution of mental states, has been confirmed once again."[29]

To revert to the false belief versus false photo conundrum, you could say that the critical factor explaining autistics' deficits in the former but not the latter is theory of mind and the abilities it confers where interpreting other people's mental states is concerned. Sally's ignorance of where her doll has been put, and Anne's and the viewer's knowledge of where Anne put it, are all such states of mind, and it is these, purely abstract, mental realities that autistics find it so difficult to grasp. Although they may be better than average at visualizing real objects, autistics are symptomatically blind where *mental* ones are concerned, and this is the critical difference. Indeed, findings such as these closely resemble those regarding vision which I mentioned in the Introduction (see p. 11). They suggest that visualizing someone's state of mind is very different from visualizing a physical scene and that completely different cognitive systems and parts of the brain may be involved in each.

Nevertheless, it can be a different case with animals. Temple Grandin is a telling case in point. She recalls that as a two-year-old child she showed the symptoms of classic autism: no speech, poor eye-contact, tantrums, appearance of deafness, no interest in people, and constant staring off into space.[30a] The psychiatrist and writer Oliver Sacks, meeting her in adult life, reported that Temple Grandin seemed largely devoid of an implicit knowledge of social conventions and of cultural pre-suppositions which most normal people accumulate throughout life on the basis of experience and encounters with others. Lacking it, she had instead to "compute" others' intentions and states of mind, to try to make formal and explicit what for the rest of us is second nature.[31]

But whatever her shortcomings where comprehension of the characteristically human mind is concerned, Temple Grandin's expertise in understanding the animal mind is so great that her services as a consultant on animal behaviour are widely sought, and she has become an acknowledged international authority on the humane handling of livestock. Indeed, in the opinion of some authorities, she has arguably done more than anyone else in the world to improve the welfare of animals in a practical way.[32] As Grandin herself puts it in a recent book, "Autism made school and social life hard, but it made animals easy." Indeed, she remarks that "Autism is a kind of way station on the road from animals to humans." Speaking of herself as an autistic, she adds that "We use our animal brains more than normal people do, because we have to. We don't have any choice. *Autistic people are closer to animals than normal people are.*"[33] According to another autistic woman, "an autistic person regards her environment the same way as an animal."[34] There is certainly evidence that autistics may have intact understanding of desire and the link between it and the simpler emotions of happiness and sadness, or states such as hunger and thirst.[27] Such observations explain why autistic children have also been described as *desire psychologists*, and, when compared with Down syndrome children matched for age and language competence, have been found to use significantly more words related to desire, but far fewer to do with cognition.[35]

Observations such as these have led some authorities to comment that "Lacking a theory of mind is in one sense akin to viewing the world as a behaviourist."[27] The founder of Behaviourism, Ivan Pavlov (1849–1936), certainly sounded somewhat like an autistic when he remarked "Does not the eternal sorrow of life consist in the fact that human beings cannot understand one another, that one person cannot enter into the internal state of another?"[36] *Behaviourism* derived its name from its dogmatic assertion that the mind was a "black box" that could not be opened and about whose internal workings science could not speculate. According to the behaviourist, B. F. Skinner (1904–90), words such as "mind" and "ideas" were "invented for the sole purpose of providing spurious explanations." And because "mental or psychic events are asserted to lack the dimensions of physical science, we have an additional reason for rejecting them." Skinner's fellow behaviourist, John B. Watson (1878–1958), proclaimed that "the time has come when psychology must discard all reference to consciousness" and be purged of "all subjective terms such as sensation, perception, image, desire, purpose, and even thinking and emotion as they are subjectively defined."[37] All that could be studied objectively was what went into the brain in the form of stimuli and what came out of it as observed behaviour. Nothing else could be said. Behaviourism was the study of behaviour, not of the mind—mind-blind psychology, if ever there was.

But a denial of the mind was not limited to behaviourist psychologists. According to George Williams, one of the most eminent of twentieth-century Darwinists:

only confusion can arise from the use of an animal-mind concept in any explanatory role in biological studies of behaviour
… Mind may be self evident to most people, but I see only a
remote possibility of its being made logically or empirically
evident…no kind of material reductionism can approach any
mental phenomenon.

Williams concludes that the "solution to the non-objectivity of mind" is
"to exclude mind from all biological discussion."[38a] Elsewhere Williams
castigates what he calls "lubricious slides into discussions of pleasure
and anxiety and other concepts proper to the mental domain" as nothing other than "flights of unreason" on the part of authors who "claim
to have provided a physical explanation of mental phenomena."[39]
Similar comments to those of Williams can be found in the work of the
ethologists, Niko Tinbergen (1907–88) and Konrad Lorenz (1903–
89). These writers concentrated on observed behaviour and mistrusted
mental terms, which were often dismissed as "anthropomorphic" (that
is, committing the error of attributing human thoughts and feelings to
animals). Such views have been perpetuated and popularized by their
pupils, such as Richard Dawkins, according to whom "Ethologists…
do not permit words such as 'fear', 'anger', 'libido' and even 'hope',
but only as formally defined intervening variables or hypothetical
constructs."[40]

   Such a conscious, intentional rejection of all things mental is certainly comparable to the involuntary and unintentional mind-blindness
of autistics, but perhaps deserves a term of its own. My suggestion
would be *anti-mentalism*. As such, the term designates a rational belief
rather than a cognitive deficit—an anti-mind theory, if you like. But
whatever you care to call it, such behaviouristic anti-mentalism was
typical of most twentieth-century Darwinists and many students of
animal behaviour. The result of such views was what you might call
evolutionary, genetic, or ethological behaviourism: "explanations" of
behaviour that went directly from the evolutionary, genetic, or ethological factors proposed to the observed behavioural result. Such an
approach neglected the mental level of explanation altogether, and at

times left you wondering why organisms should be regarded as possessing minds at all—so irrelevant did they seem to behaviour. Where human beings were concerned, evolutionary, genetic, or ethological behaviourism prompted understandable protests that such an approach was "reductionistic" and diminished people to the status of mindless robots, controlled by their genes or ethological programming to act in ways essentially no different from the ways in which an ant or an amoeba might behave.

Mentalism

Another virtue of the concept of anti-mentalism is that it implies the existence of what it negates. *Mentalism* was a term that was originally used to describe stage acts in which the performer appeared to be able to read other people's thoughts—a feat which was also called a "head-act" or "mind-reading." However, *mentalism* is also used in philosophy and psychology to describe what behaviourism attempted to rule out: the belief that the mind is real and that our subjective experience of it provides valid insights for these disciplines. This is the exact contrary of anti-mentalism and describes the essential deficit in mind-blindness: the tendency to infer, interpret and predict mental states in yourself and others—perhaps animals included—in other words, to *mind-read* or to *mentalize.*[6]

An advantage of thinking in terms of mentalism is that it allows us to dispense with the cumbersome phrase "theory of mind" along with the misleading implications it carries with it, such as the impression it gives that people's mentalistic abilities spring from a prior conceptual understanding of psychology. This is clearly not the case, because mentalism is an implicit, automatic, unconscious ability that comes as naturally to most normal people as walking or talking. And just as no one needs to study the grammar and syntax of their native tongue in school before being able to speak it competently, or learn anatomy and mechanics before being able to walk, so no normal person needs a course on theory of mind before they can interact socially with other human beings. Theory of mind, in other words, is not a consciously learnt body of propositions such as the Special Theory of Relativity or the theory of music.

Temple Grandin's attempts to compensate for her mentalistic deficit by consciously thinking "algorithmically" about human social interactions is what you might call a true "theory of mind" because it is something she has had to learn, apply intentionally, and think about conceptually:

> Since I don't have any social intuition, I rely on pure logic, like an expert computer program, to guide my behavior. I categorize rules according to their logical importance. It is a complex algorithmic decision-making tree. There is a process of using my intellect and logical decision-making for every social decision. Emotion does not guide my decision; it is pure computing... Using my system has helped me negotiate every new situation I enter.[30b]

So, paradoxically, autistics such as Grandin do have theories about the mind—or, at least, about other people's minds—because this is the only way they can compensate for the lack of the implicit, automatic, unthinking ability to understand the mind that the phrase "theory of mind" was intended to describe. However, the term "theory of mind" is too well established in the literature to be avoided entirely. So from now on I shall treat it as a phrase equivalent to mentalism, and prefer *mentalism* and *mentalistic* as the noun and adjective that refer to the same fundamental concept: human beings' ability to understand their own minds and behaviour and the minds and behaviour of others in purely abstract, mental terms. Indeed, to this extent mentalism can be seen as equivalent, not only to people-thinking as opposed to things-thinking as I mentioned earlier, but also to "mind-reading," "folk psychology," "social intelligence," "human sense,"[41] "mentalizing,"[6] and "mindness."[42]

Earlier I quoted the biologist, George Williams, and his anti-mentalistic comments. Nevertheless, and notwithstanding his radical rejection of all things mental, he nicely illustrates what I mean by mentalism when he goes on to confess that he feels "intuitively that my daughter's horse has a mind. I am even more convinced that my daughter has." Although he immediately adds that "Neither conclusion is supported by reason or evidence," even this militant anti-mentalist is forced to admit that the notion of his daughter's—and even a horse's—mind makes intuitive sense to him.[38b] Such an implicit, instinctive sense of other people's minds could be called a theory of mind, but when authorities such as Williams combine it with what is much more obviously a principled, thought-out theory against the use of mental terminology, *mentalism* seems a better term to describe it. In other words, people such as Williams can hold anti-mentalistic theories, but—unlike someone who is autistic—can still be able to practise normal mentalism understood as *an innate ability to intuit others' motives, state of mind, and feelings.*

Kanner commented that an "amazing lack of awareness of the feelings of others, who seem not to be conceived of as persons like the self, runs like a red thread through our cases"[43] and more recent authorities point out that, although individual autistic children differ in their intelligence, capacity for learning and use of language, all are abnormal in the ways in which they relate to other people.[18b] Perhaps not surprisingly then, autism has been portrayed as a disorder of empathy,[44] and more recently, *empathizing* has been suggested as another alternative to theory of mind defined as "the drive to identify another person's emotions and thoughts, and to respond to these with an appropriate emotion."[45] Clearly, this is intended to avoid exactly the same difficulties with theory of mind that we have just been looking at, and adds an emotional, implicit dimension to mind-reading understood in opposition to mind-blindness. According to this way of looking at things, the difference between the false belief and false photo test is that the Sally-Anne situation demands an ability to empathize with Sally, whereas judging the positions of moved objects does not involve any kind of empathizing.

But as Temple Grandin's remarks above again show, it is not empathizing as such that characterizes her autistic deficit, but her inability *to empathize with human beings.* As we saw, she has if anything an enhanced ability to empathize with animals and their feelings, but this seems to contribute little or nothing to her ability to understand people:

> The work I do is emotionally difficult for many people, and I am often asked how I can care about animals and be involved in slaughtering them. Perhaps because I am less emotional than other people, it is easier for me to face the idea of death… However, I am not just an objective, unfeeling observer; I have a sensory empathy for the cattle. When they remain calm I feel calm, and when something goes wrong that causes pain, I also feel their pain. I tune in to what the actual sensations are like to the cattle rather than having the idea of death rile up my emotions. My goal is to reduce suffering and improve the way farm animals are treated.[30c]

Again, cases can be found where autistics empathize to an astonishing extent not merely with animals, but even with totally inanimate or even abstract objects as the following quotation from another autistic shows:

> I remember being very upset about being introduced to the spelling concept of dropping the "e," if one exists, at the end of a word when one adds the suffix -ing. My concern over the letter was so great that I talked about it during a counselling session with a psychiatrist I was seeing at the time. He drew the letter of concern on a piece of paper and let it fall to the floor. I had to go to rescue it. I truly felt bad for this letter that was cast aside and dropped to the floor.[46a]

According to another:

> I would feel absolutely terrible if I did anything that disappointed someone or hurt someone's feelings. So I did have the ability to feel empathy and guilt; once in the third grade, for

instance, I cried uncontrollably after killing a few ants in my room. But what I lacked was an ability to predict how others would be affected by my actions (and inaction). I had difficulty seeing things from someone else's point of view.[47]

Not simply feeling empathy, but actually empathizing—albeit without any awareness of doing so—is vividly reported by another autistic:

Whenever I get a very strong emotion and I am not clear as to where it comes from, I have to consider whether someone I am in communication with is displaying a similar emotion, and I am picking it up from them. Sometimes I feel as if I am fused with that other person's emotions and can't separate myself from them.

One time when I was talking to my mother on the phone while at college, I got an overwhelming feeling of blackness when I talked to her and became very sad. Thinking about this, I realized that I didn't have anything to be terribly sad about and perhaps had fused myself with an emotion from her. I called my mother back and found out that she was terribly sad.[46b]

You could say this is *mind-blind* or *behavioural empathizing* because it lacks an insight into whose feelings are involved, and why. This in turn suggests that it is the mentalistic aspect of being able to empathize with other human beings that is lacking in autism, not simply empathy as such. To the extent that this is implied and assumed in the use of "empathizing" in this context, it could be seen—along with "theory of mind," "mentalizing," and "folk psychology"—as an alternative formulation for what I would prefer to call mentalism. Nevertheless, a recent study points out that previous research on adults has predominantly focused on cognitive empathy, effectively ignoring the role of empathic feelings. The researchers administered the Interpersonal Reactivity Index, a multi-dimensional measure of empathy, to 21 adult high-functioning autistics and 21 matched controls. The results suggested that while the autistic group scored lower on measures of cognitive empathy and theory of mind, their scores were no different from controls on a measure of empathic concern, and in fact were higher than controls on another of personal distress.[48]

A study comparing violent with non-violent paranoid schizophrenics found that "violence in paranoid patients with schizophrenia appears to be associated with the combination of hostility towards others, good mentalizing abilities and poor empathy." Furthermore, the authors speculate that "It is possible that violence in paranoid schizophrenia can be attributed, in addition to deficits in empathic abilities, to the ability to use mentalizing abilities to manipulate and deceive their victims."[49] If this is so—and we shall see later that there are good reasons for thinking that it is—then empathizing and mentalizing are clearly different things, and should not be confused. Indeed, another recent study found that empathizing appears to be essentially equivalent to *agreeableness* in the five-factor model of personality, something you would not expect to find in violent paranoiacs, however you defined "agreeable."[50]

Much the same is true of psychopaths, who, as Alfonso Troisi points out, are frequently deceitful and manipulative in order to gain personal profit. Even though they may display a glib, superficial charm, psychopaths tend to be callous, cynical, and contemptuous of the feelings, rights, and suffering of others. In other words, what characterizes their disorder is an absence of empathy. However, this lack of empathy is not associated with any other deficit of social cognition. On the contrary, psychopaths are capable of accurately assessing the costs and benefits of short-term social interactions, correctly reading others' behaviour, utilizing self-monitoring information to alter their strategies, and successfully disguising their intentions. Indeed, experimental studies have confirmed that there is no impairment in theory of mind in psychopaths. Again, as Troisi also points out, children with Williams syndrome (a rare developmental disorder caused by loss of genes from chromosome 7) have mild-to-moderate mental retardation combined with a high degree of sociability and empathy for others. Nevertheless, this remarkable degree of social development is coupled with a deficit in the ability to interpret other people's behaviour in mental terms. Despite their increased empathy and social gregariousness, individuals with Williams syndrome have mentalistic deficits. So whereas psychopaths show a profound empathic dysfunction but no indications of impairment with theory of mind, individuals with Williams syndrome show abnormally high levels of empathy combined with defective mentalism.[51] In short, psychopaths are not autistic as they would have to be if a deficit in empathy alone was what was critical in autism. Williams syndrome children, on the other hand, have mentalistic deficits comparable to those seen in autistic children, but are nonetheless highly empathic—again suggesting that a lack of empathy is not the central factor in autism. On the contrary, what all these findings argue is that the essential deficit in autism is what I am calling *mentalism*.

From attention to intention

A plausible evolutionary origin for mentalism can be found in *direction of gaze*.[52] Primates (monkeys, apes, and man) have forward-rotated eyes, often to the extent that the visual axes are practically parallel (as in the human case). The benefit of this is excellent stereoscopic vision, which would have served their ancestors well in the arboreal habitat in which primates first evolved. However, the cost is a notable reduction in the visual field, particularly when compared with the almost panoramic view enjoyed by many mammals whose eyes are placed much more to the side of the head and whose visual fields may not even overlap at the front. The result is that primates have become more social (and more vocal) so as to gain the advantage of many different pairs of eyes. Primates have also compensated for their restricted field of view by becoming sensitive to the direction of gaze of others. This is particularly important, because not only can it tell you where the others in the group are looking, it can also give useful clues about what they are seeing, and their state of mind and intentions.[53]

In other primates the outer surface of the eye is often the same colour as the rest of the face. In many species of birds the whole eye is effectively camouflaged by being the same colour as the surrounding plumage (in the case of the tern, a black cap reaching down just far enough to hide the eyes). However, human beings have a white area—the *sclera*—surrounding the iris which may have evolved to reveal direction of gaze by giving the eyes a target-like appearance with their black pupils surrounded by a coloured iris surrounded in turn by the white sclera. Indeed, a series of experiments suggest that, along with the sclera, we have evolved a dedicated expert brain system for monitoring direction of gaze using the whites of the eyes as the principal clues.[54] The more white of eye that was visible in fearful expressions, the greater was the response of the *amygdalas*. These paired, almond-like organs lie left and right deep within what has been called the emotional brain[55] and are implicated in fear responses; and, as these experiments show, respond particularly to the eyes.[56] A study of a woman with damage to the amygdalas which impaired her ability to detect fear on other people's faces found that when instructed to look at the other person's eyes, her recognition of fear became normal. Such findings suggest that normal people pay particular attention to the eyes when looking at others' faces, and especially to detect a basic warning signal such as fear.[57]

The primate researcher Daniel Povinelli points out that appreciating the idea that others "see" is fundamental to "the entire question of theory of mind—at least with respect to our human understanding of the mind"—or, in other words, to mentalism. He adds that:

> most of our social interactions begin with determination of the attentional state of our communicative partners, and from that point forward we constantly monitor their attentional focus throughout the interaction. Nothing can disrupt a social interaction more quickly than realizing that someone is no longer looking at you.[58]

Indeed, eyes are often called "the windows of the soul," and detection of another person's direction of gaze and shifts of attention have been described as "the linchpin of social cognition."[59] It has been proposed that young children first experience the "meeting of minds" which epitomizes mentalism when they shift their attention to join that of someone else as indicated by the other person's direction of gaze.[60] In other words, where the eyes lead, the mind follows, and what might at first have seemed an after-effect of social living, or a trivial detail in it—direction of gaze—now begins to take on the appearance of a central, fundamental, and strategic adaptation.

Look Me in the Eye is the title of a recent best-selling account of the author's life with Asperger's syndrome,[61] and in his original paper Asperger observed that "The characteristic peculiarities of eye gaze are never absent" in autistics. He went on, "From the first moment when an infant can properly 'look,' that is, from the third month of life, and well before there is any verbal expression, the majority of his social relations are based on eye gaze. How the small child drinks in the world with his eyes!" But with autistic children:

> there is a fundamental difference. Hardly ever does their glance fix brightly on a particular object or person as a sign of lively attention and contact... The disturbance is particularly clear when they are in conversation with others. Glance does not meet glance as it does when unity of conversational contact is established. When we talk to someone we do not only "answer" with words, but we "answer" with our look... A large part of social relationship is conducted through eye gaze, but such relationships are of no interest to the autistic child. Therefore, the child does not generally bother to look at the person who is speaking. The gaze goes past the other person or, at most, touches them incidentally in passing.[62]

Temple Grandin observes that the eyes of autistic children "seem to see everything except the one who is speaking to them,"[63] and recent research has wholly corroborated Asperger's original finding. Indeed, direction of gaze turns out to be a better measure of mentalizing ability than the standard verbal response in tests of false belief such as the Sally-Anne scenario, and is even more discriminating between autistic and non-autistic mentally handicapped children.[6d] However, the deficit is not simply a perceptual one: autistic children matched with controls show similar reflexive responses to shifts in direction of gaze in laboratory experiments. Like chimpanzees, autistic children can follow a shift in direction of another's gaze which indicates the location of an object. This rules out the possibility that autistic deficits in gaze-monitoring can be accounted for by a purely perceptual impairment in responding to eye-movements in others. But also like chimps, autistic children do not appear to interpret or understand the meaning of such shifts in mental terms such as attention or emotion[64,65] (see the box on p. 67: Do chimps interpret gaze as we do?).

Direction of gaze normally reveals the current state of an organism's attention: in other words, it reveals its probable current awareness. Furthermore, this can betray more than merely the direction in which it is looking, or even the exact target of its concern. Direction of gaze can also disclose much about an organism's state of mind. A fixed, unblinking stare at an object can reveal a high level of concern, such as when a predator is stalking prey, or prey being stalked have seen the predator and are apprehensively monitoring it. By contrast, an unfocused, drifting direction of gaze which wanders over a large area can indicate a relaxed, unconcerned frame of mind, for example on the part of prey who have not yet spotted a predator or predators who are not looking for prey. Yet again, a probing, restless scanning of an area can reveal that the organism is searching for something in a state of anxiety or anticipation, as when prey know that a predator is near by but can't tell exactly where it is, or when a predator has temporarily lost its prey but knows it to be in the immediate vicinity.

Such examples as these show what a short step it is to go from monitoring an organism's attention to beginning to detect and even predict its intention: in other words, extrapolating from its current awareness to its next likely action. Furthermore, these examples also suggest the evolutionary forces that might have been at work in bringing about such a development. A prey animal that correctly anticipated the next move of a predator, for example in predicting where and when the predator would pounce, could easily owe its life to that ability. Such a

Do chimps interpret gaze as we do?

Having established by experiment that chimpanzees and humans share a common behavioural system related to gaze-following, the primate researcher Daniel Povinelli and his co-workers asked the more central question of how this similarity might help us to understand whether or not chimpanzees appreciate what others "see." For example, in a situation in which the experimenter glanced towards something behind a partition, the apes leaned forward and looked around to the back of it, exactly as if they understood that the experimenter could not see through the partition. However, the researchers also tried to find out if chimpanzees understood the distinction between someone who could see them and someone who could not. Chimpanzees routinely beg by extending an up-turned hand towards a human and looking into their eyes, and this seemed an ideal context in which to answer the question. The researchers noticed that their chimps would often play by putting objects such as plastic buckets or bags over their heads to prevent themselves seeing, and then try to find their way around blind-folded, so to speak. Indeed, they noticed that the apes would occasionally stop and peek out, suggesting that they were fully aware of what they were doing.

This natural behaviour was used in an experiment in which a chimpanzee encountered two familiar researchers from whom they could beg, but only one of whom could see them, thanks to having their back towards the animal or being blind-folded in various ways. The finding was that the chimpanzees were just as likely to gesture to the person who could not see them as to the person who could. However, in the case of the experimenter with their back to the animal, the apes only ever gestured to the experimenter facing them. The researchers noticed that their chimpanzees would often turn and look over their shoulders at another animal behind them and so this natural behaviour was used in a new experiment in which both experimenters sat with their backs to the experimental animal, but one looked over their shoulder at it and the other did not. To the surprise of the researchers, the apes did not prefer to gesture to the person who could see them. To be absolutely sure, a final series of experiments had the experimenter holding a screen in front of their face or to the side of it, looking towards or away from the experimental animal, or looking through a screen with eye-holes as opposed to holding the same screen next to the face but with eyes clearly closed. All the results confirmed the finding that the chimpanzees were just as likely to choose the person who could not see them as the person who could, and that they were treating the conditions as problems to be solved by comparing physical postures, not by reasoning about who could see them.

However, one animal, Megan, performed much better than others, and eventually learnt the correct responses to the experimenter with eyes open or closed. According to the most parsimonious interpretation of all the experimental findings, the apes were learning a set of procedural rules as the basis for their choices in which the experimenter's bodily orientation was most important, face was less important, and eyes were least important of all. If this were true, then the frontal aspect of a person would be more important than whether the person's eyes were open. To test this, the chimp was presented with a choice between someone facing towards them with their eyes shut, and someone facing away from them but looking at them over the shoulder with open eyes. The parsimonious explanation predicted that the apes would prefer the facing-with-eyes-shut experimenter to the looking-over-the-shoulder-with-eyes-open one, and the results strikingly confirmed this. Reviewing other studies and their own experiments, Povinelli and his colleagues go on to conclude that

- chimpanzees do not interpret the pointing-like gestures of themselves or others in the manner that we do;

- although they are quite sensitive to the behaviour of others, chimpanzees do not interpret behaviour in mentalistic terms;

- chimpanzees do not draw on underlying intentions in judgements of accidental as opposed to deliberate actions.[1]

development is an obvious candidate for so-called *arms-race evolutionary escalation:* a situation in which better prediction of predators' intentions on the part of prey leads to predators having to become more resourceful in outwitting such anticipation, which leads to prey having to become even better at predicting intention, and so on, in principle ad infinitum—and in practice until both sides have become very good at monitoring and detecting the other's intentions.

Detection, prediction, and interpretation of intention are an obvious second stage in the further development of mentalism. A critical mentalistic deficit in ASD linked to failure to monitor gaze is an inability to judge and interpret others' intentions: so-called *intentionality detection.* Autistic people often fail to pick up cues directed at them in otherwise obvious and unmistakeable ways, and are poor at interpreting body language or judging the implications of others' statements and behaviour. Where language is concerned, this is because human beings normally do not use words completely literally, and expect communications to be relevant to the speaker, their state of mind, knowledge, and beliefs—including, as we have seen, false ones. Consequently autistic people tend to use language more literally than normal, and to misinterpret meanings which rely on understanding an expression relative to another person's intention or point of view. For example, a young autistic woman is said to have actually painted the flowers at an art class rather than make a painting of them, and another became alarmed when told that she would be "sleeping on the train" rather than in a bed inside the train. Again, a young man with autism and a reputation for taking things said to him literally spent all day travelling to deliver a letter he had been asked to post to a friend. As Patricia Howlin remarks, "This literal response to language can also make individuals sound abrupt or even rude at times. A student called Eric, when asked what year his birthday was by his new tutor, looked at her in incomprehension and replied with scorn, 'Well, every year of course!'."[66]

Families with autistic children who have been taught to answer the telephone sometimes report that the child will reply to the inquiry of a caller, "Is so-and-so in?" with a simple "Yes!" but then replace the receiver, evidently thinking that a correct factual response is all that is required in such a situation![67] Another common example is provided in this reminiscence from an autistic's autobiography: "During the third grade I remember a classmate telling me that he felt like a pizza. I couldn't figure out what made him feel like a pizza. Eventually I realized he meant that he felt like eating a pizza."[46c] Indeed, all failures to understand or respond to others' feelings and expressions, verbal or otherwise, are failures to interpret intention correctly—at least if we assume that the basic intention of any expressive communication is to be correctly understood. To this extent, mentalistic deficits in autistics' language and conversation skills could be seen as symptomatic of a fundamental shortcoming where interpretation of intention is concerned.

Recently brain-scanning has suggested that in order to predict others' behaviour we probably put ourselves in their shoes and unconsciously run through the same processes in our own minds as they do in theirs. So-called *mirror neurons* are known to be excited in parts of the cortex involved with the action when someone sees someone else performing an act, and shortfalls in corresponding areas might explain some mentalistic deficits in autism.[68] A sub-circuit known as the ventral pre-motor cortex appears to be involved with predicting others' behaviour, while another area called the dorsal pre-motor cortex plans the actual execution of it. Some of the brain regions involved in prediction have been found to be abnormal in the brains of people with autism, suggesting where autistics' difficulties with understanding others' intentions and predicting their behaviour may be found.[69] Specifically, a key component of the mirror-neuron system (brain area BA 44, or the so-called *pars opercularis*) has been found to be less active than normal in autistics imitating or viewing emotional expressions. However, the same area has been found to be hyper-active in schizophrenia in response to facial expression of emotion.[70]

You could sum up this and the first chapter by saying that what has emerged from our consideration of ASD is the possibility that there are two, rather than just one, cognitive systems in human beings, what I called *things-thinking* as opposed to *people-thinking*, or *mechanistic* as compared to *mentalistic* cognition. We saw in this chapter that serious deficits in mentalism characterize autism and explain the social and psychological shortcomings of people with ASD. However, the first chapter revealed that in some cases at least remarkable mechanistic skills can emerge as compensations in autistics. This suggests that rather than being unitary, human cognition resembles the situation now known to exist in relation to sight and which I briefly mentioned in the Introduction. Just as disorders such as visual agnosia and optic ataxia reveal that we have parallel, independent systems for vision, so ASD reveals that we have a similar situation with regard to cognition. In the case of vision, one system, the so-called *how system*, is concerned with manipulation of objects, but a completely different one, the *what system*, is adapted to recognizing and identifying them, and uses a completely different neural pathway to the visual cortex in the brain.[71] In a similar way, you might say that people-thinking or mentalism is a form of cognition concerned with interacting with other human beings, and with interpreting their behaviour in terms of mental factors such as intention, emotion, or belief. Things-thinking, or mechanistic cognition, on the other hand, is a system we evolved for interacting with the physical, non-human environment, and as such is independent of mentalism, explaining why astonishing mechanistic skills can occasionally appear alongside general mentalistic disability.[72]

However, we are only at the beginning of our exploration of mentalism, and readers who persevere to the end of this book will find it developing right up to the final page. In this chapter we looked at deficits in mentalism and the way in which monitoring of gaze can lead to interpretation of intention, but in the next two chapters we need to examine what happens when mentalism runs amok and proliferates to become a veritable cancer of the mind.

Chapter 3

From Gaze
to Grandeur

The mention of hyper-active mirror neurons in schizophrenia at the end of the last chapter is the first hint of the theme to which I will devote this and the next one. As we shall see, some striking contrasts begin to appear once you compare the deficient mentalism of autism with what you find in psychotic disorders such as paranoid schizophrenia, where mentalizing is taken to bizarre extremes. We can make a start by looking a bit more closely at direction of gaze.

Delusions of gaze

In his book, *The Sense of Being Stared At and Other Aspects of the Extended Mind,* Rupert Sheldrake reports that he often turns around to find "someone staring at me."[1a] He adds that, according to his own surveys of adults in Europe and in the United States, 70 to 90 per cent said that they had sensed when they were being looked at from behind. Indeed, it is the considered view of this author that such a sense of being spied on can even be derived from closed-circuit TV cameras and other types of remote imaging, and he provides many anecdotes which he believes illustrate the point. He also includes a lengthy discussion of the "evil eye" as an instance of "the fact that people do seem able to influence others by their looks."[1b]

As Sheldrake himself points out, people's awareness of being looked at by others could be explained by sensitivity to sounds or movements in their peripheral field of vision, or to other subtle sensory clues, perceived subliminally. People may often turn around but only remember the occasions when someone was looking at them, and forget all the times they turned and no one was there. Indeed, he adds that this illusion would be enhanced by the tendency for our visual systems to detect movement. As we turn around to look behind us, if someone behind us sees us moving, we are likely to attract their attention, and so our eyes meet.[1c]

In a series of laboratory experiments, subjects were repeatedly shown images for a fraction of a second separated by blanks. Sometimes the images remained the same, but sometimes they were subtly different. In the latter case, about a third of the experimental subjects reported a feeling that the image had changed before they could identify what the change was. But in control trials the same people proved that they could reliably tell when no change had occurred. According to the researcher, "this explains a lot of the belief in a sixth sense;" and he adds that "Our visual system can produce a gut feeling that something has changed even if we cannot visualize that change mentally."[2]

Yet according to Sheldrake, there is not just a sixth sense, but a seventh also—one identified with what he calls "the extended mind." Indeed, Sheldrake is even prepared to challenge the conventional scientific theory of vision seen as resulting from light being registered by cells in the retina which then transmit nerve impulses to the brain. He dismisses this as nothing more than "a dogma accepted on the authority of science." In his view, "Educated people have been brought up to believe that their minds are located inside their heads, and that all their perceptions and experiences are somehow concentrated in their brains." He goes on to "propose that vision involves a two-way process, an inward movement of light, and an outward projection of images."[1d]

Of course, there is much truth in the claim that vision—like most other perceptions, but probably much more so—involves a two-way process in the sense that what we see is demonstrably constructed by our brains somewhat in the way in which computers generate virtual images. Certainly, whatever we are conscious of seeing is not what appears directly on our retinas. On the contrary, retinal images are inverted, have a significant hole near the centre (the blind-spot) and are processed separately as left and right halves of the visual field in opposite hemispheres of the brain. Only in our subjective, mental perception are the two halves of the visual field seamlessly joined, put the right way up, and shown without any obvious sign of a blind-spot. Furthermore, there is evidence that some visual hallucinations definitely originate within the visual system itself, and represent artefacts of the visual processing mechanism projected out into the virtual reality that our brains construct.[3]

But this is evidently not what Sheldrake means. He goes on to say that "This outward perception occurs within mental fields, which I call perceptual fields."[1e] Indeed, according to Sheldrake's theory, "Mental fields that extend beyond the brain may also explain telepathy," and he adds that "our own telepathic powers are generally poor compared with those of dogs, cats, horses, parrots, and other species of mammals and birds."[1f] He speculates that "They may have a seventh sense that enables them to detect threatening intentions. They may be able to sense when a would-be killer is looking at them, even if they have not yet detected the predator through sight, smell or hearing."[1g] He adds that "This is a potentially dangerous thought. It would be much less disturbing to dismiss the sense of being stared at as an illusion—or even as a form of paranoia."[1h]

Certainly, feelings of being watched, stared at, or spied on remarkably similar to those reported by Sheldrake are common in paranoid schizophrenia. Daniel Paul Schreber (1842–1911) has been called "the most frequently quoted patient in psychiatry,"[4] and his autobiographical account of his paranoid psychosis "the most written-about document in all psychiatric literature"[5] (see the box on p. 76: The Schreber case). Schreber's book included a section in it entitled "Direction of Gaze" long before the subject had been introduced into discussions of mentalism. Writing about his psychiatrist, Schreber comments:

The Schreber case

Daniel Paul Schreber was born in Leipzig, Germany, in 1842. His father was Moritz Schreber (1808–61), a famous orthopaedist who wrote many influential books on gymnastics and child-rearing, and also gave his name to Schrebergärten—the German for what the English call "allotments" (plots of land for urban residents to till). His elder brother by three years, Gustav, was a judge, and committed suicide in 1877 following tertiary syphilis and associated mental complications.

Paul Schreber (as he was called in his lifetime) qualified as a lawyer and married in 1878, but no children survived a number of pregnancies. He first fell ill in 1884, aged 42, having stood unsuccessfully as a candidate for the *Reichstag*, and at the time was a judge presiding over the *Landgericht*, an inferior court at Chemnitz. He was admitted to the Sonnenstein Asylum and later to the Leipzig Psychiatric Clinic, but was discharged in the summer of 1885. In 1886 he returned to a similar judicial position in Leipzig to the one he had previously occupied.

In 1893 he was appointed a Presiding Judge of Appeal but shortly after was re-admitted to the Leipzig clinic, and later was transferred to the Lindenhof and later the Sonnenstein asylums. Between 1900 and 1902 he wrote his *Denkwürdigkeiten eines Nervenkranken*[1] (later translated into English as *Memoirs of My Nervous Illness*), and took legal action which eventually secured his discharge at the end of 1902, when he was 60. The *Denkwürdigkeiten* was published in 1903. In 1907 Schreber's mother died aged 92 and his wife suffered a stroke. Shortly afterwards Schreber was admitted to an asylum for the last time and died there in 1911, the year in which Sigmund Freud published an interpretation of the case.[2]

Freud is not the only author who has tried to psychoanalyse Schreber. A number of post-Freudian psychoanalysts have attempted to interpret Schreber's illness in terms of his childhood and upbringing and to portray his father as a domestic tyrant.[3] But recent biographical research has shown that there is in reality little or no evidence that Schreber's illness can be attributed to his treatment by his parents, peers, or society at large. Nevertheless, as the author of this research remarks, the newly discovered biographical material on Schreber has nothing to say either for or against the merits of Freud's own interpretation of the case, which entirely omits any discussion of the issue of Schreber's childhood and family.[4] Schreber appears to have suffered from paranoid schizophrenia, a disorder with a rate of incidence and unknown (but predominantly genetic) origin comparable to that of autism. But as we shall see in Chapter 6, Freud's central observation fits nicely with new insights into the evolutionary genetics of sex, autism, and psychosis.

I…gained the impression that Professor Fleschig had secret designs against me; this seemed confirmed when I asked him during a personal visit whether he really honestly believed that I could be cured, and he held out certain hopes, *but could no longer*—at least so it seemed to me—*look me straight in the eye.*[6a]

Another schizophrenic objected to the "eye-language" used by the judge who examined him and to the fact that "before I entered my flat somebody always had to annoy me with some meaningless glance,"[7a] while yet another described being continuously monitored by a "Watcher-Machine."[8a] Indeed, delusions of being watched, stared at, or spied on are so common in paranoid schizophrenia that Harry Stack Sullivan (1892–1949), a psychiatrist famed for treating schizophrenics, advised his colleagues to sit at the side of such a patient rather than facing them, never to look them in the eyes, and to address them in the third person![9]

Recent laboratory experiments have provided the first direct scientific evidence that people with schizophrenia are unusually sensitive to the direction of another person's gaze. Furthermore, the researchers point out that the social deficits seen in schizophrenia could be the outcome of such an over-sensitivity—particularly in preventing them making accurate inferences about what another person is likely to be thinking.[10] In other words, both excessive sensitivity and insensitivity can result in perceptual deficits. This clearly happens in the case of sensitivity to light or sound causing visual or auditory impairments, and it can just as easily occur in relation to social inferences: too much sensitivity can be as bad as too little.

Schreber also often railed at the sun, which he saw as God's eye or as a living being who spoke to him in human language. According to his psychiatrist, "the patient used to stand for a long time motionless in one place, staring into the sun, at the same time grimacing in an extraordinary way or bellowing very loudly at the sun with threats and imprecations, usually repeating endlessly one and the same phrase..."[6b] Although impossible before his illness, in the course of it Schreber believed he could look at the sun without blinking—indeed, the sun's rays visibly paled before him when he did so. Nor was Schreber the only case to show this particular symptom. There are much more recent reports of retinal damage in sun-gazing paranoid schizophrenics.[11,12] Indeed, one study suggests that Schreber's claims may have had a factual basis in the finding that a sub-group of schizophrenic patients have an abnormality in retinal neurons which reduces sensitivity to light.[13] And similar sentiments to Schreber's about the sun can even be found in psychotics with manic-depression (bipolar disorder: a diagnosis which could well have been one of schizophrenia if the patient had lived in the United States at the time rather than in England[14]):

> The sun came to have an extraordinary effect on me. It seemed to be charged with all power; not merely to symbolize God, but actually to be God. Phrases like: "Light of the World," "The Sun of Righteousness that Setteth Nevermore," etc., ran through my head without ceasing, and the mere sight of the sun was sufficient greatly to intensify this manic excitement under which I was labouring. I was impelled to address the sun as a personal god, and to evolve from it a ritual of sun worship.[15a]

At the very least, an interesting contrast emerges between autism and psychosis where monitoring gaze is concerned. As we can now begin to see, where autistics have serious deficits in monitoring and inter-preting gaze, paranoiacs show delusional excesses. Rupert Sheldrake's book on the sense of being stared at suggests that even quite normal people can believe that they are supernaturally sensitive to direction of gaze. Indeed, there are even cases where the deranged sensitivity applies to the direction of your own gaze: "I was myself a camera. The views of people that I obtained through my own eyes were being recorded elsewhere to some kind of three-dimensional film."[8b] And cases can be found of psychotic patients who share Sheldrake's theory of vision, believing that they "transmit" their visual sense so that their eyes are directed outward and touch things directly: "Upon looking at a landscape, for example, she carries away with her some of the actual material of which it is constituted."[8c]

The why and how of passion and persecution

A similar pattern of deficient response in autism but hyper-sensitivity in psychosis can be found in relation to detection of intention in para-noiacs such as Schreber. According to him, "All human activity near me, every view of nature in the garden or from my window stirs certain thoughts in me; when I then hear 'Why only' or 'Why because' spoken into my nerves, I am forced or at least stimulated in immeasurably greater degree than other human beings to contemplate the reason or purpose behind them." As a case in point, he mentions watching workmen in the asylum and adds that "I am unavoidably forced to give myself an account of the reason and purpose of every single job." The result is that:

> Being continually forced to trace the causal relation of every happening, every feeling, and every idea has given me gradu-ally deeper insight into the essence of almost all natural phe-nomena and aspects of human activity in art, science, etc., than is achieved by people who do not think it worth while to think about ordinary everyday occurrences.

Even being introduced to a "Mr. Schneider" arouses the question of "why he is called Mr. Schneider? This very peculiar question 'why' occupies my nerves automatically—particularly if the question is repeated several times—until their thinking is diverted into another direction."[6c]

Nor is this a symptom confined to Schreber. A schizophrenic named Anne is reported to be "always asking herself why, for instance, one does something in one way and not another; how one says thank you or washes oneself; which clothes one should wear, on what occasion, and why?"[16] Another who successfully cured himself of delusional thinking did so in part by asking *how?* instead of *why?*: "Why? can easily be supported by ill-reasoning. A person's answer to why he or she is being persecuted can itself be a delusional idea. Instead, one must explore How?—how he or she is being subject to others' schemes."[17]

Although these schizophrenics' compulsion to ask *why?* is a characteristically exaggerated one, it is not pathological in itself. The ability to ask why someone did—or, just as easily, did not—do something follows as a natural development of prediction of other people's intention. Once we begin to predict what people may do next, we are also bound to ask why they fail to do what we expect, or do what we did not expect. This leads us into interpretation of intention, suggesting that schizophrenics' compulsive posing of the question *why?* is only an exaggeration or overstatement of a normal, mentalistic response. Indeed, such a mentalistic concern with meaning, motive, and interpretation immediately suggests why the mother of a pair of autistic boys reports that neither of them ever used the word *why?*[18a] If this line of reasoning is correct, it was yet another manifestation of the characteristic mind-blindness of autistics and stands in striking contrast to the perpetual *whys?* addressed to themselves by schizophrenics such as Schreber. So too does the following observation by the same mother, which includes not just the whys and wherefores of mentalism but the value judgements that so often follow them in normal minds:

The boys have plenty of aggravating habits of their own, of course, but they don't whinge, compete, squabble or blame other people for their own shortcomings. They don't exaggerate minor injuries or try to get someone else into trouble… I never hear those tiresome phrases like "It's not fair" or "He started it" or "Are we nearly there?" … They may get cross with me when I thwart their desires, but they never criticize me, or anyone else.[18b]

As an adult autistic puts it:

A lot of things to me just are—not good or bad—they just exist. I often wonder why others seem to exert a lot of energy deciding whether others are good, bad, ugly or beautiful. This is a skill that I don't seem to have nor care to cultivate. This does not mean I am unaware of the difference between right and wrong or bad and good… It just seems to me that a lot of what goes on in the daily judging of others and their actions is not worth the energy expended in doing so.[19]

But contrast this non-judgemental and accepting autistic attitude with Schreber's, who remarks that:

It is demanded of me to relate to myself everything that happens or is spoken by human beings, particularly during my regular walks in the garden of the Asylum. Hence my stay in the Asylum's garden has always been very troublesome, and led in previous years to scenes of violence between myself and other patients.[6d]

And not just other inmates he might meet in the garden; Schreber carried his antagonistic attitude to others to the point of condemning even new acquaintances with reproaches he harboured against old ones:

The senior attendant of the Asylum deserves special mention. On the very day of my arrival the voices said that he was identical with my fellow lodger v. W.; he was said to have given false evidence about me in some State inquiry, either on purpose or through carelessness, and particularly to have accused me of masturbation; as a punishment for this he had now to be my servant...[6e]

The *Memoirs* is full of such recriminations and seldom mentions anyone without some kind of moral censure or personal criticism: the exact contrary of autistic unconcern with others and indifference to making judgements that I illustrated just now. Indeed, Schreber's book is itself a manifestation of the litigiousness so often found in paranoia (and exacerbated by delusions of persecution). Here we should recall that Schreber wrote his book in large part to try to secure his release in the courts, adding a legal essay on *In what circumstances can a person considered insane be detained in an Asylum against his declared will*, along with legally argued grounds for appeal. To this extent, the entire work is one of litigation and most of it is concerned with the injustice of which not just the whole human race but God himself was guilty in Schreber's judgement.

The previous quotation from Schreber illustrates another very common symptom of paranoia in the voices which he continually heard—often accusing him of wrong doing and always voicing criticisms or complaints of one kind or another. These frequently harangued him with insulting imputations, referring to him as "Miss Schreber" and enquiring "Is he not unmanned yet?" At other times he was called "The Prince of Hell" and subject to abuse too vile to be printed. Alternatively, the voices would constantly question him, not only with the insistent *whys?* mentioned just now, but with comments that someone else might easily have made, such as "What do you really mean?" or "We have had this before!"[6f] Schreber asks us to:

Imagine a human being planting himself before another and molesting him all day long with unconnected phrases such as the rays use towards me ("If only my," "This then was only," "You are to," etc.). Can one expect anything else of a person spoken to in this manner but that he would throw the other out of the house with a few fitting words of abuse? I also ought to have the right of being master in my own head against the intrusion of strangers.[6g]

Perhaps so, but Schreber's protest suggests that sensitivity to the comments of others is such an innate, evolved part of normal human mentalism that it can become pathologically sensitive, and operate without external cause, such as pain reactions in phantom limbs, or tinnitus (ringing) in the ears, or phosphenes (patches of light) in closed eyes. As such it would qualify as yet another symptom of psychosis which contrasts with the marked insensitivity to mentalism seen in autistics. Thanks to their deficits in mentalism, people with autistic tendencies not only fail to understand mental terminology in full, but are often remarkably immune to its intended effects, so that other people perceive them to be callous, self-centred, and insensitive to the wishes and needs of other people. Indeed, far from hearing imagined voices, a common complaint about autistics is that they often seem not to listen to real ones, with the result that autistics are often mistakenly thought to be deaf. According to one: "Autism makes me hear other people's words but be unable to know what the words mean. Or autism lets me speak my own words without knowing what I am saying or even thinking."[20a]

Paranoid hyper-sensitivity to voices recalls the similar sensitivity to direction of gaze mentioned just now. The researchers who first demonstrated the latter in the laboratory go on to suggest that people with schizophrenia may be "hyper-primed" to detect other people's intentions, and clearly the same could apply to what people say to schizophrenics. They add that this is consistent with several other lines of evidence that these individuals "over-perceive" other people's intentions. For example, they note that patients with schizophrenia show an enhanced tendency to link perceived intentions with consequences, and to judge the movements of objects as more affected by the actions of people than do healthy controls.[10]

Over-sensitivity to intention can take two forms, depending on whether the intention detected is positive or negative. A schizophrenic patient illustrates both in his recollection that "I was hardly out of the house when somebody prowled round me, stared at me and tried to put a cyclist in my way. A few steps on, a schoolgirl smiled at me encouragingly…"[7b] Positive over-interpretation of others' intentions underlies *erotomania*, otherwise known as *de Clérambault's syndrome* or *erotomanic type delusional disorder.*[21]*

The latter term describes how the subject delusionally believes that others are infatuated or are in love with them, and most sufferers are female.[22] In his memoirs, the painter Salvador Dalí (1904–89) recounts a memorable case of erotomania on the part of a peasant woman from his native town in Spain, Cadaques. Named Lydia, at the age of 20 she had met the Catalan writer, Eugenio d'Ors, and soon afterwards become convinced that he was in love with her, but had to conceal his passion for her in his writings. When d'Ors ignored all her letters, Lydia came to believe that the texts of his daily column in a newspaper were coded replies. And, wonderfully anticipating the concept of mentalism elaborated here, Dalí adds that:

> She would interpret d'Ors's articles as she went along with such felicitous discoveries of coincidence and plays on words that one could not fail to wonder at the bewildering imaginative violence with which the paranoiac spirit can project the image of our inner world upon the outer world, no matter where or in what form or on what pretext…elucidating it word by word in an interpretive delirium so systematic, coherent and dumbfounding that she often verged on genius![23]

However, negative over-valuation of intention is more common—particularly in men—and is seen in the delusions of persecution which are found in so many paranoid psychotics (sometimes along with erotomania). We have already seen that Schreber entertained paranoid feelings

---

* See Ian McEwan's novel, *Enduring Love,* and its useful appendices for some further striking examples to those given here.

about his psychiatrist, Professor Flechsig, remarking that *"right from the beginning the more or less definite intention existed to prevent my sleep and later my recovery from the illness resulting from the insomnia for a purpose which cannot at this stage be further specified."*[6h] But this was just the start of it. Much of Schreber's memoirs are concerned with a much more elaborate delusion of persecution involving what he termed "soul-murder":

> a plot was laid against me (…) the purpose of which was to hand me over to another human being after my nervous illness had been recognized as, or assumed to be, incurable, in such a way that my soul was handed to him, but my body—transformed into a female body…—was then left to that human being for sexual misuse and simply "forsaken," in other words left to rot.

Schreber adds that the "most disgusting" part of this plot was "that my body, after the intended transformation into a female being, was to suffer some sexual abuse, particularly as there had even been talk for some time of my being thrown to the Asylum attendants for this purpose."[6i] Schreber believed that "God himself must have known of the plan, if indeed He was not the instigator, to commit soul murder on me, and to hand over my body in the manner of a female harlot."[6j] Indeed, Schreber's delusional system centred on a universal struggle of good against evil in which Schreber himself "had to fight a sacred battle for the greatest good of mankind," and from which he says that "the picture emerges of a martyrdom which all in all I can only compare with the crucifixion of Jesus Christ."[6k]

So not just in relation to monitoring and interpretation of gaze and voice, but also in relation to imputation and interpretation of intention, paranoid schizophrenics such as Schreber show a striking contrast with autistics. Whereas autistics often ignore intention to the point of seldom if ever asking why someone did or did not do something, and certainly consistently fail to interpret other people's intentions correctly, paranoid schizophrenics do the opposite. As we have seen, Schreber compulsively questioned people's intentions with his unending *whys?*

and showed the proverbial paranoid tendency to feel persecuted by all and sundry while erotomaniacs such as Lydia manage to find hidden attentions to themselves where none was ever intended.

Conspiracies and magic

Yet another autistic deficit is found in *shared attention mechanism*. Autistic people typically do not become involved in group conversations or activities because they usually fail to understand the element of collective psychological activity that is inevitably involved.[24] Temple Grandin noticed:

> a kind of electricity that goes on between people... I have observed that when several people are together and having a good time, their speech and laughter follow a rhythm. They will all laugh together and then talk quietly until the next laughing cycle. I have always had a hard time fitting in with this rhythm, and I usually interrupt conversations without realizing my mistake. The problem is that I can't follow the rhythm.[25]

Indeed, according to Rupert Sheldrake:

> when two people are sitting talking to each other, they are not only linked through the words that are said and heard, but through body language and visual contact, through the shared environment, and so on. If they know each other well, then they are also linked by the emotional bonds between them, and by shared memories. These are all favourable conditions for telepathy, and favour the transfer of feelings, images, concepts and ideas.[1i]

Once again, paranoiacs are characteristically even more mentalistic and are given to imagining not mere telepathic communication, but concerted group activity often expressed as conspiracies against them, as the last quotation above from Schreber illustrates. To take another example, Schreber noticed that "as soon as I sit down on a bench in the garden and…close my eyes, which would in a short time lead to sleep…, *a fly, wasp or bumble-bee or a whole swarm of gnats appears* to prevent me from sleeping." Indeed, he goes on to add that he has "most stringent and convincing proofs of the fact that these beings do not fly towards me by accident, but are beings newly created for my sake each time!"[6l] Even more annoyingly, he also believed that, whenever he wished to go there himself, "some other person in my environment is sent to the lavatory—by exciting the nerves of the person concerned—in order to prevent me from emptying myself." He assures us that "this I have observed so frequently (thousands of times) and so regularly that one can exclude any thought of it being coincidence"![6m]

Paranoid delusions of conspiracy, in other words, can be seen as fantastic elaborations of the shared attention mechanism that enables normal people to understand what goes on in groups, meetings, and social gatherings of all kinds. Although autistics find appreciating what goes on in a group difficult, and often give it little serious thought or attention, paranoid psychotics pay far too much attention to groups, and tend to see conspiracies everywhere and imagine everyone intriguing behind their backs. Indeed, for paranoiacs such as Schreber, life was one vast, cosmic conspiracy implicating not just other human beings both alive and dead, but God himself.

In Schreber's case this tendency went with a readiness to attribute minds—or what he called "bemiracled residues of former human souls"—to birds and trees and generally to mentalize—he would have called it to "spiritualize"—the whole world—not so much theory of mind as *theology of mind.* According to the language of the souls he heard speaking to him, Schreber was called "the seer of spirits," and he saw them everywhere, not merely in animals and plants, but in the heavens. The sun's rays were by turns the "nerves of God" or "God's spermatozoa," and in an extraordinary projection of the material basis of his mind "it appeared that nerves—probably taken from my body—were strung over the whole heavenly vault."[6n]

Indeed, not merely in the external world, but in his own self,

Schreber found other minds. This was graphically portrayed by his delusion that on one occasion 240 Benedictine Monks, led by a Father whose name sounded like Starkiewicz, suddenly moved into his head. Among other souls who invaded Schreber's person was a group which consisted mainly of former members of the Saxonia Students' Corps—not to mention relatives, friends, former colleagues and doctors who had treated him in the past.[6o] And it was not just in his mind, but in his body too, that he felt the presence of these other minds. He noticed that:

> friendly souls always tended more towards the region of my sexual organs (of the abdomen etc.) where they did little damage and hardly molested me, whereas inimical souls always aspired towards my head, on which they wanted to inflict some damage, and sat particularly on my left ear in a highly disturbing manner.[6p]

Schreber underlines the essentially human character of these presences within him and the mentalistic quality of his interpretation of them when he adds that "I saw…'little men' innumerable times with my mind's eye and heard their voices." And just in case anyone should think him incapable of distinguishing the mental from the physical he adds in a footnote to this sentence: "Of course one can *not* see with the *bodily* eye what goes on inside one's own body, nor on certain parts of its surface, for instance on the top of the head or on the back, but—as in my case—one can see it *with one's mind's eye*…"—or, as I would prefer to put it, *mentalistically*.[6q]

Another way of describing this tendency to mentalize to excess is what has been called *magical ideation*. The Magical Ideation Scale developed at the University of Wisconsin presents a questionnaire asking the respondent to agree or disagree with a list of statements. These range from what you might call commonplace superstition (such as "Horoscopes are right too often for it to be a coincidence") to some with a distinctly delusional tone, themselves ranging from the erotomanic ("I sometimes have the passing thought that strangers are in love with me") to the more conventionally paranoid ("I have sometimes sensed an evil presence around me"). Also included are many sentiments endorsed by conventional religions ("I have wondered whether the spirits of the dead can influence the living"); belief in the paranormal ("I think I could learn to read other people's minds if I wanted to"); or even extra-terrestrial life ("The government refuses to tell us the truth about flying saucers").[26] Students who scored high on the scale also showed more psychotic symptoms than students with lower scores, and in a study of psychiatric patients those with schizophrenia had a higher magical ideation score than non-schizophrenic patients or normal controls. A longitudinal study of 7800 students revealed that students who scored high on magical ideation in college showed more symptoms of schizotypy and other schizophrenia-related disorders a decade later, and also reported more psychotic experiences than others. Ten years later, the number of people who had developed some form of psychosis was significantly greater in the group that had scored high on magical ideation.[27] Two different studies of first-onset symptoms in people developing schizophrenia found that the great majority reported pre-occupation with metaphysical, supernatural, or philosophical issues,[28,29] and other authorities conclude that belief in paranormal and mystical experiences, or admitting to a strong sixth sense, are regularly found to occur in individuals with milder schizophrenic personality disorders.[30]

These findings make complete sense if you consider the fact that mentalistic thinking, although perfectly true and applicable in its own, proper psychological setting, inevitably becomes delusional if substituted for mechanistic cognition of the physical world. We have already seen how easily even erstwhile scientific writers such as Sheldrake can begin to credit ideas such as the evil eye and sixth—or, in his case, even seventh[1j]—senses in relation to vision and attention. However, intention can even more easily be extended beyond its proper, purely mental domain. Another of the statements from the Magical Ideation Questionnaire reads, "I have felt that I might cause something to happen just by thinking about it too much." Schreber illustrates the extreme culmination of this kind of thinking when we find him vastly overstating his own influence on things, for example in his claim that:

> the weather is now to a certain extent dependent on *my* actions and thoughts; as soon as I indulge in thinking nothing, or in other words stop an activity which proves the existence of the human mind such as playing chess in the garden, the wind arises at once.

He concluded that *"everything that happens is in reference to me."*[6r] Other schizophrenics claim that "When my eyes are bright blue, the sky gets blue," or that "all the clocks of the world feel my pulse," while another recalls that "I really thought the world was turning around me... I referred everything to myself as if it were made for me..."[7c]

Such *delusions of reference* as they are often called can be seen as an exaggeration of the normal belief in yourself as the agent responsible for your own intentions. They result from extension of the fundamental mentalistic sense of your own responsibility for your conscious acts outwards on to acts and events which in reality cannot be caused by your own mind, intention, or behaviour. Furthermore, such interpretations of intention have a foundation in reality. A case in point might be inadvertently to distract someone's attention so that they do something they did not intend, say drop something, or bungle something that they would normally do perfectly well. In these circumstances you may not have directly intended the accident, but mentalistically you feel responsible because you know that your intervention—albeit quite innocent—probably contributed to the outcome. And from real situations such as this it is but a short step to begin to think as Schreber evidently did that just about everything that happened around him did so in some way or another in connection with himself. Indeed, even normal people have been found to over-estimate the extent to which they can control random events (such as thinking that you have more control over the outcome if you throw dice yourself rather than have someone else throw them for you).[31] Looked at from this point of view, Schreber's delusions of reference are—as with so many of his symptoms—not so much pathologically unprecedented as extreme exaggerations of normal mentalism.

But of course, intentions can also be retrospectively regretted, and repudiated, particularly if the outcome was less than or contrary to what was intended. For most people, such miscarried intentions become the subjects of private recrimination, personal sorrow, and ultimately perhaps selective amnesia—or at least some degree of self-vindication. We tend to say things such as, "I didn't really mean to do it," "That wasn't what I actually intended," or "I would never have wanted this to happen." But here again Schreber shows the process of self-excuse in an extreme form when he asserts that, where he is concerned:

> Plates simply break in two without any rough handling, or objects which the servants or others present or even I myself hold (for instance my chessmen, my pen, my cigar-holder etc.) are suddenly flung to the floor, where those that are breakable naturally break into pieces. All this is due to miracles; for this reason the damage caused is made the topic of conversation by people around, usually some time afterwards.[6s]

The sense of self in ASD and psychosis

This appeal to miraculous intervention to explain his own clumsiness or contrariness illustrates the extent to which magical, mentalistic thinking can produce bizarre fantasies and severe alienation from reality—something all the more noticeable when the delusions in question lack the fig-leaves of conventional credulity or the vestments of traditional religious belief as they so starkly do in the Schreber case. Indeed, such delusions of reference sometimes border on true megalomania, with schizophrenics claiming that "everything from the largest to the smallest is contained in me."[8] Authorities comment that "The self is identified with the All. The patient is not just someone else (Christ, Napoleon, etc.) but simply the All. His own life is experienced as the life of the whole world, his strength is world-sustaining and world-vitalizing."[7d]

Schreber believed that he "became in a way for God the only human being, or simply the human being around whom everything turns, to whom everything that happens must be related and who therefore, from his own point of view, must also relate all things to himself."[6t] Schreber, in other words, was not merely the centre of his own little world; he believed himself to be crucially central to the entire cosmos. In manic-depressive (bipolar) psychotics similar feelings are commonly found in manic periods. The case I quoted from earlier shows that not just delusions about the sun, but about the self also parallel those seen in paranoid psychotics such as Schreber:

> I feel so close to God, so inspired by His Spirit that in a sense I am God. I see the future, plan the Universe, save mankind; I am utterly and completely immortal; I am even male and female. The whole Universe, animate and inanimate, past, present and future is within me. All nature and life, all spirits, are cooperating and connected with me; all things are possible. I am in a sense identical with all spirits from God to Satan. I reconcile Good and Evil and create light, darkness, worlds, universes.[15b]

Delusions of grandeur seldom get much grander, and megalomania could hardly be more megalomanic than this!

Autistics, by contrast, typically exhibit a diminished sense of self. For example, autistic children typically make pronoun-reversal errors, referring to themselves as "you" and their mothers as "I" or "me." However, language-impaired controls, such as sufferers from Down syndrome, do not make comparable errors, despite their poor speech competence.[32] Again, three autistic young men with normal IQ who could pass tests of false belief (such as the Sally-Anne scenario) but nevertheless had varying degrees of mentalistic impairment were asked to record their thoughts at particular but unpredictable moments during a normal day (cued by a special device they carried with them). Each enjoyed participating, but only the least impaired boy quickly took to the idea of reporting his inner mental states; the second least impaired was only able to do so after four sessions; and the most impaired never satisfied the experimenters' criteria for understanding the instructions. Instead, this individual persisted in only recording his purely physical actions, never his inner mental state. What struck the authors of this study about the boys' reports was that all three described inner experience which was literal and visual, and appeared to lack verbal or other imagery. There was little or nothing in the way of introspective commentary on the events described that reflected the subjects' own reactions. Such findings appear to be in line with other studies which suggest that when children are able to report their own mental states they are also able to report the psychological states of others, but that when they cannot report and understand the mental states of others, they do not report those states in themselves.[33] In other words, "It is impossible to build up a sense of oneself without a good theory of other people's minds."[34a]

According to another account, "Autobiographies of individuals with autism hint at disturbances of self-consciousness. Just as sleep-walkers can carry out many complex actions without being fully conscious of carrying them out, so children with autism go about their daily routines without full awareness of their own feelings and thoughts."[35] Indeed, the following excerpt from a published autobiography of an autistic explicitly uses the symbolism of sleep-walking and hypnotism:

> my first words were the meaningless echoes of the conversation of those around me…ninety-nine per cent of my verbal repertoire was a stored-up collection of literal dictionary definitions of stock phrases…before I'd ever known a want of my own,… my first "wants" were copies of those seen in others (a lot of which came from TV)…every facial expression or pose was a cartoon reflection of those around me. Nothing was connected to self. Without the barest foundations of self I was like a subject under hypnosis, totally susceptible to any programming or reprogramming without question or personal identification… Like someone sleep-walking or sleep-talking, I imitated the sounds and movements of others—an involuntary compulsive impressionist.[20b]

A study of so-called Asperger savants mentioned earlier (see pp. 26–27) observes that even so well-known and famous a writer as Hans Christian Andersen operated through a false self and had very little of a real or core self. The poet William Butler Yeats, who has also been diagnosed as an Asperger savant, remarked that "My character is so little myself that all my life it has thwarted me. It has affected my poems, my true self, no more than the character of a dancer affects the movements of a dance."[34b] According to the autobiography of a woman diagnosed with Asperger's syndrome at the age of 42, "One of the best ways of understanding what autism is like is to imagine yourself as a perpetual onlooker. Much of the time life is like a video, a moving film I can observe but cannot reach. The world passes in front of me shielded by glass."[36] Temple Grandin comments that "Using my visualization ability, I observe myself from a distance. I call this my little scientist in the corner, as if I'm a little bird watching my own behaviour from up high." She adds that this has also been reported by other people with autism and that Asperger noted that autistic children constantly observe themselves.[37]

The mother of two autistic boys I quoted earlier regarding their lack of *whys?* reports that both her sons showed "an indifference or aversion to photographs or films of themselves." Of the one called George she recounts that he "used to narrate the story of his own life as it was happening always in the third person." Examples are: "He jumped into the bath with a tremendous splash; 'Where can Daddy be?' exclaimed George anxiously… He clutched his spoon tightly. The sausage bounced off the plate, but he caught it." She adds that her all-time favourite was when he was eating a McDonald's hamburger. "He pulled out the slimy, khaki slice of dill pickle and handed it to me, saying, 'Mum, this is my conscience!'."[18c]

Another autistic's autobiography gives an account of being bullied and beaten by another child to the extent that she discovered on returning home that her face was "criss-crossed and bleeding from thousands of little scratches." Her reaction, though, was to stand in front of the mirror for a long time looking at her face, which she thought "looked interesting." The same writer adds that "The vague sense of my body that I did have meant that I wasn't particularly aware whether I was dirty, or how my clothes were sitting. I didn't feel it."[38]

However, a lack of self-awareness need not always seem pathological. On the contrary, people on the autistic spectrum can seem selfless in the best sense of the term, and can possess a winning simplicity of character and disarming straightforwardness that is only otherwise seen in young, unspoilt children, whose minimum level of self-awareness they have retained into adult life. Reminiscing about the French writer and political activist, Simone Weil (1909–43), who has been posthumously proposed as an Asperger savant, an acquaintance said that "everything about her emanated a feeling of total frankness and forgetfulness of self, revealing a nobility of soul that was certainly at the root of the emotions she inspired in us."[34c] A similar, unaffected and guileless humility can be seen in other historical cases retrospectively diagnosed as autistics, such as the Franciscan friar, Brother Juniper, or the Blessed Fools of Russia.[39] Autistic selflessness, it would seem, is not simply a sometimes striking symptom of the disorder but in the right circumstances can be a qualification for beatification—be it religious or secular.

The author I quoted just now who talks of sleep-walking also remarks that "Autism makes me feel sometimes that I have no self at all, and I feel so overwhelmed by the presence of other people that I cannot find myself." But she adds, "Autism can also make me so totally aware of myself that it is like the whole world around me becomes irrelevant and disappears."[20c] Normal people can have a sense of their own selves alongside one of other people's, but in autism this seems to be difficult: either you find yourself and lose the others, or find the others and lose yourself. This can also show itself as a need for others to provide you with a sense of self. For example, it is said of A. J. Ayer, the autistic British philosopher I mentioned earlier, that he always wanted to be the centre of attention, and liked to perform in front of an audience and bask in its admiration. The playwright, John Osborne, described him as the most selfish, superficial, and obtuse man he had ever met;

but another playwright described him perhaps more perceptively as "a Narcissus incapable of seeing himself." Fitzgerald quotes Ayer saying: "I am famous, therefore I exist," and argues that this shows that his sense of self depended on the admiration of others.[34d]

Tony Attwood, a leading clinician and writer on Asperger's syndrome, points out that some Asperger's cases over-compensate by going into what he terms *God mode* and becoming "an omnipotent person who never makes a mistake, cannot be wrong and whose intelligence must be worshipped."[40] However, this metaphoric God mode is very different from the much more literal one of psychotics such as Schreber, who explicitly compared himself to Jesus Christ, the Virgin Mary, and believed that he exercised a fascination over God himself.[6u] In the psychotic case, you see true narcissism, with autobiographical accounts recalling moments when "My thoughts…were all of Me: how fascinating is Me… I looked at Me in the mirror. 'You enchanted one!' said I, 'You're my Companion, my Familiar, my Lover, my wilding sweetheart—I love you!'."[41] In autism, by contrast, you seldom find narcissism with such a secure sense of self. Indeed, there are even rare cases where an autistic lack of self and a psychotic excess can be found alternating in the same person:

> I have…an immense difficulty with maintaining eye contact in conversation: when I look at somebody speaking to me I almost become lost and I have difficulties processing what they are saying; I have similar difficulties putting together my thoughts if I am supposed to be looking at somebody, such as my therapist or psychiatrist. As a result, I do not have a strong sense of an emotional self, and I believe I resemble my dad in this manner, who does not emote very often. When I become manic, I suddenly feel comfortable engaging with people in conversation. These episodes always feel like miracles and lead to my thinking I have answers to all of life's problems and am the second coming of Jesus, which I understand is similar to a thought disorder that people with schizophrenia have.[42]

In other words, here is a remarkable case of autistic and manic tendencies alternating in the same individual, with the characteristic diminution of the sense of self associated with gaze-avoidance, but something like true megalomania supervening during manic phases.

Chapter 4

Cancers
of the Mind

In the last chapter we saw that four symptomatic deficits in autism—gaze-monitoring, interpretation of intention, shared attention, and sense of self and personal agency—each had its pathologically exaggerated equivalent in psychotics such as Schreber. In this chapter we shall see that this pattern reveals something fundamental about psychosis which has been glimpsed before but which only emerges clearly when contrasted with the situation in autism. If autism can be thought of as mind-blindness, then psychoses such as Schreber's could be seen as *cancers of the mind*: malignant mental tumours that attack the core functions which make up mentalism and grow uncontrollably, eventually destroying the mind itself.

Memory, self-deception, and candour

There are two different types of memories: factual or *semantic* ones (such as remembering that Paris is the capital of France), and *episodic* or personal ones (such as recalling a visit you made to Paris).[1] Essentially the difference is that between *knowing* and *remembering*.[2] Recent experiences related to the self are consolidated into long-term *autobiographical memory*. Access to recent episodic memories rapidly degrades and most are lost within 24 hours of formation. Only those memories integrated at the time or consolidated later—possibly during sleep—remain accessible and then become true autobiographical memories.[3] Indeed, Conway comments that:

> autobiographical memory is dominated by the "force" or "demand" of coherence. A stable, integrated, self with a confirmatory past that yields a consistent and rich life story constitutes a self that is able to operate effectively, achieve goals, and relate to others in productive ways. A coherent self will have high self-esteem and a strong positive sense of well being, both powerful predictors of physical health. Thus, the benefits of coherence may then be considerable.[4]

We have already encountered *coherence* in connection with the weak central-coherence that is characteristic of the autistic style of thinking (see pp. 48–50). Another way of interpreting the remarks just quoted would be to say that episodic/autobiographical memory could be seen as inherently *mentalistic,* while semantic, factual memory was much more *mechanistic.* In laboratory tests individuals from the higher-functioning end of the autism spectrum show characteristic deficits in episodic/autobiographical memory—those involving personal identification with events. However, they reveal no such deficits in relation to semantic memory as tested in tasks such as rote memory, cued recall, and recognition memory.[5]

On the contrary, autistic subjects typically have superior recall for true as opposed to false memories. A common way of testing this is to ask subjects to memorize a random list of words on a similar subject and then later to require them to identify the original words from a differently ordered list containing some new words with similar associations to the original ones. So, for example, a list that originally included words associated with sleep and including *bed* might be re-ordered and include *pillow* instead on the retest. In tasks such as this autistics are significantly less likely to make the mistake of thinking that the newly introduced lure-words were in the original list. However, the ASD subjects achieve normal rates of recall for the previously studied words, and therefore demonstrate greater discrimination between true and false memories than the control group. Commenting on one such study, the researchers conclude that "The autistic spectrum disorder group appeared to be relying on a highly literal form of memory, missing out misattributions resulting in false recognition responses."[6] In another study, although Asperger's subjects were described as making significantly fewer *remember responses* (that is, episodic recollections) than did matched normal control subjects, they made more *know responses* (semantic recollections). Furthermore, we have already seen that remarkable rote memory can often be found in autism, and almost always in autistic savants, some of whom have amazing powers of recollection in connection with things such as sports, history, or literature (see pp. 27–29). Yet despite such feats of factual memory, "the main conclusion is that there is indeed episodic memory impairment in adults with Asperger's syndrome."[7] Other writers describe autistics as being unable to remember *themselves* performing actions, participating in events or possessing knowledge and strategies, suggesting that the same is true of autistics' autobiographical memory. Indeed, with Conway's perceptive comment quoted just now in mind, you could see this as yet another aspect of weak central-coherence in autism: a mentalistic deficit in which autobiographical memory was much less central and coherent with the self than normal.

The same pattern of hyperbolic expression of a normal aspect of mentalism which we noted in relation to things such as gaze and intention in the previous chapter is found in relation to memory in paranoid psychotics such as Schreber, who often fabricate complex and colourful autobiographies that do not simply border on the delusional, but cross over it into manifest insanity.[8] Indeed, Schreber's very title, *Memoirs of My Nervous Illness*, immediately reminds us that the entire book is one long account of the episodic/autobiographical memories of one particular person, whose recollections are so intimately intertwined with his delusions that they are often impossible to disentangle. Here, perhaps the most striking example is Schreber's extreme embellishment of the normal mentalistic ability to include yourself in episodic and autobiographical memories. This shows itself in his delusion that he was the only real human being alive, and that others were "fleetingly improvised"—mere allusions to human beings.[9a] Many if not most of these people were clearly real persons whom Schreber encountered, but their reduction to mere ciphers underlines the central role that Schreber's own self always plays in the *Memoirs*. Others may be remembered, but they are recalled only in reference to Schreber himself, and appear to have little other significance apart from their connection with him. Another schizophrenic recalls that people "were mere empty skins" or marionettes on a stage,[10a] while others describe them as "puppets," "manikins," or "automatons."[11a] Where autistics typically fail to include themselves in their episodic memories, psychotics such as Schreber have difficulty including anyone *but* themselves!

A sense of your own central place in your own history allows not only mental time-travel into the past, but into the future too. If you can recall yourself as the principal actor in what has already happened to you, you can also easily imagine yourself as the author of actions yet to take place, and rehearse scenarios of as-yet-unrecorded autobiographical events. But just as we might predict, autistics also show characteristic deficits here: not only are they unlikely to travel mentally into their own past, they are if anything even less likely to travel into the future in this respect and often show characteristic deficits in imagination as a result.[12]

Yet as we might also expect, psychotics such as Schreber show the exact contrary tendency where mental time-travel is concerned. Going beyond mere memory of his own lifetime and time-travel into his own past, Schreber came to believe that his encounter with his psychiatrist, Dr Flechsig—definitely a real episode in his past—had historical precedents reaching back much further. He "concluded that at one time something had happened between perhaps earlier generations of the Flechsig and Schreber families." Schreber then goes on to name the individuals involved, some of whom he imagined to have lived in the previous century.[9b] Here not just autobiographical memory, but history itself is transformed in a manner that is wholly and centrally coherent with Schreber's beliefs about himself and his role in the greater scheme of things. And as far as time-travel into the future was concerned, we have already seen (and shall see in more detail later) that Schreber harboured bizarre fantasies about a cosmic conspiracy centring on himself which involved his transformation into a woman who would then give birth to a new race which would re-populate the world!

One reason why Schreber wrote the book and thought it to be so important was that he believed that through his personal experiences he had gained unique insights into reality denied to others, and the title of his book might be rendered as his *Great Thoughts* rather than simply his *Memoirs*.[13] Schreber's self-confessed aim was "solely to further knowledge of truth" and he believed himself "infinitely closer to the truth than human beings who have not received divine revelation." Nor did he consider himself unduly credulous, remarking that he had belonged to the category of doubters where religion was concerned, at least "until divine revelation taught me better."[9c] Indeed, he adds that:

> Whoever knew me intimately in my earlier life will bear witness that I had been a person of calm nature, without passion, clear-thinking and sober, whose individual gift lay much more in the direction of cool intellectual criticism than in the creative activity of an unbounded imagination.

Not surprisingly then, he goes on to remark that "It seems psychologically impossible that *I* suffer only from hallucinations," and adds that "I can claim two qualities for myself without reservation, namely *absolute truthfulness and more than usually keen powers of observation*."[9d]

If central-coherence is a function associated with mentalism as suggested earlier, it is notable that Schreber himself makes an extreme claim for it when he remarks with emphasis that "*every single nerve of intellect represents the total mental individuality of a human being*." Indeed, he adds that "the sum total of recollections is as it were inscribed on each single nerve of intellect."[9e] According to the schizophrenic playwright, Antonin Artaud (1895–1948):

> the brain wants to say too many things which it thinks of all at once, ten thoughts instead of one rush towards the exit, the brain sees the whole thought at once with all its circumstances,

and it also sees all the points of view it could take and all the forms with which it could invest them...[14]

According to some authorities, comments such as this illustrate the *over-inclusiveness* that characterizes schizophrenic thinking. This has been described as a failure to maintain boundaries and to generalize to excess.[15,16] Concordant with this, recent neurological research suggests that many symptoms of psychosis can be seen as involving higher connectivity of some aspects of cognition, especially for thought processes involving language. Brain-imaging suggests that delusional symptoms and hallucinations in schizophrenia involve dysfunctions in brain areas that impair bottom-up processing, giving greater perceptual control to top-down mechanisms, and other studies show that schizophrenia involves greater impairments in local as opposed to global processing of stimuli, with enhanced global-processing advantages for some tasks.[17] This is the exact opposite to the local over-connectivity with global under-connectivity of brain functions seen in autism and mentioned in a previous chapter (see pp. 47–49), and indeed as long ago as 1964 Rimland suggested that autism and schizophrenia represent problems of under-associative and over-associative brain function.[18]

In Schreber's case, his psychiatrist remarked that "the patient is filled with pathological ideas, which are woven into a complete system, more or less fixed, and not amenable to correction by objective evidence and judgement of circumstances as they really are." He adds that "these delusional ideas...are developed and motivated with remarkable clarity and logical precision." Later in the same report he refers to "a structure of ideas so fantastically elaborated and developed and so far removed from the usual trends of thought that it is hardly possible to sketch them briefly..."[9f] Schreber's delusional system, in other words, was as pathologically over-inclusive as it was chronically immune to criticism and refutation. The whole was so much greater than the sum of its parts that no detail could possibly contradict or undermine it: central-coherence with a vengeance!

For a writer who owes most of his justly deserved fame to his beautifully written account of his delusional system and its consequences for his life, Schreber's view of himself as infinitely closer to the truth than other human beings represents a very high level of self-deception. Furthermore, you could see this as another striking contrast between autism and psychosis. Where paranoiacs such as Schreber are prone to extreme self-deception and wildly erroneous perception resulting in the bizarre delusional thinking that usually typifies the untreated condition, autistics are often pathologically literal and truthful. Where psychotics can be found admitting to have been "artful little liars" even at the age of five or six,[11b] autistics are very much "truth-seekers,"[19] and tend to be immune to many commonplace contemporary prejudices. While "pretence and equivocation are greatly used by schizophrenics,"[20a] Oliver Sacks comments on "the touching simplicity and ingenuousness" of Temple Grandin's writing and "her incapacity for evasion or artifice of any kind."[21] Grandin herself remarks that:

> Autistic people tend to have difficulty lying because of the complex emotions involved in deception. I become extremely anxious when I have to tell a little white lie on the spur of the moment. To be able to tell the smallest fib, I have to rehearse it many times in my mind. I run video simulations of all the different things the other person might ask. If the other person comes up with an unexpected question, I panic. Being deceptive while interacting with someone is extremely difficult unless I have fully rehearsed all possible responses. Lying is very anxiety-provoking because it requires rapid interpretations of subtle social cues to determine whether the other person is really being deceived.[22a]

As other writers have pointed out, successful lying relies not just on competence in understanding false-belief situations, but real skill in exploiting and manipulating them, and this, as we have already seen, autistics notoriously lack (see pp. 51–52). Perhaps not surprisingly then, brain-imaging reveals that there is more brain activity when lying than when telling the truth. Areas activated when lying are predominantly left hemisphere ones involved in attention, error-detection, and voluntary movement (specifically, the anterior cingulate cortex and pre-frontal and pre-motor cortices).[23]

Difficulty with the mental skills involved with deception might partly explain why autistics tend to be such poor liars, and it would certainly explain why articulate autistics speak of themselves as defiant "in the face of orthodoxy" and as despising and loathing "the system of the world, with its fashions and trends and flimsy ideas and philosophies, its media and social conditioning." Indeed, the writer quoted here reports that he would sometimes make the mistake of bringing this superficiality to the attention of odd individuals:

> "Have you noticed how false everyone is?" I would start. "The way they change depending on whose company they are in? They talk one way when they are on their own, and a completely different way when they're with their friends—sometimes even altering their feelings and beliefs to suit."[24a]

He concludes, "It's because they're scared of being themselves, you see"—something that we have already seen autistics are most decidedly not.[24b] A consequence of such candour is that autistics represent a unique challenge to the rest of the human race:

> Autism, with its indifference to cultural values, implies an existential critique of society. It questions some of its most valued concepts... Society is challenged and humbled by the sheer existence of people who are unmoved by values that it takes for granted.[25a]

Like aliens who have lived unsuspected on Earth, "These mysterious, impossible, enchanting beings will always be among us, unwitting yardsticks for our own moral behaviour, uncomprehending challengers of our definition of what it means to be human."[26a]

Hyper-mentalism

Nevertheless, it would be wrong to conclude that everything that goes on in the psychotic mind by contrast to the autistic one is simply self-deceiving and delusional. On the contrary, Bleuler noted that schizophrenics who seem totally withdrawn and uninterested in their environment nevertheless "pick up an astounding amount of information from snatches of conversation about the personal lives of their doctors and care personnel, and about tensions among them"[11c]—something seldom if ever reported of autistics. The psychiatrist Randolph Nesse notes that "those who have worked with schizophrenics know the eerie feeling of being with someone whose intuitions are acutely tuned to the subtlest unintentional cues, even while the person is incapable of accurate empathic understanding."[27] Other authorities comment regarding the case-histories of psychotics that:

> Reported experience of "telepathic" contact with another person close by...may well indicate a genuine hyper-awareness of "leaked" social signals which are then interpreted, rightly or wrongly, as having psychological meaning... Anyone who has interacted with psychotics will know of their uncanny capacity to respond to subtle social cues, believed to have been concealed from them.[28a]

The same writer concludes that "the underlying quality of schizophrenia is not a defect at all, but an exquisite sensitivity of the nervous system, which...gets translated into an *appearance* of deficit..."[29] A psychotherapist comments that people with a suspicious, "paranoid style" of thinking "are also conspicuously hyper-sensitive and hyper-alert. These people are exceedingly, nervously sensitive to anything out of the ordinary or unexpected."[30]

First-person accounts of psychotics concur. According to one:

> Schizophrenia is a disease of information. And undergoing a psychotic break was like turning on a faucet to a torrent of

details, which overwhelmed my life... Although my sense of perception remained unaffected, everything I saw and heard took on a halo of meaning that had to be interpreted before I knew how to act. An advertising banner revealed a secret message only I could read. The layout of a store display conveyed a secret clue. A leaf fell and in its falling spoke: nothing was too small to act as a courier of meaning.[31]

In the words of another:

> It seems accurate to me that many delusions arise from a person's over-analyzing and articulating ideas, followed by making a series of loose associations between them. While most people in their "right mind" would consider these ideas and connections everyday coincidences or minor irrelevancies, the psychotic individual often obsesses over them and tries to find a deeper meaning.[32]

Another schizophrenic remarks that "Every single thing 'means' something," adding that "I have a sense that everything is vivid and important... There is a connection to everything that happens—no coincidences."[11d] A Canadian woman in remission from schizophrenia remarks how when she was ill "The walk of a stranger on the street could be a 'sign' to me which I must interpret. Every face in the windows of a passing streetcar would be engraved on my mind, all of them concentrating on me and trying to pass me some sort of message."[33] A recovered patient added, "Today I can see clearly how things really are; but then I always thought something unusual was up, even on the most trivial occasion. It was a real illness."[10b]

Furthermore, there are experimental studies which suggest that such subjective impressions are by no means always delusional. For example, one carefully controlled study found that paranoid patients even when on medication are demonstrably better than normal controls in interpreting non-verbal cues—at least where the resulting expressions are genuine and where the situation is one of expectation of an electric shock. With simulated expressions, normal subjects performed better than paranoid ones, but as the experimenter herself points out, this is just what you would expect if you thought that paranoiacs have a special sensitivity to non-verbal cues.[34] And as the earlier discussion of autistics' limitations where deceit is concerned would suggest, children diagnosed with a rare form of childhood-onset schizophrenia showed enhanced performance by comparison to autistic children and normal controls in a task involving deception of others.[35] Positive associations have also been reported between measures of empathy and milder, so-called schizotypy.[36,37] Again, a test of divergent thinking in which subjects had to invent uses for a range of conventional and ambiguous objects showed that the schizotypical group performed particularly well in comparison with schizophrenics and normal controls, activating much more of the right pre-frontal cortex in doing so.[38] Indeed, such mildly psychotic tendencies have been associated with enhanced social-emotional creativity and imagination in general[28,39]—a point to which I will return in the concluding chapter.

In everyday speech we are likely—perhaps jokingly, perhaps not—to suggest that someone is being "paranoid" if we think that they are being over-sensitive to someone else's behaviour or expressions and consequently finding motives or meanings where there are none. In other words, you could say that in such instances we are suggesting that whoever is being "paranoid" is reading too much into someone else's mind, rather than too little, as autistics typically do. In genuine paranoia such excessive mentalizing means that although paranoid schizophrenics may indeed be more sensitive to expressions of others' states of mind in certain respects, they are nevertheless as likely to over-interpret them erroneously as autistics are likely to under-interpret them erroneously. Interestingly then, brain-imaging studies of individuals clinically at risk of psychosis show differences in brain activation associated with more pronounced processing of emotionally neutral facial expressions. In fact, the study suggests that such a tendency to over-react to neutral stimuli might be a biological risk-indicator for psychosis.[40] So not just in the everyday meaning of "being paranoid," but in brain reactions too, there may be some truth in the idea that paranoia involves a pathological over-reaction to harmless stimuli.

Laboratory studies certainly suggest that "patients with delusions of persecution might over-attribute intentions and causes to the actions of agents."[41] A recent study of schizophrenics used similar computer-animated triangles and other simple figures to those employed in the study of autistics' mentalistic abilities that I mentioned in the second chapter (see p. 53). This was the first study of schizophrenia to use a task that required real-time theory of mind abilities in which participants were asked to monitor a moving, dynamic display as it unfolded in front of them. Some of the animated sequences had a simple storyline, but others were random. The experimenters report that "Typically, low accuracy scores on the random animations arose from individuals reading too much into the animation sequence," and conclude that "a tendency to over-interpretation, i.e., seeing meaning where none exists, is consistent with current conceptualisations of 'paranoia'."[42]

We have already seen that you could describe autistics as having an impoverished theory of mind ability characterized by symptomatic deficits in mentalism. If you wanted a single term for this, you could describe autism as *hypo-mentalistic:* meaning that the disorder characteristically features serious under-development of mentalism. However, my discussion of the case of Schreber suggests that paranoia in particular (and perhaps psychosis in general) could correspondingly be seen as *hyper-mentalism*—in other words as having too much theory of mind and manifesting excessive mentalistic tendencies.[43]*

An important point is that hyper-mentalism in psychosis, like hypo-mentalism in autism, will inevitably produce mentalistic deficits understood as failures to mentalize normally. People with so-called *positive*

---

* Strictly speaking, the term ought to be *super-mentalism*—or more correctly still, *super-mentality*—given that the root *mens* is Latin and not Greek like the prefix *hyper-* (or possibly even *hyper-psychism*, if we were to substitute the corresponding Greek root). But *super-mentality*—like *hyper-psychism* for that matter—would arouse the wrong associations in English speakers, and there are a number of good precedents (such as *sociology*, to name but one). Finally, the large number of other coinages using the same prefix that approximate to hyper-mentalism (many of them cited in the main text) made its choice unavoidable.

symptoms of schizophrenia (in other words, hallucinations, delusions, and paranoia) have been described as having a "hyper-theory of mind" understood as "an impaired theory of mind due to an over-attribution of knowledge to others that will result in inaccurate inferences about others' mental states."[44] In the same way that a teacher who had a hyper-active child in the class would not be likely to find that child doing extra homework, we should not assume that hyper-mentalism is simply normal mentalizing, plus some more. On the contrary, excessive mentalizing will result in outcomes that can at times look very like autistic deficits, such as avoidance of social contact, misunderstanding of others' intentions, emotions, or expressions, inability to appreciate humour or irony, and misuse or under-use of mentalistic language. But whereas autistic deficits in mentalism will be the result of an inability to mentalize to a normal extent, psychotic deficits may be expected to show the exact contrary pathology: a tendency to mentalize to excess, to be over-sensitive to purely mental factors, and to apply mentalism in inappropriate circumstances or to improper ends.

Again, autistics can often feel that people are against them and that they are being persecuted, just as paranoid psychotics do. But the only laboratory study undertaken at the time of writing which compared Asperger's with paranoid patients and normal controls found that the low-level paranoid symptoms of the autistic group arose as a consequence of different mechanisms to those involved in psychotic delusions.[45] Furthermore, a study comparing 25 people with a diagnosis of Asperger's syndrome with 18 normal controls concluded that "The paranoia observed in Asperger syndrome therefore does not appear to stem from the same factors as seen in the paranoia of people with a diagnosis of schizophrenia." On the contrary, the authors sensibly suggest that "the paranoia seen in Asperger syndrome is of a different 'quality' to that observed in schizophrenia…it may stem from a confusion of not understanding the subtleties of social interactions and social rules" rather than being seen as part of a "plot" against them.[46] Tony Attwood, a leading authority of Asperger's syndrome I have cited a number of times before, points out that:

A person with Asperger's syndrome may develop what appears to be signs of paranoia, but this may be an understandable response to very real social experiences. Children with Asperger's syndrome encounter a greater degree of deliberate and provocative teasing than their peers. Once another child has deliberately teased the child with Asperger's syndrome, any subsequent confusing interaction with that child can cause the child with Asperger's syndrome to make the assumption that the interaction was intentionally hostile. This can eventually lead to long-term feelings of persecution and the expectation that people will have malicious intent.[47a]

Although a recent report found verbal—but no non-verbal—theory of mind deficits in schizophrenics with persecutory delusions,[48] an earlier study that looked specifically at paranoia concluded that theory of mind deficits were not causal or specific to paranoid delusions. Instead, its authors suggested that such delusions may be secondary effects resulting from information-processing overload in schizophrenics.[49] Autistic "paranoia," in other words, is hypo-mentalistic, and often reinforced by the very real mistreatment and misunderstanding autistics meet with at the hands of other people. Psychotic paranoia, on the other hand, is hyper-mentalistic in over-interpreting other people's behaviour to provide apparent evidence of plots, conspiracies, and bad intentions that simply do not exist.

A study that used schizophrenics as a control group when it examined mentalistic skills in Asperger's syndrome explicitly stated that the schizophrenics' social impairment "does not appear to result from an impaired theory of mind."[50] Another study found that although higher scores on a single dimension of mild schizophrenic tendencies were associated with poorer theory of mind ability, no association was found between theory of mind and either total ratings of schizophrenic tendencies or traits analogous to the symptoms of schizophrenia. Furthermore, the same study pointed out that it could be argued that poor scores on mentalistic tasks are related to "general deficits in attention or motivation, lower IQ, higher doses of antipsychotic medication, poor memory, and/or greater severity of illness."[51] Indeed, a recent meta-analysis of 32 studies of theory of mind in schizophrenia concluded that a comparison of autistic and psychotic mentalism from this point of view might be an interesting topic for future research.[52] At the very least, this establishes that a hyper-mentalistic interpretation of psychotic deficits in mentalism is still an open question, and that we cannot jump to the conclusion that it has already been refuted.

On the contrary, even extreme negative symptoms of schizophrenia, such as catatonic rigidity and withdrawal, might be interpreted in terms of hyper-mentalism. Sass comments that "manifestations of hypertrophied self-consciousness" like delusions of being watched:

> are not likely to facilitate normal forms of pragmatic and social activity, which may help to explain why some schizophrenics seem to move in such a stiff or awkward way. One schizophrenic patient complained, "None of my movements come automatically to me now. I've been thinking too much about them, even walking properly, talking properly and smoking—doing anything. Before they would be able to come automatically.

Indeed, Sass goes on to mention a case described by Arieti in which such inhibitions led ultimately to catatonic paralysis. The patient spent so much time thinking about what he was doing that in the end he was unable to do anything and felt himself "solidifying" and "assuming statuesque positions"![11e] Of course, a single case does not prove that others are the same, but inhibition and paralysis of thought and action thanks to excessive mentalizing are commonly reported by schizophrenics, so the suggestion that hyper-mentalism is the root cause of such negative symptoms is not as unwarranted as it may seem. The proposition certainly fits the finding by brain researchers that, in sport for example, thinking about a move slows down its execution.[53] And it may not be coincidental that "attention deficit"—the opposite of the excessive attention directed to activity in the case quoted here—is linked to "hyper-activity" in describing ADHD (attention deficit hyper-activity disorder), a disorder that shares many similarities with those on the autistic spectrum.

Another negative symptom that Sass suggests may be an outcome of what I would term hyper-mentalism is a lack of sense of self in psychotics. We have already seen that something similar is found in autistics, but Sass points out that, "far from involving diminished capacity for self-conscious awareness" as is so often assumed, the disturbance in the sense of self seen in schizophrenics "is actually associated with an *exaggerated* self-consciousness" or "hyper-reflexivity."[54] Sass portrays schizophrenic individuals as "hyper-alert," having "hyper-awareness"[11f] and remarks of schizophrenics that "what entraps them… is a condition of hyper-intentionality, with exaggerated wilfulness and self-reference."[11g] Laing describes the "unembodied self" of the schizophrenic as "hyper-conscious" and developing a relationship with itself "which can become very complex"[20b]—or, in other words, highly mentalistically elaborated. He reports a case in point as lacking a sense of self because the patient was always asking himself whether it was *he* who really wanted to do the things he did,[11h] and another in which the subject insists that "his 'self' and his 'personality' were two quite separate things."[20c] Another psychotic remarked: "When I am ill I lose the sense of where I am. I feel 'I' can sit in the chair, and yet my body is hurtling out and somersaulting about 3 feet in front of me." Other patients report difficulty with distinguishing self from others: "Gradually I can no longer distinguish how much of myself is in me, and how much is already in others. I am a conglomeration, a monstrosity, modelled anew each day."[55] Sass quotes a schizophrenic remarking that "My downfall was insight… Too much insight can be very dangerous, because you can tear your mind apart." On another occasion the same patient added, "Well, look at the word 'analysis.' That means to break apart. When it turns upon the self, the mind would rip apart"[56]—and inevitably take the self with it.

By way of contrast, Attwood quotes a retired actor with Asperger's syndrome who remarked that it was only in his adult years that he developed his identity.[47b] The comment is particularly insightful in illustrating what is perhaps the most fundamental contrast between autistics and psychotics where sense of identity is concerned. Where autistics may fail to acquire a normal sense of self in the first place because of their arrested mental development, psychotics who report a lack of identity might be expected to have acquired it in the normal way, but then to have gone beyond it. Both may look sometimes superficially similar in their quest for confirmation of their sense of self, but in the case of the autistics this will result from a deficit that seeks a remedy, whereas in that of psychotics it will be the outcome of an overblown or over-elaborated self-concept that needs constant re-affirmation and re-inflation. And where autistics who lack a sense of self may come to rely on others to provide it, psychotics characteristically do it for themselves, vainly attempting to reinforce a sense of self by mentalizing to excess: "When I suddenly realized I hadn't been thinking about myself I was frightened to death. The unreality feeling came. I must never forget myself for a single instant. I watch the clock and keep busy or I won't know who I am."[20d]

Mental functions such as inhibition, self-control, and self-awareness are known to be mediated by the front part of the brain: specifically, the *pre-frontal cortex.* In a previous chapter I pointed out that this was also the part of the brain that can be inhibited by magnetism to produce autistic-savant-like skills in some normal volunteers (see pp. 28, 31). Deficits in executive frontal brain functions such as planning and prioritizing have been seen as fundamental to autism,[57] and in the first part of this chapter we saw that this was certainly true with regard to self-awareness and autobiographical memory. By contrast, we also saw just now that the right pre-frontal cortex was more active than normal in divergent thinking in people with milder schizophrenic tendencies. Delusions could be seen as extreme divergences in thinking, and so it is perhaps significant that brain-scanning studies point to an association between distortion of reality and hyper-activity of the medial pre-frontal cortex in patients with schizophrenia and similar disorders.[58] Moreover, a new computational model suggests that a neurological system critical to the activity of the pre-frontal cortex (the GABA, or *gamma-aminobutyric* one) is dysfunctional in psychotics thanks to moving into the so-called *H*—or hyper-active—mode. Furthermore, the same explanation appears to work for substance-induced psychosis and for epileptics who have schizophrenia-like symptoms. The author suggests that one of the consequences of the brain abnormality in schizophrenia would be hyper-excitability of this part of the cortex—just as we might suppose if hyper-mentalism were indeed the fundamental pathology in psychosis.[59] Although such studies are still in their infancy and much remains to be established about the functioning and physiology of the brain in both autistic and psychotic disorders, these particular findings hint that ultimately it might be possible to found both the imputed hypo-mentalism of autism and the parallel hyper-mentalism of psychosis on brain systems such as these. And clearly, if this were to be true, both qualitative extremes of mentalism could be traced to quantifiable differences in the brain and set on sound physical foundations.

A further case in point might be bipolar/manic-depressive disorder. This seems distinctly hyper-mentalistic to the extent that its distinguishing symptom—extremes of affect—is manifestly a pathological exaggeration of a normal aspect of mentalism. Manic delight when your team wins and abject depression when it loses are completely normal mental reactions. What makes such responses pathological in bipolar disorder is the extreme to which they are taken and the lack of real causes for them. But this again could be seen as characteristically hyper-mentalistic (and the converse of autism, where such normal emotional responses are often muted, or absent altogether). Moreover, you could see both mania and depression as pathological exaggerations of normal mind-reading. When people say they are "in the mood" for something, what they mean is that they are reading their own minds as positively disposed towards the thing in question; conversely, when they say they are "not in the mood" a negative reading of their state of mind has been taken. In mania and depression such normal exercises in assessing your own mental state are taken to extremes—almost as if the brain's mood-indicator had become hyper-sensitive, so that it indicated vastly greater swings in either direction. If so, the fundamental pathology would once again be quantitative: pathologically amplifying a normal exercise in inwardly directed mentalism into the bizarre exaggerations seen in bipolar disorder (and perhaps involving neurological systems comparable to that mentioned just now—although not necessarily located in the pre-frontal cortex). In any event, a recent study of almost 5000 hospitalized patients found that up to 23 per cent of those diagnosed bipolar reported hallucinations, and other reports suggest that between a half and three-quarters of manic-depressives experience some kind of psychotic symptom. Indeed, one study based on self-report questionnaires put the lifetime incidence of psychotic symptoms among manic-depressives as high as 90 per cent.[60,61,62] At the very least, such findings indicate that bipolar disorder might be much closer to schizophrenia than once supposed, even if the exact relation of the two psychoses remains unclear.

Where age of onset is concerned, the concepts of hypo- and hyper-mentalism neatly explain why autism is a disorder with an invariable onset in childhood, whereas classical schizophrenia is very much an adult-onset (or at the very least, a late adolescent) one, with childhood-onset schizophrenia being very rare (and even then appearing later than autism at about the age of eight).[63] The reason could simply be that no one could develop the characteristic hyper-mentalism of a psychosis without first developing a more normal level of mentalism—evidently something which usually takes the whole of childhood and the greater part of adolescence to achieve. Indeed, schizophrenics appear to have an ability to mentalize right up to their first breakdown,[64] and if they had failed to acquire a normal theory of mind in childhood they would have come to the attention of clinicians long before the onset of their illness.[65] Clearly, this is predictable if psychosis represents a pathological extension of mentalism far beyond the normal range: you would have to acquire normal mentalizing ability before it could become pathologically over-developed. But if autistics are symptomatically hypo-mentalistic, this would imply that they had never completed the normal process of mental development, but stopped short long before at some point in childhood (or perhaps regressed back to it). In any event, autistic symptoms would show in childhood and psychotic ones would not be seen fully developed until later—which is exactly what we normally find. In other words, here would be the reason why in the past at least people thought of autism only in relation to childhood, and of schizophrenia and other psychoses almost exclusively in relation to adult life.

Rupert Sheldrake's concept of what he calls "the extended mind" is another instance of what I would prefer to term hyper-mentalism. According to him, "Our minds are extended into the world around us, linking us to everything we see." This leads him to believe that "unexplained human abilities such as telepathy, the sense of being stared at and premonition are not paranormal but normal, part of our biological nature." Instead of thinking of minds as confined to brains, he suggests that "they involve extended fields of influence that stretch out far beyond brains and bodies" giving credence to reports of remote viewing, psychic spying and clairvoyance.[66] He adds that in another of his books, *Dogs that Know when Their Owners Are Coming Home,* he claimed that these unexplained powers are widely distributed in the animal kingdom. Such extensions of mental activity to other species, and such belief in "mental fields" extending out from the mind in time and space, eminently portray the concept of hyper-mentalism as clearly as the behaviourist's denial of the mind illustrates that of anti-mentalism (see pp. 56–57). Indeed, as schools of psychology, behaviourism and parapsychology stand at opposite ends on the continuum of mentalism: behaviourism at its hypo-mentalistic extreme and parapsychology at its hyper-mentalistic one.

Another common symptom of schizophrenia closely related to telepathy is *thought-insertion* or *thought-control:* the feeling that other people are responsible for, or are in some way controlling, what you are thinking. Once again, this is a pathological extension of the truth. Other people do indeed place thoughts in our minds, and the people and things we interact with do control our thinking to some extent. This book, for instance, is an attempt to insert thoughts into the reader's mind (I hope a successful one); and doing something such as driving a car does claim a person's attention and does indeed control their thinking, for example to the extent that it obliges them to pay attention to traffic signals. But in psychosis the mechanistic basis of such thought-insertion or control is neglected, and thoughts in themselves are believed to be transmitted independent of words spoken or printed on a page, while external forces or agents are imagined to control the mind directly. Such hyper-mentalism can then all too easily generate secondary hyper-mentalizing in response. In the words of one unusually insightful schizophrenic:

> By delving into the backstage, behind-the-scenes working of my thinking, I was assuring myself that I was in control of my own thoughts. I had to reassure myself that I was not being toyed with telepathically by someone else—that it was I who was minding my own business, that I really did have a mind of my own.[67]

Magic and religion

With the fore-going in mind, you could see religion along with magic and superstitious thinking in general as the normal, socially acceptable expression of hyper-mentalism in human culture. To the extent that magic and superstition are cultural, you could see them as contagious cancers of the mind: something that a person catches by contact with others whose minds are already infected. Indeed, where one religion or superstition becomes dominant in a society, we would be justified in calling it not just a cancerous contagion of the mind, but a mental epidemic. And of course, in a culture where everyone is hyper-mentalistic in certain respects, such madness becomes normal, and escapes recognition for what it is. On the contrary, in a mad-house taken over by the inmates, only the sane seem abnormal!

Magic invites credulity for miracles and supernatural intervention in the form of the belief that prayers, rituals, or spells can affect physical reality and bring about the fulfilment of wishes—or, in other words, that mere mental factors such as intentions and expressions can change the real world. Superstition is based on the belief that things are not what they seem, and that behind apparent chance events or manifest appearances lurks a deeper, more psychologically significant reality that can be interpreted in typical mentalistic terms such as intention, meaning, guilt, or justice. Experiment reveals that most people entertain highly anthropomorphic expectations about their gods, however much this may conflict with their explicit beliefs. Specifically, people expect their gods' minds to work much like human ones, displaying the same processes of perception, memory, reasoning, and motivation. People remember stories best when they include a combination of counter-intuitive physical feats (for example, ones in which characters go through walls or move instantaneously) and plausibly human psychological features (such as perceptions, thoughts, and intentions).[68] Religion applies mentalistic thinking to the entire world and maintains that beyond immediate appearances life has a moral and ethical dimension often represented in divine judgement and retribution in an after-life, heaven, or hell. As a result, reality as a whole—and not just social reality—becomes peopled with divine agents who can be influenced in mentalistic ways analogous to those in which ordinary humans can be: through supplication (prayer), flattery (praise), generosity (sacrifice), apology (confession), restitution (penance), visitation (pilgrimage), and lobbying (intercession via saints, angels, or other deities). Accommodation for deities is provided in temples, churches, and chapels; and entertainment added in the form of sacred music, dramas, and processions. Indeed, some religions even claim to have quasi-legal, mutually binding contracts with their deity such as can only otherwise exist between human agents, such as the Old and New Covenants of Judaism and Christianity respectively; and several regard God as the author of their sacred book and guarantor of their claims to territorial sovereignty and racial integrity. In this way, all manner of personal and collective fears, failings, and frustrations beyond the remedy of mere mortals can be redressed, and a mentalistic adaptation could become the foundation for the evolution of religion. As Schreber perceptively commented:

> the legends and poetry of all peoples literally swarm with the activities of ghosts, elves, goblins, etc., and it seems…nonsensical to assume that in all of them one is dealing simply

with deliberate inventions of human imagination without any foundation in real fact.[9g]

The real fact, however, was the evolution of mentalism as a means of inter-personal communication, and the foundation of all this was its primeval inflation into an imaginary means of influencing reality as a whole (see the box below: Religion versus science).

Religion versus science

If there are indeed two parallel cognitive systems, mentalistic and mechanistic cognition as proposed here, a notable contrast between them is that historically mentalism appears to have undergone an extraordinary primeval inflation in the form of magic, superstition, and religion, while mechanistic understanding of nature had to wait until modern times to transform the world. Presumably the reason for this is that although mechanistic skills evolved in parallel with mentalistic ones, mechanistic thinking in the form of scientific and technological theorizing required the prior evolution of literacy and numeracy—not to mention mathematics and technological developments such as the telescope.

However, religion also seems to have evolved from primitive animism to modern monotheisms via totemism and polytheism. *Animism* attributed minds to objects, places, and natural phenomena in the form of a belief in spirits who inhabited these things. *Totemism* extended the concept of an animal mind to invest entire species with spiritual affinities to social groups such as clans or tribes. *Polytheism* peopled heaven with human deities of all kinds, often comprising entire dynasties of divinities whose human faculties and even frailties are often wonderfully apparent in the great literary works describing them such as *The Iliad, Ramayana,* or *Mahabharata.* But it is in *monotheism* that the purely mentalistic attributes of the deity are developed to an extreme degree. Hence human gaze-monitoring becomes divine *omnipresence* by means of which God sees all things; human mind-reading becomes divine *omniscience* by way of which God knows every thought and intention; and psychological agency becomes divine *omnipotence* by way of which God can do any and all things. The mentalistic sense of being a unique self that consciousness confers on normal human beings (if not necessarily on autistics) becomes the belief in the uniqueness of one God, and the denial of all others. Literacy creates the opportunity for sacred texts, not simply *about* the deity but ultimately authored—or at least endorsed—by the deity, and for the prescription of moral codes and the anathematization of heresies. And along with this goes the idea of God as a just judge, corrector of all wrongs, and punisher of evil, which epitomizes his role as the ultimate expression of the moral dimension of mentalism. In short, God emerges in the evolution of religion as the being with the supreme mentality and the ultimate theory of mind—hyper-mentalism incarnate!

Magic, superstition, and religion are extensions of mentalism into regions where it does not actually apply: the physical, material world which is the proper domain of mechanistic cognition. The consequence is that a conflict between mentalism and mechanistic thinking was inevitable and unavoidable once science and technology began to develop and reclaim territory lost to mentalism, such as astronomy, where the Copernican revolution replaced traditional astrology and Aristotelian cosmology. The next great conflict occurred—and, in some places at least, is still going on—when Darwin discovered a mechanistic alternative to biblical creation mythology. However, a third and perhaps definitive conflict seems inevitable now that, thanks to research into autism and technological advances such as brain-scanning, mentalism itself is coming under mechanistic scrutiny. Where once the mind inflated to comprehend all things in terms of mental agency, now mechanistic cause-and-effect at the level of genes, neuro-anatomy, and brain physiology seems poised to claim the mind as its ultimate prize!

In his *Natural History of Religion* David Hume (1711–76) observed that there is a:

> universal tendency among mankind to conceive all beings like themselves, and to transfer to every object, those qualities, with which they are familiarly acquainted, and of which they are intimately conscious. We find human faces in the moon, armies in the clouds; and by a natural propensity, if not corrected by experience and reflection, ascribe malice or good-will to every thing, that hurts or pleases us. Hence…trees, mountains and streams are personified, and the inanimate parts of nature acquire sentiment and passion.[69a]

Indeed, Hume adds that even "philosophers cannot exempt themselves from this natural frailty; but have often ascribed…to inanimate matter the horror of a vacuum, sympathies, antipathies, and other affections of human nature."[69b]

But the question remains of why human beings should so compulsively and routinely mentalize nature. A recent suggestion is that we see apparent people everywhere because it is vital to see actual people wherever they may be. And not just people: "it is better for a hiker to mistake a boulder for a bear than to mistake a bear for a boulder."[69c] In other words, to the extent that hyper-mentalism means attributing human-like minds to objects or organisms that in reality lack them, it is entirely normal, and the occasional false alarms, so to speak, are more than compensated for by the importance of not missing a real occurrence:

> when we see something as alive and humanlike, we can take precautions. If we see it as alive we can, for example, stalk it or flee. If we see it as humanlike, we can try to establish a social relationship. If it turns out not to be alive or humanlike we usually lose little by having thought it was. This practice thus yields more in occasional big successes than it costs in frequent little failures. In short,…"better safe than sorry."[69d]

Exactly the same reasoning explains other pathological mental states such as anxiety attacks or phobias. In these cases too, the better-safe-than-sorry principle applies and explains why, even though there may be so many false alarms, the fear/phobia system is nevertheless more useful if set for too much sensitivity than it would be if set for too little. For some individuals at the extreme end of the sensitivity setting this may mean chronic, disabling anxiety or irrational phobias, and much the same could be true of mentalism. It may be that paranoid schizophrenics such as Schreber represent only the extreme end of a normal distribution, with everyone having some tendency to over-mentalize in some situations but few taking it to such lengths as he did. Mentalism, in other words, like anxiety or phobias, may be a naturally selected tendency that would only become pathological in cases such as Schreber's where it far exceeded its normal bounds.

Nevertheless, if a greater tendency to belief in magic, superstition, and religion can be found among psychotics such as Schreber, the same reasoning suggests that it should be found less among autistics. Interestingly in this respect, the issue of autistics' attitude to religion and belief in God is raised by the case of a Scottish eighteenth-century autistic, Hugh Blair of Borgue (1708/9–65), who lived at a time when religious observance was much more important than it is in many places today. Hugh's difficulties brought him to the attention of the courts with the result that detailed documentation about him has been unusually well preserved. In their retrospective analysis of the legal proceedings that provide much of the evidence on which the diagnosis of Blair's autism is based, Houston and Frith comment that:

> It follows that a lack of theory of mind restricts a religious sense… For this reason the question posed by the judges: "Did Hugh Blair have a sense of God?" can be interpreted as analogous to the question posed by modern psychologists: "Did Hugh Blair have a theory of mind?"

Their answer is that his behaviour suggested that Hugh appreciated religious feelings and participated in the proper religious activities.

Nevertheless, they point out that the final verdict of the court implies that the judges did not believe that Hugh had the same sense of God as other members of the community, and conclude that this matches their interpretation of Hugh having a diminished awareness of mental states.[25b]

Up to the present, there have not been any systematic studies of autistics' religious feelings or beliefs, but one paper has been published that considered the evidence in autobiographical accounts such as those I quoted in the last chapter. The author concludes that religion in autism is entirely different from normal experience, and that God is perceived more as a principle than as a mental agent. Instead, God is seen as a force responsible for organizing the cosmos in an orderly fashion, or is reduced to the equivalent of scientific logic itself. She adds that a sense of inter-personal relations between the worshipper and the deity and of emotional dependency on an intentional agent who has control over the individual is noticeably absent in autistic accounts of religion. This writer comes to the conclusion that because autistics have difficulty interpreting the meaning attached to social behaviour and therefore probably cannot rely on a theory of mind to explain their experiences, their religious beliefs cannot attach to core representations of mental agency. Consequently, supernatural agents such as God are perceived as behavioural rather than intentional agents.[70] Indeed, the mother with two autistic sons who I have cited before remarks that her boys "don't turn to God as a way of navigating life's difficulties," adding that when one of them "was (inappropriately) attending a mainstream primary school, his report simply said, 'Religious Knowledge: not applicable'."[71]

Although hardly a typical autistic, Kim Peek (see pp. 27–28), is worth quoting in this context. His father comments that his son attended a Mormon seminary five times a week for 20 years and graduated with 20 diplomas. Yet he adds that, "Because of his reasoning limitations, I think his religion is what he's read and heard, not what he contemplates and tries to reason about. He is purely fact-oriented, so he doesn't normally express his feelings about faith or religious doctrines." An amusing example of Kim Peek's literalness in this respect is the occasion when, out with his father, an inebriated stranger stopped him and said, "My son, Jesus walks with you." "No," Kim shot back, "this is my father!" When asked by Dustin Hoffman if he believed in God, Kim replied, "In God there is mystery. In my heart there is mystery. Two mysteries make one belief. To know oneself is to know God. Thank you." When asked if he prayed, his answer was: "God is almighty. He knows my mind. Thank you."[72]

Where more typical cases are concerned, an account of the religious belief of one high-functioning autistic observes that the person concerned, "Simply could not cope with spirituality when it was seen as the collective considerations of others;" adding that, "owing to the specific nature of his cognitive and emotional impairments he had found it very difficult to engage either in the theological and/or the philosophical debate that occurred in the traditional construction of religious practice."[73] Observations such as this explain why Tony Attwood points out that clinicians need to be aware of the qualitative and functional differences between a special interest in the supernatural on the part of a high-functioning autistic "and the early signs of schizophrenia."[47c]

We saw earlier that Albert Einstein has been suspected of having notable autistic tendencies (see p. 26). In this context it is worth pointing out that in a recent book Richard Dawkins introduced the term *Einsteinian religion* to distinguish between the great physicist's purely metaphorical invocations of the deity and true *supernatural religion.*[74] Dawkins makes this distinction because, although Einstein famously made remarks to the effect that God does not play dice with the universe and that, although subtle, the Lord is not perverse, he also explicitly denied belief in a personal God, and admitted only to being 'a deeply religious non-believer.' Indeed, Einstein explicitly added that 'I have never imputed to Nature a purpose or goal, or anything that could be understood as anthropomorphic,' and insisted that "The idea of a personal God is quite alien to me and seems even naïve."[74a] But another way of making the same point would be to say that Einstein's religious thinking—like that of the typical autistic—was notably *hypo-mentalistic* rather than hyper-mentalistic, and to the extent that it was based on scientific insight, perhaps even what you could call *mechanistic.*

Indeed, *quantum mechanistic* might seem justified in the case of Temple Grandin. Despite declaring herself to be first and foremost a "hard-brained scientist,"[75] she rationalizes her belief that "humans have greater amounts of soul because they have more microtubules where single electrons could dance, according to the rules of quantum theory":[22b]

> In all the years I have worked in slaughter plants, I have intuitively felt that I must never misbehave near the kill chute. Doing something bad, like mistreating an animal, could have dire consequences. An entangled subatomic particle could get me. I would never even know it, but the steering linkage in my car could break if it contained the mate to a particle I disturbed by doing something bad.[22c]

Grandin recounts incidents when power transformers blew up and other electrical outages occurred as she arrived at slaughter houses where cattle were abused, or equipment failed because a plant manager shouted at her angrily, and again suggests that "bad karma" may have started "a resonance in an entangled pair of subatomic particles within wiring or steel." She adds that "These were all weird breakdowns of things that usually never break," and asks whether this "could just be random chance" or "some sort of cosmic consciousness of God."[22d]

Of course, you could call this superstition rather than religion, and I suggested earlier that superstition is another manifestation of hypermentalism. Nevertheless, a comparison of Temple Grandin's remarkable book *Animals in Translation* with Sheldrake's *Dogs that Know when Their Owners Are Coming Home* mentioned earlier reveals that Grandin is by far the more objective of the two, and although attributing remarkable cognitive abilities—and even genius—to some animals, denies that they are telepathic, or capable of pre-cognition or any other kind of extra-sensory perception (ESP). On the contrary, in an apparent reference to Sheldrake she specifically says that "a lot of people think animals have ESP... There's even a scientist in England who's written books about ESP. But they don't have ESP, they just have sensitive sensory apparatus."[76]

Again, the fact that no less a behaviourist than B. F. Skinner once published a paper entitled "'Superstition' in the pigeon"[77] suggests that the situation with regard to apparent superstitious thinking in autistics may be more subtle than it seems. The irony of this is of course the fact that in this paper—and despite the inverted commas around the word superstition—Skinner appears to attribute a highly mentalistic attribute to a laboratory animal which is supposed to lack any kind of mind, at least according to the anti-mentalistic nostrums of behaviourism (see pp. 56–63). Skinner used the term "superstition" to describe the widely replicated finding that laboratory animals can become spontaneously and accidentally conditioned by otherwise random or freak stimuli that might occur in association with a reward. For example, if a hungry pigeon is placed in a cage and receives food at random intervals unlinked to any particular behaviour, the pigeon is likely to become conditioned to keep repeating whatever it happened to be doing when the first reward arrived. And of course, once this apparent link is established and the animal begins to repeat the reinforced behaviour more frequently, the more likely it is to become even further reinforced by subsequent rewards occurring in connection with it. In fact, Skinner's experiments showed that an interval between reinforcements of about 15 seconds was the optimal one and that one as long as a minute was much less so.[77]

It was of course the apparently compulsive repetition of the reinforced behaviour that made Skinner think of superstition—along with the fact that the experimenter knew that there was in reality no connection whatsoever between the behaviour and the reward that had occasioned it. Indeed, the superstitious pigeon was so intuitively appealing to audiences that Skinner frequently used it as a classroom demonstration that was—and apparently still is in the words of one authority—"a consistent crowd-pleaser."[78] In terms of the concepts being developed in the course of this book, you could see the pigeon's superstition as *mechanistic*, rather than mentalistic: it would be purely behaviourally superstitious—superstition without any mental content whatsoever. But equally, whatever could happen in a pigeon in this respect could just as easily—perhaps even more easily—occur in a human being. As Skinner himself pointed out:

> There are many analogies in human behavior. Rituals for changing one's luck at cards are good examples. A few accidental connections between a ritual and favorable consequences suffice to set up and maintain the behavior in spite of many unreinforced instances. The bowler who has released a ball down the alley but continues to behave as if he were controlling it by twisting and turning his arm and shoulder is another case in point. These behaviors have, of course, no real effect upon one's luck or upon a ball half way down an alley, just as in the present case the food would appear as often as it does if the pigeon did nothing—or, more correctly speaking, did something else.[77a]

In other words, if a pigeon can exhibit what I would call *mechanistic superstition*, then so too can a human being, and the sporting or card-playing examples cited immediately above underline the mechanistic aspect because they relate to mechanical actions carried out on objects or imagined to influence them. The mother of the two autistic boys I quoted above on the lack of religious feeling in her sons adds that:

> Autistic children…don't collude in magic because it involves the use of mentalizing skills they simply don't possess… To appreciate magic, you need a firm grasp of what's normal, what's expected. Autists, who see the world in disconnected detail rather than as a coherent whole, lack that overview of normality.[26b]

To the best of my knowledge, no one has ever investigated the superstitions of autistics in any systematic way, but we have already seen that impressions of their religious beliefs suggest that they fit the pattern we might predict and are less mentalistic and much more mechanistic than normal. Again, we saw earlier in this chapter that many autistic people lack a sense of personal agency and as a result fail to connect events that happen around them to their own internal mental states. As a result, autistics might be predicted to be even more likely to exhibit superstitious behaviour than normal people. Indeed, to the extent that an autistic might be severely hypo-mentalistic, they might be as prone to superstitious behaviour as one of Skinner's pigeons.

The reason for this would be that, whereas a normal person might be able to relate events around them to their own and others' motives, knowledge, state of mind, skills, and abilities, an autistic might simply observe them happening without reference to themselves or others, rather as we saw exemplified by the three young men mentioned in the previous chapter (see pp. 92–93). Lacking an ability to interpret such events in terms of their own or others' mental states, an autistic might be all the more likely to attribute them to luck, God, or any other arbitrary factor that seemed credible. For example, autistic children often do not understand the difference between justified knowledge and a mere guess, and the case is recorded of an intelligent autistic boy of 12 who answered questions by saying he knew certain things "By telepathy."[79] Belief in—or perhaps it would be more accurate to say *invocation of*—telepathy is thus not necessarily evidence of what I am calling hyper-mentalism. In this case it looks more like a convenient excuse, rather than a piece of mental insight. Indeed, high-functioning Asperger's cases in particular might be especially prone to attribute certain events to such external agencies and to try to close the gap, so to speak, between their own minds and those of others by use of socially accepted symbolism, such as that of conventional religion, traditional superstition, or parapsychology.

Mental metastasis

An implication of this line of reasoning is that, if autistics are hypo-mentalistic even when they are religious or superstitious, psychotics might be correspondingly *hypo-mechanistic*. If there are indeed two parallel cognitive systems—what I am calling mentalistic and mechanistic cognition—and if deficits in mentalism sometimes go with remarkable mechanistic skills in autism, you might wonder to what extent hyper-mentalistic psychotics also tended to show mechanistic short-comings. We also saw that autistics often have superior sensory abilities, and where visual acuity is concerned, psychotics have been reported to have deficits in vision that symmetrically balance the enhancements found in autism.[80] Some psychotic patients report that they have deficits in "sensory discrimination," along with "poor neuro-muscular co-ordination" and "sensorimotor activity," thanks to domination by "central-symbolic, particularly verbal activity" serving the "ideological level," which "is the most highly developed" in schizophrenics.[81] As another psychotic put it, "I'd like a pack of cards with four suits—morals, phantasy, reality—I'd like to get rid of the reality suit."[11i] According to one psychiatric authority, "the mentally sane person…is subjectively certain and not to be corrected when speaking about her own mental states"—that is, when speaking *mentalistically*. However, "The patient with delusions differs…in so far as he speaks with subjective certainty and incorrigibly about facts which do not lie within the scope of his mentality: things, events, other persons, in short, the external world." Psychotic delusions can therefore be defined as "*statements about external reality which are uttered like statements about a mental state, i.e., with subjective certainty and incorrigible by others.*"[82]

As this book went to press, a study using brain imaging revealed that, by comparison to normal controls, paranoid patients attribute intention to purely physical causality and, as the authors put it, could be described as "treating things like persons." The authors propose that mentalism in paranoid patients might malfunction because it is over-active from the start "and thus is not well suited to distinguish between mental and physical states." On the contrary, they conclude that—just as I argue here—detection of intention becomes "hyper-active in the paranoid interpretation of the physical world."[83]

In other words, delusional thinking is hyper-mentalistic not simply in the sense of going beyond normal mentalism, but in encroaching on non-mental, mechanistic reality. Schizophrenics have been found to have impaired visual-spatial and maths abilities, relative to their verbal skills, and to be especially poor at solving practical and commonsensical problems.[84] Again, one study found that carriers of a genetic tendency to psychosis in their near relatives showed impairments in verbal memory and in visual and spatial abilities. A separate study concluded that a relative superiority of verbal to spatial skills—or what I would call mentalistic to mechanistic cognition—represents a cognitive asymmetry characteristic of schizophrenia.[85,86] Indeed, even depression has been linked to deficits in spatial memory to the extent that depressed patients have been found to perform significantly less well than healthy controls in video games demanding good spatial recall.[87]

Hyper-mentalism, in conclusion, is not simply a malignancy of the mind understood as excessive mentalizing within its proper inter- and intra-personal realm. As in actual cancers, the disease becomes really dangerous when it advances to the stage of *metastasis*: the spread of the malignancy to other parts of the body. In this case metastatic mentalism invades mechanistic cognition as well so that, not simply mentalizing functions, but the mind as a whole becomes cancerous, and reason and reality are put at risk.

Chapter 5

The Battle of the Sexes in the Brain

In the last two chapters we saw that a remarkable pattern was emerging when we compared autistic and psychotic symptoms. Not only could we make a case for psychoses such as paranoid schizophrenia being the hyper-mentalistic equivalent of autistic hypo-mentalism, but we also saw that individual symptoms could often be portrayed as opposites. In this chapter I want to consider the possible genetic, evolutionary, and neuro-anatomical explanations for such an extraordinary antithesis of symptoms. But before we look at that, we should begin with the more general issue of the heritability of mental illnesses such as autism and schizophrenia.

Strange inheritance

Although claims have been made that autism "knows no racial, ethnic, or social boundaries" and that "Family income, lifestyle, and educational levels do not affect the chance of autism's occurrence,"[1] Kanner himself clearly thought differently. In his very first account, he commented regarding his cases of autism that *"They all come of highly intelligent families,"*[2a] adding in 1949 that his "search for unsophisticated parents of autistic children had remained unsuccessful to date."[3] He went on to assert that "For the most part, the parents, grand-parents, and collaterals are persons strongly preoccupied with abstractions of a scientific, literary, or artistic nature, and limited in genuine interest in people."[2b.] Indeed, in his second paper on autism a year later, he added that "Nine of the twenty families are represented either in *Who's Who in America* or in *American Men of Science*, or both."[4] We have already seen that Asperger also noticed that his cases often came from families in which the father's profession was a technical or engineering one, and today there is good evidence that both Kanner and Asperger were right in thinking that parental characteristics do indeed contribute to the risk of autism.[5]

An astonishing example of the possibility that both fathers and mothers may contribute to the likelihood that a child will be diagnosed autistic can be found in the reported incidence of these disorders in Silicon Valley (Santa Clara County, California). In 1993 there were 4911 diagnosed cases of autism. In 1999 the figure passed 10,000, and in 2001 there were 15,441 cases, with new ones added at seven per day, 85 per cent of them children. Furthermore, such hot-spots for autism are not limited to California: comparable findings are reported from the Cambridge area in England. Given that employment in Silicon Valley and around Cambridge is primarily in electronic engineering and computing, and that equal-opportunity employment means that many children born there will have both parents in these industries, so-called *assortative mating* has been suggested as the most likely explanation. This is the finding that likes attract, and that people tend to marry partners who have much in common with themselves. In other words, it looks as if mentalistic deficits in "things people" with engineering skills are being compounded in their children by inheritance of these deficits from both parents.[5,6] Studies to confirm this conclusion are currently under way, and the first results suggest that mothers of children with autism are indeed more likely to have a more technological turn of mind than normal.[7]

Although autism has been described as one of the most heritable of all psychiatric conditions,[8] it is not one that obeys the laws of inheritance discovered by Mendel. These state that individuals inherit a complete set of genes from each parent, and that genes can be *dominant* or *recessive*. Normally, both copies of a particular gene (or *allele*) are expressed.

However, recessive genes are different: they are not expressed if paired with a non-recessive allele from the other parent. But if a child inherits the same recessive gene from each parent, it is expressed, since there is no alternative non-recessive allele present. This explains how many deleterious genes survive: they are only expressed—and therefore subject to natural selection—in the rare instances when a person has two copies of them. However, when inherited as just a single copy—which will happen in the vast majority of cases—they are not expressed and so escape selection. Dominant genes, by contrast, are always fully expressed, even when inherited as a single allele. The result is a complex, but highly regular and predictable pattern of inheritance which medical genetics has fully explored. Yet autism does not fit the Mendelian model, and if genes for it exist, they do not behave like classic dominants or recessives.

Nevertheless, autism does seem to run in families. If one of two identical twins is autistic there is a 60 per cent chance that the other will also be, and there is an 86 per cent chance that the other will have some symptoms of autism. Again, there is a 1-in-20 risk of a second child in a family being autistic if one is already, while the risk of a third also being autistic after two previous children have been diagnosed is 1-in-3. Recent research based on 3000 twin pairs aged seven to nine suggests that core symptoms of autism such as social deficits, communicative difficulties, and rigid or repetitive behaviour are only loosely linked (at least in childhood). Indeed, 59 per cent showed only social impairments, and 10 per cent showed deficits in only one of these three core symptoms that would satisfy a diagnosis of autism. The same study added that there may be many individuals with isolated deficits of an autistic nature that do not quite meet diagnostic criteria but who nevertheless have difficulties of comparable severity to those who do.[9] Finally, family and twin studies have shown that relatives of autistics show increased rates of more broadly defined, sub-clinical autistic traits with incidences approaching 50 per cent in first degree relatives.[9,10*]

---

*   The claim that rates of incidence are similar for all ethnic and racial groups is also dubious. Evidence exists suggesting a lower than normal incidence among American Indians and Hispanics and an increased one among African Americans.[11]

Similar findings relate to the heritability of schizophrenia. Like autism, it is indisputably heritable, yet also like autism, schizophrenia does not obey Mendel's laws of inheritance. Nevertheless, there is a 48 per cent probability that if one of a pair of identical twins has the condition, so will the other; and there is also a 45 per cent chance that if both of a child's parents have schizophrenia a child of theirs will also develop it. The figure for fraternal twins is 17 per cent, and the risk factor for a child in a family having schizophrenia if a sibling has it is 9 per cent.[12]

Schizophrenia, like autism, poses another paradox because, along with this high degree of heritability, it manifestly damages individuals' survival and reproductive success. So how could the genes responsible evolve? Nevertheless—and again like autism—schizophrenia persists at a prevalence of about 1 per cent across all human cultures. A recently proposed solution is that genetic liability to schizophrenia has evolved as a consequence of selection for human traits involving social cognition, creativity, and language[13,14]—or what I would call mentalism. According to this hypothesis, genes that increase risk of schizophrenia have been subject to positive selection in the evolution of human beings thanks to their key role in mentalistic cognition. Recently, Crespi, Summers, and Dorus evaluated this hypothesis by screening human and primate genes for evidence of positive selection. They found statistically significant evidence for positive selection on 26 of 80 genes mediating liability to schizophrenia, including some which exhibit some of the best-supported functional and genetic links to this disorder. Previous studies indicated that recent positive selection in humans has driven the evolution of a suite of additional genes linked with schizophrenia risk, and variants of three genes associated with schizophrenia have recently been linked with measures of creativity. Taken together, the authors conclude that these findings provide evolutionary and genetic support for the hypothesis that schizophrenia represents "the illness that made us human."[15]

Or at least, half of what makes us human. If I am right about mentalism being only one of two systems that run side-by-side in normal cognition, the other half of what makes us human is mechanistic cognitive skill, and it is not hard to see why this should have evolved. As we have already seen, there is a statistically significant link between autism and engineering, with Asperger's syndrome being colloquially known as *The Engineer's Disorder*. If so, this in itself:

> might also help to explain why a condition like autism persists in the gene pool: the very same genes that lead an individual to have a child with autism can lead to superior functioning in the domain of folk physics. Engineering and related folk physics skills have transformed the way in which our species live (*sic*), without question for the better. Indeed, without such skills, Homo sapiens would still be pre-industrial.[16]

In other words, while the genes that can produce psychoses such as schizophrenia appear to underlie the mentalistic skills of people people, the mechanistic abilities of things people might be explained by genes that could predispose to autism. As Temple Grandin points out:

> If all the genes and other factors that cause autism were eliminated, the world would be populated by very social people who accomplish very little. The really social people are not motivated enough by "making things" to spend the time necessary to create great art, beautiful music or master-works of engineering that require attention to detail. It's just not part of their mindset. Yet, that's often where people with ASD excel.[17]

Part of the paradox of why severe mental illnesses such as autism and schizophrenia have genetic causes may therefore lie in the fact that the very same genes that can produce these pathological conditions also underpin the twin cognitive systems on which human pre-eminence as a species relies: mentalistic and mechanistic cognition. One gave us our society, culture, language, and ability to empathize and interact with other people's minds. The other gave us science, technology, and all the manual, mechanical, and technical skills on which our civilizations depend. If this view is correct, autism and psychoses such as schizophrenia are indeed the price we pay for these critical cognitive adaptations.

The extreme male brain

Another possible solution to the genetic paradox of autism at least is that autism represents an exaggeration of a perfectly normal type of development, in this case, that of male mentality. Reasons for thinking this may be so were apparent from the beginning when both Kanner and Asperger noticed that what they were each independently describing as autism was much more prevalent in males than in females. In fact, Asperger originally believed that his syndrome never occurred in girls before puberty.[18] Nor were such initial impressions misleading: rates of incidence of the disorder are four to five times higher in males than in females and higher still in Asperger's syndrome.[19] According to some estimates, males exceed females by 10-to-1 or more at the highest functioning end of the autistic spectrum associated with Asperger's syndrome.[20-22] Indeed, in his original report Hans Asperger suggested that autism may represent an extreme development of the normal male brain: "The autistic personality is an extreme variant of male intelligence... Boys...tend to have a gift for logical ability, abstraction, precise thinking and formulating, and for independent scientific investigation. In the autistic individual, the male pattern is exaggerated to the extreme."[23]

If this were so, we might expect early developmental influences, ultimately controlled by genes and mediated by hormones, to account for the development of autism. Testosterone is the principal hormone involved in male sexual differentiation before birth, and there is now good evidence that it affects brain development in ways that could predispose to autism. For example, a recent study carried out at the age of 12 months found that girls made significantly more eye-contact than boys and that the amount of eye-contact in both sexes was related to exposure to foetal testosterone.[24] A similar study found that girls had a considerably larger vocabulary than boys at 18 and 24 months, and that this difference was related to foetal testosterone exposure, suggesting that it might be involved in shaping the neural mechanisms underlying both eye-contact and language ability.[25] More recently still, further findings suggest that pre-natal exposure to male sex hormones is associated with poorer quality of social relationships and more restricted interests, particularly in boys.[26]

Experiments with babies only a day old show that from birth girls attend more to social stimuli, such as faces and voices, than do boys, who attend more to non-social, spatial stimuli, such as mobiles or traffic.[27] Babies with autism show an even more marked lack of interest in faces than normal males, and here it may be significant that autistics process visual information about faces in the same part of the brain normally used for objects alone, rather than in the specialized face-recognition and reaction region found in normal people.[28,29] Normally girls develop social skills sooner than boys, and studies suggest average female superiority in language skills, social judgement, empathy, and co-operation. Most girls develop language earlier than most boys, and by 18 months there can be a huge difference between boys and girls, with some children still not yet speaking and others with vocabularies of up to 600 words.[27]

Women on average perform better at verbal tasks than do men. For example, they can generally name twice as many synonyms for a word than can the average man, and women can usually generate longer lists of words beginning with the same letter. As these findings might suggest, language-associated cortical areas are proportionately larger in the female brain.[30] Women activate more brain regions on difficult verbal tasks than do men, who by contrast to women only activate the right cortex on challenging spatial tasks.[31] At birth, the right hemisphere is normally larger in males, whereas the corpus callosum is larger in females, and its size is linked to verbal intelligence.[32] This may be why brain-imaging of a rhyming task showed that men activated only the left hemisphere (specifically, Broca's area), whereas women activated both left and right sides of the brain. Such differences in laterality between the sexes may also explain why men but not women usually suffer verbal deficits following left hemisphere stroke.[33]

Women are also superior to men in perceptual speed as measured, for example,' in finding matching items; fine-motor co-ordination (such as that involved in needle-work); pretend play in childhood; and arithmetic. Male superiority is normally found in mathematical reasoning, especially geometry and logic. Indeed, at the highest level male mathematicians outnumber female 13-to-1. Men also normally excel in embedded- and rotated-figure tasks.[34,35] Interestingly in this respect, female-to-male transsexuals who receive testosterone injections in preparation for their sex-change operations have been reported to show large increases in rotational ability.[36] One such sex-change patient recorded the following impressions after three months of testosterone treatments:

> I have problems expressing myself, I stumble over my words. Your use of language becomes less broad, more direct and concise...you become more concrete... I think less; I act faster, without thinking... The visual is so strong...when walking in the streets I absorb the things around me... It gives a euphoric feeling. I do miss, however, the overall picture. Now I have to do one thing at a time; I used to be able to do different things simultaneously... I can't make fine hand movements anymore; I let things fall out of my hands... My fantasy life has diminished strongly... I would have liked to keep that. I am becoming clumsy, more blinkered. I didn't ask for this; it just happens.[37a]

Another recent finding that may have a similar explanation is the fact that women carrying male foetuses improve their performance on difficult cognitive tasks involving working memory and spatial ability, but not on any other tests. Although the factor responsible could not be determined and is unlikely to have been foetal testosterone, some other similar product of the foetus/placenta is almost certainly the cause.[38] By contrast, *androgen deprivation* is a male sex hormone-reducing therapy sometimes used to treat prostate cancer in men. Subjects given cognitive tests after therapy showed slightly improved verbal fluency but reduced ability to recall images, suggesting that their skills in these respects had been shifted towards the female pole of cognitive ability.[39]

Males are generally superior in most (but not all) spatial skills, and in target-directed motor skills, irrespective of practice. Where navigation is concerned, recent experiments found that men travel about 20 per cent further in virtual mazes than women do. Furthermore, women take approximately 30 per cent longer to orientate themselves, and are more likely than the men to be wrong when they do. Out of an equal number of males and females using a virtual maze for real-life navigation, only 1 of 17 subjects who got completely lost was male.[40] One possible explanation is that male and female brains simply do not work the same way in such situations. Brain-imaging recently demonstrated that on exiting a virtual 3-D maze women activate the right parietal cortex and right pre-frontal cortex, whereas men trigger the left hippocampus alone.[41]

In the case of geography, boys always win the National Geography Bee, which tests American children in grades 4 to 8 on their knowledge of places around the world,[42] and male college students can locate almost twice as many countries on an unlabelled map of the world as female students can.[43] In general, men—but not boys—seem to navigate preferentially by vector (that is, directions with distances), whereas women—but not girls—normally prefer to use landmarks.[44] The fact that this difference only appears after puberty suggests that it is an evolved, innate one mediated by sex hormones. Furthermore, such evolved sex-differences in cognition would have made sense in our ancestral environment to the extent that vegetarian food of the kind typically collected by women in primal hunter-gatherer societies is indeed often best located by reference to fixed landmarks. However, game that is being pursued by hunters can take off in any direction, and may well dictate a novel, cross-country return to base, rather than one using well-known paths. Such cross-country navigation demands exactly the kind of spatial sense at which men excel, and studies of women's greater ability to remember the location of objects closer to home also fits the predictions from the hunter-gatherer model.[45] Indeed, remarkable geographical and navigation skills are also occasionally found in autistic savants, suggesting that these are yet another aspect of mechanistic cognition.[46]

Again, tool-making and missile-throwing ability would certainly have benefited primeval males more than females in most instances, and such skills would probably have been critically involved with males' success in conflicts both with other males and in hunting. According to an experimental archaeologist who has been making stone tools for 37 years, the basic skills needed for making such tools are mainly visual, spatial, and manual, and specifically: good hand–eye co-ordination; a good sense of geometry; patience; an ability to "get the feel of a stone;" and crucially "an appreciation of angles and pressure points." He adds that "You have…to see inside the stone."[47] At the very least, this would explain why visualizing, mechanical/manual, and throwing skills all seem to be aspects of male cognitive proficiency today—not to mention why they are also found in connection with superior vector-navigating ability and geographical expertise. Certainly, today the average man does better than the average woman on most—but not all—tests of mechanical skill, notwithstanding the fact that women generally appear to be more dextrous than men.[37]

Standard IQ tests usually exclude any items that show large sex differences simply because they are designed to test populations of both sexes.[48] The result, of course, is that sex differences in cognition are systematically ignored or underestimated by such measures.[34a] Nevertheless, on a broad range of tests (spatial, verbal, maths, and memory) sex was found to account for 69 per cent of the variance in scores (compared to 9 per cent for ethnicity and 1 per cent for socioeconomic status).[49] Where mechanical skills are concerned, some special aptitude tests reveal a marked superiority in male performance. For example, US Air Force aptitude tests for mechanical comprehension show that the average male performance exceeds that of 80 per cent of females,[50] and in the top 10 per cent of mechanical reasoning ability males outnumber females by approximately 8-to-1.[51]

Such findings fit neatly with my earlier point about genes that may predispose to autism being useful to the human race in terms of their connection with mechanistic cognition once you note that a more mechanistic mind may have benefited primeval males more than females—as it still seems to do today in many instances. If men in our evolutionary past were more concerned with hunting, tool-making, and cross-country navigation as it seems that they probably were—and definitely still are in modern hunter-gatherer societies—the male propensity to autism might be easy to explain as one inevitable extreme of a normal, bell-shaped curve of mechanistic-mindedness. In other words, while some males might be deficient in mechanistic cognitive tendencies, some might have them to such an extreme extent that they would manifest the symptoms related to autism. Indeed, this would be particularly likely if, as I suggested we saw earlier, mechanistic excellence might normally go with deficits in mentalism (see pp. 45–57).

Nevertheless, appealing and almost certainly partly true as this theory is, it does have one or two notable weaknesses. One is the fact that autism is not heritable in the way in which classical sex-linked genetic illnesses such as colour-blindness or haemophilia are. Another is that, if autism were simply an extreme male-brain disorder, you would expect the males to be more severely affected and suppose that the more high-functioning, Asperger cases included more females, simply because their autistic tendencies were milder. But as I pointed out just now, the facts are exactly the opposite: the sex-ratio imbalance is far higher at the high-functioning end of the autistic spectrum, and much lower at the more severely affected end. If autism is just the extreme end of a continuum of normal male cognitive development, how can this be explained?

Genomic imprinting

Following on his comments about his own autistic tendencies that I quoted at the beginning (see pp. 34–35), Hamilton adds that "It is known now how autists, for all that they cannot do in the way of human relationships, detect better out of confusing minimal sketches on paper the true, physical 3-D objects an artist worked from, than do ordinary un-handicapped socialites." He concluded—evidently with himself in mind—that "so may some kinds of autists, unaffected by all the propaganda they have failed to hear, see further into the true shapes that underlie social phenomena."[52]

The true shape that Hamilton saw underlying social phenomena has been popularized as the so-called "selfish gene" view of evolution. According to this way of looking at things, organisms in general and people in particular are nothing more than the bio-degradable packaging of their genes. Such a view is mechanistic to the extent that it makes the transmission of genes the ultimate factor in evolution. People often misunderstand it to think that Hamilton's essential insight also puts genes in the driving seat, so to speak, but the truth is that organisms which move need brains to control their movement because genes as such could never do it on their own. Another analogy is to see organisms as acting as the *agents* of their genes. Looked at from this perspective, genes build bodies and brains to act for and on behalf of them. But they have to give those agents the necessary independence and expertise they need to complete their mission. In the human case, cognitive skills underpin the expertise that people need to acquire, and so genes build brains with mentalistic and mechanistic abilities to solve the problems posed by the human and natural environments respectively. Like passengers on a plane, genes sit quietly in their sex-cell precursor seats and leave it to the aircrew on the cerebral flight-deck to do the skilful part by delivering them safely to their destination: the next generation.[53a]

One of the most stunning insights to be derived from this selfish-gene view of evolution relates to so-called *genomic imprinting*. Even though a child inherits half its DNA from each parent, we now know that certain genes are only expressed if they come from one parent rather than the other. This in itself is a remarkable finding, because having two copies of every gene normally ensures that if one is defective, the other can compensate. Relying on just one seems dangerous, to say the least, particularly in view of the fact that most imprinted genes are expressed in the placenta before birth and in the brain afterwards. Given that the placenta is a key organ in pre-natal development and that the brain is absolutely critical later—particularly in a species such as ours—such a situation seems maladaptive, to say the least. But the whole point of the selfish gene view is that evolution is not about building the best designed bodies or most well adapted organisms. On the contrary, according to this insight, evolution is all about the survival of genes, and this can have some paradoxical consequences, one of the most paradoxical of which is imprinting.[53]

The classic example is a gene called *IGF2* which codes for a growth hormone (insulin-like growth factor 2), and is only normally expressed from the father's gene. If the mother's *IGF2* gene is also expressed, *Beckwith-Wiedemann syndrome* results. Beckwith-Wiedemann babies are one-and-a-half times normal birth-weight and show excessive growth during adolescence along with other over-growth symptoms, such as tumours. Normally the mother's copy of the *IGF2* gene is silenced, or *imprinted*. But if both copies of this gene are silenced, the result is the opposite: the pre- and post-natal growth retardation of *Silver-Russell syndrome*. Beckwith-Wiedemann and Silver-Russell are *genomic sister syndromes*.[54] These are disorders in which duplications or deletions in imprinted or sex chromosome genes result in paired disorders with contrasting symptoms. In the case of *IGF2:*

- father's copy expressed, mother's imprinted = just enough (normality)

- both father's and mother's copies imprinted = none (Silver-Russell syndrome)

- both father's and mother's copies expressed = twice as much (Beckwith-Wiedemann syndrome).

In the case of *IGF2*, the underlying logic of the pattern of imprinting reflects the contrasting costs and benefits of growth to the mother as opposed to the father. Larger size is normally advantageous to mammals (at least when it falls within the normal range), and in the case of human beings, larger babies live longer, suffer less disease, and have better all-round health; while coronary heart disease, stroke, and non-insulin dependent diabetes are associated with low birth-weight.[55] Taller men do better in most occupations, are preferred by women, and tend to have more sexual partners and children than shorter ones.[56] Although the mother's genes in her children benefit from their growth to exactly the same extent as the father's, only the mother pays the cost. In the tangible terms of a child's birth-weight, the mother's contribution is billions of times greater than the father's, which is only a single sperm! Intangible costs are much the same: in sub-Saharan Africa, a woman has about a 1-in-100 risk of death in childbirth and a staggering 1-in-21 lifetime risk of death from all causes relating to pregnancy, childbirth, or abortion.[57] Although the risk of dying during childbirth for a modern Western woman is about 1-in-10,000, the figures for Africa probably reflect the reality for much of human evolution—and, of course, the risk for men everywhere and throughout history has been exactly zero. However you look at it, a mother's obligatory biological investment in her offspring exceeds that of the father by a huge amount.

As a result, paternally-active genes favour growth much more than maternally active ones, and are particularly strongly expressed in the *placenta*—an organ primarily designed to extract resources from the mother. Indeed, an abnormal conceptus with a double set of paternal genes and without any genes whatsoever from the mother results in a massive proliferation of the placenta without any associated foetus.[58] The human placenta is the most invasive of all mammalian placentas, and in some cases can be so invasive that it perforates the uterus, killing the mother. The fact that anaemic mothers have heavier placentas than non-anaemic ones despite giving birth to lower-weight babies suggests that the placenta can actively respond to deficits in the mother's provision of nutrients by becoming larger. Cells originating in the placenta aggressively widen the mother's arteries that feed it by breaking down their walls and weakening them, so that they sag and distend, thereby increasing blood supply to the cavities that the placenta excavates to receive it. Fine, tree-like capillaries fill these spaces and directly absorb nutrients from the mother's blood and return wastes to it. Paternally active genes in the foetus/placenta also drive up the mother's blood pressure and blood-sugar levels to the benefit of the foetus, but also with potentially serious long-term consequences for the mother's health—selfish genes indeed![59]

Conflict between maternal and paternal genes can continue after birth. *Prader-Willi syndrome* affects about 1 in 15,000 births, and is caused by the loss or silencing of genes inherited from the father on chromosome 15 through receiving both copies of this chromosome from the mother, or losing part of the paternal copy.[60] Symptoms listed include lack of appetite, poor suckling ability, a weak cry, inactivity and sleepiness, high pain threshold, and reduced tendency to vomit.[61] By contrast to Prader-Willi, in its sister disorder, *Angelman syndrome,* only the paternal chromosome 15 is present in its entirety, and the critical maternal genes involved in Prader-Willi syndrome are missing.[60] Symptoms include prolonged suckling, hyper-activity and frequent waking.

Although both Prader-Willi and Angelman children are retarded, Angelman retardation is usually much more severe, and—as in the most severe cases of autism—speech is absent. Whereas Prader-Willi patients have a high pain threshold (and often damage themselves as a result), Angelman patients have a low pleasure threshold to the extent that frequent paroxysms of laughter is listed as a major diagnostic feature and the condition is sometimes known as "Happy Puppet Syndrome."[62] Again, whereas Prader-Willi children with two copies of their mother's chromosome 15 are almost always diagnosed as psychotic, Angelman cases are much more likely to be diagnosed as autistic in their behaviour and are more severely retarded (often having no language).[63] Indeed, there is a striking contrast where appetite is concerned: Prader-Willi children, although poor sucklers at first, become indiscriminate and uncontrollable foragers for food, and obese as a result.[64] This poses a sharp contrast to the norm in autism, where remarkably fastidious food preferences are often found, and the outcome is more likely to be some measure of malnutrition—seldom if ever obesity (see table on p. 148). On the contrary, between 18 and 23 per cent of anorexia cases also have symptoms of Asperger's syndrome, and concerns about food intake can be the starting point for diagnosis for this autistic condition.[65]

Diametrically different symptoms of Angelman and Prader-Willi syndromes

Angelman syndrome	Prader-Willi syndrome
prolonged suckling	poor suckling
frequent crying	weak crying
hyper-active/sleepless	inactive/sleepy
low pleasure threshold	high pain threshold
tendency to autism	tendency to psychosis

You could see the prolonged suckling, hyper-activity, and frequent waking of Angelman syndrome as embodying every mother's worst fear, and not coincidentally associated with paternally expressed genes. The suppression of paternal and the enhancement of maternal genes in Prader-Willi children, on the other hand, could be seen as explaining why, despite being seriously retarded, these children make much less demand on the mother thanks to their lethargy, sleepiness, weak cry, and poor suckling. Indeed, even the indiscriminate food-foraging and obesity of older Prader-Willi children can be seen to conform to this interpretation. This is because, when these traits evolved in primal hunter-gatherer pre-history, they would have made children more in-dependent of the mother's resources (principally breast-milk) and more likely to survive periods of prolonged neglect by her thanks to their fat reserves.[64] And in any event, Angelman and Prader-Willi syndromes graphically illustrate the potentially contradictory effects of imprinted genes: failures can result in everything or nothing, with the critical something poised precariously in between.[53b]

Imprinting and the brain

In previous chapters I argued that many of the most striking symptoms of psychotic illnesses such as paranoid schizophrenia could be seen as the exact opposite of those found in autism. As we saw, the clear implication is that, rather than being totally unconnected, autism and psychosis now begin to look as if they could represent poles of a continuum of mentalism stretching from the extreme hypo-mentalism of autistic mind-blindness to the bizarre hyper-mentalism of paranoid psychotics such as Schreber. But now we can begin to see a further remarkable similarity: this is that this pattern of diametrically opposed extremes of pathology can also be seen in Prader-Willi and Angelman syndromes. Furthermore, the fact that some Angelman cases are diagnosed autistic and some Prader-Willi ones are psychotic suggests that a similar pattern of oppositely expressed parentally active genes might underlie autism and psychosis as a whole, making them not just genomic, but psychiatric sister disorders.[54]

A further pair of sister syndromes that I have not mentioned so far can be found in relation to reading. *Dyslexia* describes difficulty in learning to read despite adequate intelligence and opportunity, and is found in about 1-in-20 primary-school age children, with a prevalence in boys about four times that in girls. As many as 70–80 per cent of schizophrenics were found to exhibit a significant number of dyslexic language traits in one study, and the neuro-anatomical and cognitive correlates of dyslexia are similar to those found in both schizophrenia and schizotypal personality disorder.[66]

Hyperlexia is essentially the opposite of dyslexia. The term describes the spontaneous and precocious mastery of reading in children, usually before the age of three, and in conjunction with impairments of verbal communication. Hyperlexics typically can read more or less anything, but cannot necessarily understand what they are reading. An early account of the phenomenon in relation to autistic savantism termed such precocious reading or speaking ability without much understanding *pseudo-verbal*.[46] Hyperlexia is a rare condition, found almost exclusively in conjunction with autism, and we have already encountered one famous hyperlexic in the person of Kim Peek, the savant role-model for the film *Rain Man* (see pp. 27–28). Like Kim Peek, hyperlexic children often show significant impairments in reading comprehension, especially in relation to the more mentalistic aspects of language, such as irony, metaphor, or humour. Indeed, to the extent that reading words is a purely mechanistic skill now performed by computers but that understanding what they mean is a mentalistic one only fully developed in normal human beings, you could see hyperlexia as representing an extreme of the pattern of preserved mechanistic but impaired mentalistic cognition found in autism as a whole. And as this association would lead you to expect, hyperlexic children show enhanced visual-spatial abilities like those typically found associated with autism.[66] In other words, whereas autistics are sometimes hyperlexic, schizophrenics are more likely to be dyslexic: another diametrically-opposed set of symptoms to add to the list (see table, p. 151).

Certainly, the association of dyslexia with schizophrenia, and hyperlexia with autism along with all the other symptoms listed in the table, provides striking support for the theory that psychosis and autism represent opposite disorders arrayed on a continuous mentalistic spectrum. Like autism, dyslexia is a highly heritable trait, and genome scans have provided strong evidence for the involvement of sites on chromosomes 2, 6, 7, 13, and 18. Dyslexia has also been noted in three of four children from the same family with a maternal duplication of part of chromosome 15, and the South Carolina Autism Project found abnormalities in the same region to be the most important common feature in the first hundred cases it studied.[67] More recent studies have confirmed this finding in greater detail and added evidence for a link with savant skills.[68] Furthermore, this same stretch of chromosome 15 is critically implicated in Angelman and Prader-Willi syndromes.

However, because a large number of genes on many different chromosomes appear to be involved, and because gene expression related to parent of origin can vary from gene to gene and tissue to tissue in the same individual, the range of symptoms in autism and psychosis can be expected to be much greater than in Prader-Willi and Angelman syndromes, explaining why the antithetical features listed in the table—which is by no means exhaustive—are usually only found in some cases. Again, autism is common in Rett, Turner's, and Fragile X syndromes, in tuberous sclerosis and more rarely in numerous other

Diametrically different characteristics of autism and psychosis

Autism/Asperger's syndrome	Psychosis/Paranoid schizophrenia
gaze-monitoring deficits	delusions of being watched/spied on
apparent deafness/insensitivity to voices	hallucination of and hyper-sensitivity to voices
intentionality deficits	erotomania/delusions of persecution
shared-attention deficits	delusions of conspiracy
theory of mind deficits	magical ideation/delusions of reference
deficit in sense of personal agency/episodic memory	megalomania/delusions of grandeur
literalness/inability to deceive	delusional self-deception
pathological single-mindedness	pathological ambivalence
early onset	adult onset
visual/spatial skills and enhanced visual acuity	visual/spatial deficits and reduced visual acuity
some hyperlexic	some dyslexic
local brain over-connectivity with global under-connectivity	local brain under-connectivity with global over-connectivity

conditions.[69] Autistic disorders can also be environmentally induced by pre-natal thalidomide, or viral infection, and by ethanol or valproic acid poisoning in pregnancy. Valproic acid (sodium valproate) is an anti-convulsant and mood-stabilizing drug which affects gene expression and when administered to pregnant mice or rats in early foetal development induces an equivalent of autism in these animals. Indeed, all of these factors could mediate genetic effects within the individuals concerned via the same kind of genomic imprinting that also accounts for Angelman and Prader-Willi syndromes.

Even the fact that autism is more likely to be found in the children of older fathers than those of younger ones or of older mothers can be explained in the same way.[70] Unlike men, who produce sperm continuously throughout their lifetimes in a 14-stage process taking approximately 72 days, women copy all their DNA long before birth, where it remains sequestered in the precursors to what will later be released as mature egg cells during ovulation in adult life. Genomic imprints are re-set each time a gene is copied into an egg or sperm cell. The very same *IGF2* gene that a man inherited from his mother with her maternal imprint could be passed on by him in a paternally active form in one of his sperm. The likelihood that imprinting errors could occur increases with the number of times that a cell divides. A mature woman's egg cells have gone through only 20-odd cell divisions, all but the last of them before her birth. But a man aged 30 produces sperm that are the result of almost 400, and one of 50 sperm cells which have gone through more than twice that number of divisions.[71] This in itself could well explain why older fathers are more likely to have autistic children than younger ones. However, autism is not the only psychiatric disorder in which paternal but not maternal age has been implicated. The other notable one is schizophrenia and related disorders.[72] Of course, this could be a coincidence, but if not it does suggest an intriguing possibility. This is that autism and psychotic illnesses such as schizophrenia may be sister disorders related to faulty genomic imprinting. Imprinting errors in one direction might result in autism, but those in the opposite direction might predispose to schizophrenia in later life.

Excepting the placenta, most imprinted genes are expressed in the brain, and in mice there is arresting evidence that maternally and paternally expressed genes play very different roles in brain-development. This is because it is now possible to produce mice in the laboratory that express mainly the father's or the mother's genes, and to stain cells in such a way that you can see exactly where the paternal or maternal genes are going in the developing body. The result is striking: foetal mice with a father but no mother are larger than normal and have a bigger placenta but reduced brains. Those with a mother and no father are the opposite—they are smaller than usual, have reduced placentas, but have larger brains than normal.[73] Naturally-occurring abnormal human foetuses with a double set of the mother's genes and one of the father's (rather than a single set from each parent) are small except for the head, show a retardation of growth, and have small placentas. By contrast, those with a double set of their father's genes and a single set of the mother's are well grown except for the head and have a large placenta.[58,74]

In mice, cells with only maternal genes are found in large numbers in the cerebral cortex (and the underlying striatum) and in the fore brain, but very few are found in the so-called limbic system[75]— especially in the hypothalamus (of which, more in a moment). This is true of mature, fully-grown mice but even more so of foetuses, where there is a complete absence of maternal cells in the hypothalamus. In both cases, mother-only cells are found to be particularly clustered in the frontal lobes of the cortex. Father-only cells, by contrast, are the exact opposite: these are found in the hypothalamus and limbic system, but not in the cerebral cortex. The few that are found in the forebrain tissue of embryos do not proliferate and are subsequently eliminated. However, no such difference is found in the brain-stem, which appears to be equally the work of maternal and paternal genes.[76]

In human beings, the *hypothalamus* is concerned with basic drives and appetites such as hunger, thirst, sex, and aggression, and with emotional responses such as pleasure, pain, and fear.[75] Consequently, some kind of developmental defect in the hypothalamus was suspected in Prader-Willi and Angelman syndromes from the beginning.[61] The hypothalamus also regulates the production of pituitary growth hormones, which, along with adrenal, thyroid, and sex hormones, either directly or indirectly control growth. The pituitary is sometimes called the master endocrine gland of the body, but is itself under the control of the hypothalamus, both neurologically and chemically. Neurologically, the posterior pituitary is just a part of the hypothalamus that protrudes from the brain and is not a gland in its own right.[77]

From this point of view, you could see the hypothalamus as

performing a role in the brain analogous to that of *IGF2* in the genome. Like *IGF2*, the hypothalamus is concerned with growth and consumption of resources and, again like it, mammalian mothers appear to place imprints on the genes that build it, just as they do the *IGF2* gene. Presumably this is because imprinting these genes limits the growth that would result if the genes for building the hypothalamus from both parents were expressed. And significantly in this respect, the development of the hypothalamus is impaired in Prader-Willi syndrome where, as we have just seen, maternal genes are disproportionately expressed at the expense of paternal ones.[78] Cells in the embryonic hypothalamus are critical for later development, and the sizes of its cell populations in the foetus could provide a prediction of subsequent neuro-hormonal activity during later life.[79] In other words, imprinted genes that control the growth of nerve cells in the development of the foetal brain could indirectly determine body size: according to this way of looking at it, fathers would want more, but mothers would want less.

But what of the neo-cortex, and why should maternal genes be preferentially expressed there—and why most of all in the frontal part? An obvious suggestion is the finding to which I have already alluded that the frontal part of the neo-cortex is critically concerned with impulse-control and inhibition of lower centres, such as the hypothalamus. Frontal brain volumes are larger in women, and the difference in the average volume of the orbito-frontal cortex between men and women accounts for about half of the variation in antisocial behaviour between the sexes.[80] Reduced frontal volume is associated with antisocial behaviour and psychopathy,[31] and as we saw, both brain-scanning studies and new computational models of the pre-frontal cortex suggest that this part of the brain is hyper-active in a wide range of psychotic disorders (see pp. 115–116).

If maternal genes are exclusively expressed in the pre-frontal cortex we might be justified in thinking of it as a critical part of the *maternal* brain. Indeed, a recent brain-imaging study showed that women have a significantly larger proportion of overall cortical matter compared to men. If so, then we could see the hypothalamus, amygdala, and other parts of the lower brain as *paternal* for parallel reasons: paternal genes are mainly expressed there, and these regions are also proportionately larger in men.[81] Furthermore, we can now begin to see that the relation between the two is reminiscent of that between paternally active and maternally active genes. As I pointed out earlier, the paternal brain could be seen as serving the father's genetic interest in the offspring's growth and consumption of resources, but as we can also now see, the maternal brain—and the pre-frontal cortex in particular—could equally be seen as serving maternal genetic self-interest to the extent that it is able to inhibit, control, and contain the paternal brain.

An example might be dieting. The parts of your brain that make you hungry and seek the gratification of eating are in the hypothalamus and limbic system built by your father's genes. But the parts of your brain that make you worry about the consequences of eating and able—perhaps—to resist temptation are all in the cortex constructed by maternal genes. And of course, it is the mother who has to provide food for a hungry baby during lactation, and also normally the mother (and her female relatives) who has a vested biological interest in sharing out food resources among her offspring throughout childhood thanks to the fact that all her children carry half her genes. Could this be one of the reasons why her genes build the cortical, inhibitory brain?

Because the mother's genes are equally present in all her offspring, her genetic self-interest is best served by co-operation and family unity. Any net benefit from social behaviour among her offspring is also a benefit to the ultimate reproductive success of her genes invested in all of them. Thanks to gestation and lactation, the mother is biologically the prime nurturer, and so it serves her interests to be able to nurture, educate, and instruct her children—for example to teach them their "mother-tongue" and then use it to programme their thinking in ways she approves. By these means the mother can indoctrinate, condition, and socialize her offspring in behaviour that is likely to benefit her equitable genetic investment in all of them. Here a top-down, contextual, holistic, and verbal cognitive style—a *mentalistic* one, in my term—might be particularly useful in influencing a child's social interaction with its siblings, peers, and parents. This would make a child much more likely to see things from its mother's point of view—particularly to see them in a family context—and perhaps less likely to act impulsively on the promptings of its paternal brain.[53c,82]

We saw earlier that sex differences in cognition make sense in evolutionary terms and that in primal hunter-gatherer societies it would probably have promoted a woman's survival and reproductive success to be more mentalistic than a man. One area where this might have been especially important is in relation to a woman's own children. A major function of mentalism in everyday life is to manage and manipulate other people—for example, by naming, blaming and shaming—and very often mentalism can be an alternative to more physical means. In raising their own children, it could have paid ancestral women to use mentalistic measures whenever possible for this reason alone. This is because making or preventing a child doing something merely by a word, look, or gesture—by mentalistic means, in other words—is not merely energetically less costly than physically intervening, but is much less dangerous (not to mention more efficient because such expressions can often be directed to more than one recipient simultaneously). Manhandling a child always carries the danger of inflicting injury, however slight, and in really serious confrontations verbal and emotional substitutes for physical contact could prevent otherwise potentially serious injury. Forceful but purely mental expressions of maternal wishes could nevertheless be very effective, and so selection may have favoured mothers who could substitute verbal, emotional, and gestural expressions for more directly physical ones. And even though such substitutions may have had only marginal and minimal effects, natural selection, relentlessly working over the millennia, would gradually preserve them if their overall effect were (on average and all other things being equal) to promote the survival of the genes responsible for them.

Indeed, children too would have benefited to the extent that a child is physically smaller and weaker than its mother. Lacking an ability to influence its parent by more direct physical means, children who could use mentalistic ploys such as facial, emotional, and verbal expressions might also have marginally promoted their own survival and reproductive success if the effect of that was to secure them more parental investment, or avoid risk of injury. Tears, temper-tantrums, and cries of distress, in other words, could be as effective in their own way on a child's parent as any kind of physical compulsion that one adult could use against another.[83] To this extent, both mothers and children may have had converging evolutionary interests in avoiding mindless violence and substituting the purely mental conflicts that are now so deeply woven into the fabric of family life that psychotherapists have been able to make a vocation of trying to unravel them.

Mother's baby—father's? Maybe!

The father, on the other hand, need make no obligatory biological contribution to his offspring beyond a single sperm, and other children of the same mother need not share his genes: *Mother's baby—father's? Maybe!* As a result, we have seen that the father's genes build parts of the brain that tend to motivate self-interested, instinctual, and non-social behaviour: the limbic system. The father's genetic self-interest is not necessarily served by his child seeing things its mother's way—for example, in making sacrifices for siblings to which its paternal genes may not be related in any way whatsoever. The verbal and mentalis-tic deficits of autism would be explained by the fact that the paternal brain—alias the limbic system—"eludes the grasp of the intellect be-cause its animalist, primitive structure makes it impossible to commu-nicate in verbal terms."[75a]

According to such a selfish-gene view of the matter, autism could be the consequence of the failure of the maternal brain in this respect and the notable impulsiveness, compulsiveness, and contrariness of au-tistics the inevitable result of the paternal brain's corresponding suc-cess. The striking social deficits seen in autism would seem to fit the idea that paternal genetic self-interest underlies the disorder because autistic children seem perversely committed to doing things their own way, in their own time, and for their own selves. If they can learn at all, they usually refuse to do so in the way adults think they should, and inevitably pose a severe challenge to any care-giver (who in our evolutionary past would predominantly have been the mother and her relatives). Certainly, the reduced empathy, uncooperativeness and insistence of routine seen in autism hardly contribute to easy parenting. Indeed, there is evidence that in experimental animals failure to cope with change is a central characteristic of paternal brain lesions, and a persuasive case can be made for the limbic system being centrally involved in the problems associated with autism.[84]

The same reasoning would certainly explain why the mentalistic brain systems that malfunction in autism seem to be critical to a child's social interaction with its mother.[85,86] Indeed, when paternal brain centres such as the hypothalamus and amygdala are active in dreams, aggressive impulses on the part of the dreamer emerge. However, when what I am calling maternal brain centres are activated in dreaming (the forebrain and neo-cortex), aggressive impulses are inhibited and co-operative and pro-social ones expressed.[87] As you would predict if autism was indeed caused by enhanced expression of the father's genes, proliferative over-growth (inclusions) of the placenta are found at three times the normal rate in autism,[88] and studies suggest that autistics—and males in particular—are heavier than normal at birth and have elevated levels of growth hormones such as IGF2,[89] confirming that they are indeed predisposed to consume more than usual of the mother's resources.[90] Again, there is evidence that autistics by contrast to psychotics show early brain growth during gestation at the expense of the mother.[66]

Seeing the paternal brain in this way would also explain the notable exception to autistic mentalistic deficits we noted at the beginning in relation to empathizing with animals (see pp. 54–55). A leading authority on the limbic system, Paul D. MacLean, described what I am calling the paternal brain as *paleo-mammalian* by contrast to the *neo-mammalian* cerebral cortex. By this he meant that we share a limbic system with all mammals, but our large neo-cortex—or what I am calling the maternal brain—only with higher primates, such as monkeys and apes.[91] If this older mammalian part of the brain predominates in certain critical respects in autism, it is perhaps not surprising that autistics such as Temple Grandin show such an astonishing ability to relate to cattle, horses, dogs, and other mammals.[92]

The limbic system has also been called *the emotional brain*,[93] and seeing it as having evolved in conflict with the maternal or neo-cortical brain would also readily explain yet another set of symptoms of schizophrenia that at first sight appear difficult to understand in terms of hyper-mentalism. What I have in mind here is the apathy, "affective flattening," and *anhedonia* (or lack of feelings of pleasure) so frequently found in schizophrenics. These all make perfect sense once you notice that the brain's pleasure, motivational, and emotional-response centres are all located in the limbic brain, where they serve to promote the self-assertion, consumption, and instinctive behaviour that so obviously benefits the individual's paternal genome. Furthermore, the same insight explains why such centres might also be suppressed by the maternally made neo-cortex, as my earlier example of the conflict involved in dieting suggested. The negative symptoms of schizophrenia, such as apathy and loss of emotion and pleasure reactions, could easily be understood as pathological extensions of such mental conflicts. Indeed, we have already seen schizophrenics attributing their motor-inhibition and catatonia to excessive mentalizing (see p. 113–114), and now we are considering the neo-cortex as the prime exponent of mentalism and the limbic system as its major adversary. To use a cold-war analogy, you could think of the neo-cortex as a huge cognitive jammer broadcasting the voice of the mother at ever greater amplitude to drown out the instincts clamouring for gratification in the paternal brain.[53d] To make the same point another way, you could say that if the social deficits of autism register the success of paternal genes as I suggested just now, then the negative symptoms of schizophrenia could be seen as exemplifying the corresponding triumph of the maternal genome in suppressing the lower, limbic brain. And to the extent that autistic deficits could be described as hypo-mentalistic, such negative symptoms of schizophrenia could be understood correspondingly as *hyper-mentalistic*.

Finally, the fact that all fathers are male explains why you could mistake autism for an extreme male brain disorder. But because both males and females have both paternal and maternal brains as I am calling them you can easily account for the fact that females as well as males can suffer from autism. More high-functioning autistics might be expected to be male if only their paternal brain were affected—perhaps driven to an extreme early in development by male sex hormones such as testosterone which we have already seen appear to be a factor in vulnerability to autism (see p. 34). The intact intelligence and verbal abilities of high-functioning, Asperger autistics would therefore be the result of predominantly normal maternal brain development, while the occasional appearance of mechanistic savant skills could be explained by an enhancement of characteristically male cognitive skills associated with an extreme paternal brain.

But if the balance between maternal and paternal parts of the brain was also an issue, you could imagine that another factor predisposing to autism might be under-development of the maternal brain: that is, the neo-cortex and perhaps the frontal lobes in particular. As we have seen, women averagely have more cortical grey matter, and we have already noted that areas of the pre-frontal cortex are also normally more developed in women.[81,94] Given the reliance of higher brain functions such as intelligence, language, and inhibition on the neo-cortex, you could readily understand why a combination of deficits in these maternal brain areas combined with excesses in the paternal ones might result in a more severe disability. Again, because all mothers are female, you could understand why deficits in the maternal brain might be especially important where females were concerned, and this could partly explain why the sex ratio is much less skewed in the male direction at the severe end of the autistic spectrum. In other words, whereas you would expect mainly males to be affected by paternal brain preponderance, both sexes—but perhaps females in particular—might be affected by severe maternal brain deficits whose relative effect would be emphasis of paternal brain tendencies of the kind seen in classical (Kanner's) autism. Indeed, if maternal brain deficits showed themselves in reduced intelligence and language ability, then you would expect to find more of such female autistics among the most severely affected of both sexes—just as you do.

Chapter 6

Sex and Psychosis

In the last chapter I showed how the strange genetics of autism and psychosis might be explicable in terms of imprinted genes and their effects on brain development. However, imprinted genes are not the whole story. In this chapter we need to look at another factor that operates in a similar, but subtly different way: sex chromosomes. As we shall see, here ultimately may lie the explanation of the most bizarre of Schreber's delusions: his belief that he was turning into a woman!

The X in psychosis

Another factor influencing the incidence of autism in relation to sex is the fact that female mammals get a so-called X sex chromosome from each parent (they are XX), but males receive an X from the mother and a Y from the father (making them XY). In *Turner's syndrome*, part or all of one X chromosome is missing (although the exact genetic configuration can be very complex, involving mixing of cells with different sex chromosome components).[1] The incidence of autism is vastly greater than normal in Turner's patients who resemble normal males in having got their one and only X from the mother. Indeed, their vulnerability to autism is also greater than in those Turner's cases where the X comes from the father—in other words, those who would have been female had they also received an X from their mother.[2,3a]

Because normal females have two X chromosomes, one of them is largely inactivated in each cell of the body, and this can lead to some surprising effects. A striking example is a pair of identical female twins, one of whom is an accomplished athlete while the other is wheelchair bound thanks to Duchenne Muscular Dystrophy (DMD). DMD is a genetic disorder, and identical twins share all their genes, so how can this be explained? The answer lies in X-inactivation and in the fact that the process is seemingly random and occurs early in development. Subsequent cell divisions retain the original inactivation, and so it is quite possible that when a fertilized human ovum splits to produce two identical twins, one may inherit a different pattern of X-chromosome expression to the other, and this appears to be the explanation in this case. DMD could only have been present on one X, and only one twin was unlucky enough to inherit the cells that expressed it, leaving the other unaffected thanks to expressing the other X chromosome.[4]

Nevertheless, even though X-inactivation is usually random, a study of 30 XX females with autism found X-inactivation to be notably skewed in favour of one X rather than the other.[5] Although no apparent preference for one or the other X chromosome was discovered in this rather small sample, the fact that skewed X-inactivation was found to be associated with autism in females suggests that such factors in gene expression could indeed play a role in the disorder. Further evidence that this might be the case comes from Rett syndrome, a childhood-onset neurological disorder that overlaps with autism in its symptoms and features impairment of language, mental retardation, seizures, peculiarities of head growth, loss of gross motor skills, and repetitive hand movements. However, Rett syndrome is almost exclusively diagnosed in females and appears to be caused by mutations on the X chromosome that affect the expression of its genes.[6,7]

In Turner's cases there is a significantly lower incidence of schizophrenia and bipolar disorder compared to normal, XX females.[8] However, in the case of so-called *super females* with three complete copies of the X chromosome—otherwise known as *X-trisomy*—increased rates of schizophrenia have been reported. So too have low birth-weight, length, and head size—something that is reminiscent of maternal-imprinting effects.[7] Imaging studies show that XXX females exhibit three features of brain anatomy characteristic of schizophrenia: reduced brain volume and enlarged ventricles; reduced asymmetry of the pre-frontal and temporal lobes; and a reduction in amygdala size. The smaller brains, reduced asymmetries, and smaller amygdalas of X-trisomy females suggest that their increased X chromosome gene dosage results in a brain anatomically skewed towards a more female type.

Klinefelter syndrome is caused by the presence of an additional X chromosome along with an existing X and Y (as in a normal male), so sufferers are XXY. Turner's syndrome and Klinefelter syndrome pose a striking contrast with regard to verbal and visual-spatial skills, with Turner's syndrome characterized by good verbal skills but greatly impaired visual-spatial abilities and Klinefelter syndrome individuals impaired verbally but with visual-spatial abilities spared. These syndromes also involve notably different associations with psychiatric disorders, as Turner's syndrome individuals exhibit an elevated incidence of autism and autistic traits, but Klinefelter syndrome involves a four- to ten-fold increase in liability to psychosis.[7] Psychosis in Klinefelter syndrome normally involves a relatively high incidence of auditory hallucinations and paranoia like that found in female psychotics, along with the later age of onset that is also typical of the disorder in women. As in X-trisomy, Klinefelter syndrome patients exhibit aspects of brain anatomy similar to those in schizophrenia. X-trisomy and Klinefelter syndrome involve parallel effects on brain anatomy and liability to psychosis that are presumably due in both cases to the extra X chromosome. Thus, in both XXX and XXY sex chromosome configurations, the presence of an additional X results in brain features similar to those found in schizophrenia, along with notably increased vulnerability to psychosis. In other words, the presence of an additional X chromosome makes its bearer more female in brain structure and cognition (as well as being less prone to autism).

According to this theory, the differences between male and females in brain anatomy and cognition tend to parallel the differences between normal individuals and those exhibiting full-blown psychosis or milder psychotic tendencies. In the previous chapter we saw that there is something to be said for the view that autism is a disorder featuring an enhancement of what I called the paternal brain at the expense of the maternal brain. However, if psychoses such as paranoid schizophrenia can indeed be seen as the hyper-mentalistic equivalent of autistic hypo-mentalism, then it suggests that, just as autism may represent extreme paternal brain tendencies, so such psychoses ought to go with an extreme *maternal* brain.[9]

We have already seen that Prader-Willi syndrome is caused by enhanced maternal and/or reduced paternal gene-expression, whereas Angelman is the other way round: reduced expression of maternal and/or enhanced expression of paternal genes (see pp. 147–148). If so, autism and psychosis may be similar: although the two disorders have until now seemed unrelated, genetically they may be sister syndromes as the diametrically different pattern of symptoms listed in the table on page 151 suggests. Certainly, this possibility is supported by the variant of Prader-Willi syndrome mentioned earlier in which two copies of the mother's chromosome 15 are present, without any from the father (so-called *uni-parental disomy* or UPD). Quite apart from any link with dyslexia, and by contrast to the variant of the syndrome in which only paternal genes are deleted, the majority of maternal UPD cases become psychotic in adulthood, implying that the duplication of this maternal part of the individual's genome is the likely explanation.[10] Indeed, at the time of writing this was the only example known of such a direct relationship between a specific genetic abnormality and psychotic illness.[11,12] The finding of high rates of psychosis in Prader-Willi syndrome with maternal UPD supports the suggestion that psychosis may result from the excessive expression of maternal genes, and/or reduced expression of paternal ones. Moreover, Prader-Willi maternal UPD cases exhibit less severe impairments in social behaviour than those with deletion of paternal genes.[13,14] Prader-Willi syndrome maternal UPD also involves stronger disruptions in visual-spatial abilities, as indicated by mathematical and 3-D visualization performance, and these patients lack the notably enhanced skill in doing jigsaw puzzles found in many cases of paternal deletion.[15] Taken together, these findings suggest that Prader-Willi maternal UPD cases exhibit better social and language functioning than deletion cases, but worse visual-spatial ability. This is a pattern consistent with increased effects from maternally expressed imprinted genes which as we saw earlier can be expected to favour language and social skills by contrast to paternally active ones, which can be predicted to favour visual, spatial, and maths skills.

In the previous chapter we also saw that Beckwith-Wiedemann and Silver-Russell syndromes have been recognized as another example of genomic sister syndromes which, like Prader-Willi and Angelman syndromes, are driven by opposite disruptions of imprinting for the same or overlapping genes. In Beckwith-Wiedemann, paternally-active *IGF2* is over-expressed, and one of the few studies to examine neuro-development in this syndrome found almost 7 per cent of 87 cases to be suffering from an autistic disorder—just as we might predict if enhanced paternal gene expression was a factor in autism.[16] Where Silver-Russell syndrome is concerned, the only systematic study conducted to date found relatively preserved verbal skills along with deficits in mathematical and visual-spatial ability. This finding fits with the pattern of superior mentalistic as compared to mechanistic skills found in schizophrenic disorders mentioned at the end of Chapter 4 and with that described above for Prader-Willi and Angelman syndromes (see table, p. 148). In other words, more maternal and/or less paternal gene expression is associated with more mentalistic skills and a tendency to psychosis. On the other hand, less maternal and/or more paternal gene expression goes with more mechanistic cognition and increased vulnerability to autism.

While whole brain size is reduced in schizophrenia because of reductions in grey matter (neurons) and reduced and altered white matter (nerve fibres), brain size in autism is increased during early development thanks to a striking growth spurt between birth and age four, an acceleration driven mainly by increases in white matter volume. However, after about age four, brain growth in autism levels off, so that adult brain size is not notably increased on average. Remarkably, a recent study of Asperger's syndrome showed that grey matter volume did not decrease with age between 15 and 50 as it does substantially in normal individuals. These findings suggest that autism and schizophrenia exhibit divergent patterns of grey matter loss, with little to no loss in autism, moderate loss in normal development, and high rates of loss in schizophrenia.[9]

The differences in brain size and development between autistic and schizophrenic individuals are paralleled by differences in birth-weight. As I mentioned earlier, autistics have higher birth-weight and expression of growth hormones such as IGF2 compared to controls, but schizophrenics have consistently lower weight at birth, and it has been suggested that foetal growth restriction, mediated by imprinting effects, contributes to the development of schizophrenia. Foetal and neo-natal brain growth, especially deposition of brain fatty acids, is the single most metabolically costly event during pregnancy and early post-natal life. Mothers bear most of this cost, and indeed, during the latest stages of pregnancy mothers metabolize their own brain fat for transfer to the foetus, which can trigger post-partum psychosis. According to the theory proposed here, the contrasting patterns of brain size, growth, and birth-weight in psychosis and autism are mediated by effects of paternal versus maternal genes, with paternal genes driving the acquisition of increased brain fatty acids. Indeed, human babies exhibit by far the highest average body fat content of any mammal, and this may represent an adaptation to fuel rapid, sustained brain growth driven by the conflicting interests of the parentally active genes of both parents.[3b] Again, there is a suggestion that schizophrenics may have less cancer than normal despite the fact that they smoke much more, while autistics are more prone to cancer despite smoking less.[17] As the tumours often found associated with Beckwith-Wiedemann syndrome suggest, the reason for this could be that paternally expressed imprinted genes tend to promote the development of cancer—which is another form of over-growth—while many maternally expressed genes act as tumour-suppressors and reduce cancer risk[9,18] (see the box on p. 167).

Side-effects of genetic conflict

As explained in the main text, paternally active genes tend to favour growth, while maternally active ones tend to restrict it. If autistic spectrum disorders are indeed the result of imbalances in favour of the expression of the father's genes by contrast to the mother's, the following growth effects associated with autism, both before and after birth, are explained:

- highly proliferative placentation

- increased head size, brain size, and cortical thickness

- elevated levels of growth hormones such as IGF2

- higher birth-weight in male autistics

- faster body growth

- a 100-fold greater risk of neurofibromatosis (benign nerve-tissue tumours)

- genetic alterations relating to the PI3K (phosphatidylinositol 3-kinase) pathway resulting in greater vulnerability to cancer (despite the fact that autistics smoke less).

However, if psychotic illnesses such as schizophrenia are indeed associated with the opposite situation of increased maternal gene expression relative to paternal, the following findings associated with psychosis immediately make sense:

- intra-uterine growth restriction, placental under-growth, and higher incidence of foetal hypoxia (oxygen starvation)

- low birth-weight

- low levels of brain growth-factors

- smaller brain size, thinner cortex, smaller hippocampus and amygdala

- decreased risk of cancer among schizophrenics (despite increased smoking) and their first-order relatives

- reduced expression of growth factors and decreased stem cell proliferation

- reduced thresholds for apoptosis (programmed cell death, for example if a cell becomes pre-cancerous) and evidence of increased expression of tumour-suppressor genes in schizophrenics.[1-3]

Finally, if X chromosome genes are also implicated in psychosis, and if, as suggested in this chapter, sex-determination is in part an expression of genetic conflict between male and female genes, sex ratio deviations in autism and psychosis are predictable. Claims have already been made that engineers have more sons and which invoke the extreme male brain theory of autism.[4] But unlike the extreme male brain theory, the imprinted brain theory suggested here also predicts that psychotic women should give birth to more daughters, and at least where female schizophrenics are concerned, this expectation appears to be confirmed.[5]

Psychosis, poverty, and pathogens

The role of maternal genes in restricting growth might also explain why there is now firm evidence that environmental factors can be implicated in causing schizophrenia. Studies of the Dutch wartime famine and of the Chinese famine of 1959–61 reported increased incidence of schizophrenia among children born just after the events.[19,20] Again, a study of two million Swedish children born between 1963 and 1983 revealed a significant link between schizophrenia and poverty in childhood. Those with four out of five measured indicators of hardship had an almost three-fold greater risk of schizophrenia than those with none.[21] A possible explanation is that maternal starvation has the same effect as maternally active genes in restricting growth, and according to the hypothesis advanced here, also predisposes towards the risk of psychosis in later life: nurture—or the lack of it—via nature, so to speak.

Furthermore, a study of *IGF2* expression in children born during the Dutch wartime famine provided the first evidence that transient environmental conditions early in human gestation can affect the expression of such imprinted genes.[22] Although this effect was found among those with normal birth-weight who were exposed to famine early in gestation but was not found among those with low birth-weight unrelated to *IGF2* expression exposed to famine late in gestation, the finding suggests that more direct effects cannot be ruled out in principle. On the contrary, it establishes a strong precedent for thinking that environmental factors could directly or indirectly affect gene expression in accordance with the theory set out here.

The suggestion that severe deficits in nutrition such as those associated with maternal starvation during pregnancy might have pathological consequences where development is concerned is hardly surprising. But if that were true, the theory proposed here would have the contrary, very counter-intuitive implication. This is that environmental influences which enhanced growth might predispose towards autism, perhaps by way of increasing the expression of genes such as *IGF2*—in other words, by the mechanism mentioned in the previous paragraph, but in the opposite direction. This in itself might explain quite a lot of the so-called "autism epidemic" of recent years. Growth-enhancement thanks to higher standards of living in developed countries could be predicted to predispose towards milder forms of autism such as Asperger's syndrome. Indeed, birth-weights of new-born babies in Vienna rose an unprecedented amount (from a mean of 3 kg to a peak of 3.3 kg) during the 1920s, and perhaps this partly explains why Asperger was to discover the syndrome named after him during the next couple of decades.[23] Again, critics of Kanner's original description of autism have pointed out that he portrayed it as an "upper class" disorder but that later research, particularly in Sweden (the Gothenburg studies), contradicted this and found no clear link to social class.[24] However, it might simply be that during the 1940s the heavier birth-weight effect was mainly seen among better-off people in the USA, but that by the 1980s it had spread to just about everyone in welfare-state Sweden—and today to most people in modern Western societies, where obesity,

rather than under-nourishment, has become the primary health problem related to food intake.

Another counter-intuitive prediction of the theory is that if all this
is true, then the so-called "autism epidemic" should go with a parallel decline in psychosis. At the very least, improving living conditions
should make maternal starvation during pregnancy much less likely, and
this alone ought to reduce the incidence of schizophrenia, albeit perhaps only marginally, and any other environmental or social factors
should work the same way—especially if those factors are influential in
increasing the incidence of ASD. Here it may be significant to note that
a decline in schizophrenia has indeed been reported in many Western
countries. Bleuler himself noticed that schizophrenia was becoming
milder during the twentieth century, and other authorities were asking
"Where have all the catatonics gone?" First-admission rates for schizophrenia show a considerable decrease in England beginning in about
1960, and those for Scotland a decline of 57 per cent, with falls of 37
per cent also reported in Denmark and New Zealand, and 9 per cent
in Australia.[25] A recent study in Canada showed a 42 per cent decrease
in the number of first-admission schizophrenia cases over 20 years, and
the same study found that annual inpatient prevalence rates decreased
by 52 per cent between 1986 and 1996, with no corresponding change
in outpatient rates, regardless of sex. Although what the author called
"total major affective disorders" rose, this was due to an increase in
major depression, not bipolar disorder (which is now not thought to be
so different from schizophrenia, as we have seen above, pp. 116–117).[26]
Admittedly, part of this must be accounted for by the fact that (as I also
pointed out earlier) ASD was often mistaken for schizophrenia in the
past—perhaps particularly childhood-onset schizophrenia. But the decrease in adolescent- and adult-onset schizophrenia seems too large to
be accounted for by simply supposing that what was once called a psychosis is now more likely to be diagnosed as a form of autism. Indeed,
the fact that any reduction at all has been noticed seems significant, and
is certainly predicted by the theory outlined here.

Where schizophrenia is concerned, there are suspicions that the
protozoan parasite *Toxoplasma gondii* may sometimes be a contributing

factor to the development of the illness.[27] People infected with *T. gondii* (between 15 and 80 per cent, depending on the population) are three times more likely to suffer from schizophrenia than those not infected, and so too are cat-owners. The significance of the latter may lie in the fact that the parasite can only complete the reproductive phase of its life-cycle inside a cat. It achieves this by causing its principal carriers, rats and mice, to lose their fear of cats, and so be much more likely to be eaten by one. Inside the rodent's brain, the parasite attacks the amygdala, which plays the same role in triggering fear-reactions that it does in humans. But when infected rats are treated with anti-psychotic drugs like those given to human schizophrenics the rats' fear of felines returns. Men with *Toxoplasma* infection tend to be more reckless than normal, and infected people of both sexes are almost three times more likely to be involved in car accidents, and have measurably slowed reaction times.[28,29] Indeed, there is also some evidence that reduced activity of the amygdala may represent a general feature of schizophrenia-like conditions.[30]

We have already seen that in mice only paternal genes are expressed in limbic system components such as the amygdala and hypothalamus. This finding, combined with the suspicions about *T. gondii* and schizophrenia in humans, suggests the intriguing possibility that an explanation may lie in the parasite suppressing paternal brain systems such as the amygdala to produce an overall preponderance of maternal brain function, which we have already seen could be the fundamental basis of psychosis in general and of schizophrenia in particular. Indeed, given its known affinity for the limbic system, much the same might be said for the other suspected infectious cause of schizophrenia: *Cytomegalovirus* (CMV).[31] In other words, genetic conflict might explain infectious causes of schizophrenia too, but in a somewhat different way to that involving imprinted and X chromosome genes. In the case of *Toxoplasma* or CMV infection, the genetic conflict would be between the genes of the parasite and those of the host, but the effect would be much the same: a deficit in a key paternal brain system, predisposing to psychosis.

Handedness, belief, and the brain

Each cerebral hemisphere is in the main linked to the opposite side of the body. In other words, the left motor cortex controls the right side of the body, and the right cortex the left. People normally show a dominance of one hemisphere over the other. Nine out of ten people are right-handed, meaning that the left, verbal, more mentalistic hemisphere is normally dominant, but as the findings above might suggest, left-handedness is more common in ASD, with 18–20 per cent of sufferers being left-handed. Women appear to be less lateralized than men, and therefore to show a more balanced development. Compared to males, females are less likely to be left-handed, but left-handers of either sex are more likely to score high on maths, musical and drawing ability, and chess. And as the facts about brain laterality would suggest, left-handed people have on average better spatial ability, and are more common in visual arts occupations, and in architecture and engineering.

The tendency towards the more spatial, right side at the expense of the verbal, left hemisphere in autism may be due simply to a faster, earlier pattern of brain development that is the exact opposite of that seen in schizophrenia. Indeed, this shift in the timing of development appears directly analogous to the overgrowth syndromes typical of imbalances towards paternal-gene expression effects in placental and foetal growth. By contrast, schizophrenia involves reduced structural and functional asymmetry in the brain, and this reduced lateralization is associated with slower brain development, left hemisphere dysfunction, diminished left hemisphere specialization for language, and an increase in the extent of symptoms such as delusions. Similar patterns have been detected in healthy individuals, in whom the degree of schizotypical cognition is positively associated with mixed handedness and other evidence of reduced cerebral lateralization.[9]

During gestation, hands develop early, at much the same time as sexual differentiation, and along with the brain and heart. The relative length of the fingers is fixed by 14 weeks, and reflects hormonal influences in the womb. In men, the ring finger or fourth digit tends to be longer than the index finger or second digit, but in women the lengths of these fingers tends to be more similar. A low ratio like that found in men correlates with masculinity, autism, left-handedness and musical ability, while a high ratio correlates with femininity, vulnerability to breast cancer, high female but low male fertility and schizophrenic tendencies in both sexes.[32-36]

Schizophrenic men tend to have a ratio of index- to ring-finger length that resembles the generality of women more than it does that of men—an effect related to pre-natal exposure to sex hormones and the reverse of the situation found in autistics.[36,37] We have seen that erotomania appears to be a predominantly female pathology, and although there is a slightly higher incidence of schizophrenia overall in men, women do in fact suffer more paranoid delusions and hallucinations than do men, particularly in late-onset cases. Rates of incidence of schizophrenia among family members of women with the disorder are higher than those among family members of men with schizophrenia.[38] Again, in a previous chapter I suggested that religion, magic, and superstition could be understood as normal, socially legitimated expressions of hyper-mentalism. I also pointed out that the so-called magical ideation which underlies all three has also been linked to schizophrenic tendencies. The clear implication of the argument being developed in this chapter is that if X chromosome and maternally active genes play the role in psychosis that paternal genes and the absence of a second X chromosome seem to play in autism, XX women should be found to be more religious, superstitious, and magically minded than XY men.

Although men show more belief in UFOs (unidentified flying objects) and extraordinary life forms such as the Loch Ness monster and both sexes believe in witchcraft to the same extent, women usually show stronger belief than men in ESP (especially telepathy and precognition) and in superstition (specifically, in astrology, ghosts, psychic healing, and re-incarnation).[39] *Self-transcendence* is one well-validated personality measure of mystical tendencies on which women have been found to score 18 per cent higher than men,[40] and many other measures show a comparable sex difference in attitudes towards the supernatural.

According to one study, 79 per cent of women believed in a range of paranormal phenomena, as against 59 per cent of men, and sex has been identified as the only significant demographic variable found in such studies. The explanation may be that "it is women who arguably have the greater sensitivity to human personal relationships—and who, as every contemporary survey shows, tend to be surest that the scientific picture of the world is incomplete."[41] If we add that science is incomplete because it is notably hypo-mentalistic—and even anti-mentalistic—we can begin to see why the alternative to the mechanistic, scientific view of reality should so often be seen as the mentalistic and indeed hyper-mentalistic one enshrined in magic, superstition, and religion.

Furthermore, we can now begin to understand why sociological research shows that women are more religious than men and why throughout recorded history religious movements have recruited women far more successfully than men (except of course for those that excluded women from membership). Denominational yearbooks and available religious census data show that in every sizeable religious group in the Western world women outnumber men, usually by a considerable margin.[42] Sociologists are clearly at a loss to say why this should be so, and recently have even despaired of their stock-in-trade explanation that women are only more religious than men because they are nurtured to be so.[43] However, the finding that women are generally speaking also more mentalistic than men in their cognitive style easily explains why they should also be more religious. If religion is indeed institutionalized, collective, and legitimated hyper-mentalism as I suggested earlier, it follows that we would expect the more mentalistic of the two sexes to be the more religious too, and the evidence is that they indeed are.

Nevertheless, there is an important difference between a mentalistic—or even hyper-mentalistic—maternal brain in a man and the same brain in a woman. Because all mothers are female, a maternal brain in a woman is in harmony with her sex in a way in which such a brain in a man is not. By the same reasoning, the hyper-mentalism I am attributing to paranoia suggests the prediction that in a man such a tendency could go with some measure of inner conflict relating to his sexual identity.

Of course, you could make a parallel prediction in relation to autism: even if this is indeed an extreme *paternal* brain rather than extreme *male* brain disorder, the fact that all fathers are male would nevertheless suggest that female autistics might experience an equivalent conflict. At the very least, there is now good evidence of some measure of physical masculinization—or at least de-feminization—in autistic women. A medical questionnaire completed by 54 women with ASD (along with 74 mothers of children with autism and 183 mothers of typically developing ones) found that compared to the controls, significantly more women with an autism spectrum disorder reported anorexia; hirsutism (superfluous hair on the face and body); sexual preference for either or neither sex; irregular menstrual cycle and dysmenorrhoea (painful menstruation); polycystic ovary syndrome (an endocrine disturbance in which the ovaries produce atypically high levels of male hormones); severe acne; epilepsy; Tom-boy tendencies; and a family history of ovarian, uterine, and prostate cancers, tumours, or growths (some of which have been linked to higher levels of testosterone).[44]

Such findings fit those cited in the previous chapter relating to the extreme male brain theory of autism and the apparent effects of uterine testosterone (see pp. 138–139), but the extent to which they might also indicate internal psychological conflict is unclear. In any event, we also saw that autistics are symptomatically mind-blind, not just to the minds of others, but also to their own minds, and this suggests that inner conflict over sexual identity might be less likely to be expressed, particularly in the most severe, Kanner-type cases where we have already seen the sex ratio of incidence is much less skewed towards males. And another factor—significantly reported by the world's most famous female autistic, Temple Grandin—might be her belief that autistics are much less ambivalent than normal. In her view:

An autistic person's feelings are direct and open, just like animal feelings. We don't hide our feelings, and we aren't ambivalent. I can't even imagine what it would be like to have feelings of love and hate for the same person... There's so much psychodrama in normal people's lives. Animals never have psychodrama.[45]

At the very least, the severe verbal deficits usually seen in Kanner's autism mean that, even if present, female sufferers are much less likely to be able to verbalize such a conflict. But the conflict could still be there nevertheless (albeit not mentalized), and might be an important factor in explaining the greater severity of the disorder. In other words, male autistics would, according to this reasoning, tend to manifest less severe symptoms—exactly as they indeed do if we recall the extreme male preponderance seen in so-called "high-functioning," Asperger autism.

In the contrasting case of male psychotics, we might also predict some measures of feminization or de-masculinization comparable to the contrary effects reported above in female autistics. And recalling Temple Grandin's comment about "psychodrama" being absent in autistics, we might note that it is strikingly obvious in many psychotics, and predict that the conflict between the individual's sex and their feminized brain might be expected to be associated with more severe—even psychodramatic—symptoms. In other words, if autistic symptoms correlate with higher pre-natal exposure to testosterone, psychotic ones may do so to reduced androgens and/or increased female hormones such as oestrogen before birth. A review of the latest findings concludes that the evidence supports the hypothesis that oestrogen plays a protective role in female brain development before birth, and "contributes to a less severe course and expression of schizophrenia in women than in men," just as this hypothesis would suggest. Indeed, the same author explicitly mentions feminizations and/or de-masculinization of males by sex steroid hormones as a possible predisposing factor to male schizophrenia,[46] while others note that in terms of development of the frontal cortex to the amygdala, schizophrenic men show evidence of feminization.[47]

Paranoia and homosexuality

As we have seen, psychotics such as Schreber have bizarrely over-elaborated psyches, and so we might expect such cases to express the conflict clearly—particularly if, as in his case, the individual were also verbally very fluent. Indeed, Schreber remarks that "My sleep is often disturbed by dreams" whose "tendentious content" he described as "'being retained on the side of men' in contrast to cultivating 'feminine feelings.'" Elsewhere he remarks in connection with the cosmic conspiracy that he believed existed to turn him into a woman for purposes of "sexual misuse" that:

> one may imagine how my whole sense of manliness and manly honor, my entire moral being, rose against it…it was my duty to fight now and then to prove my manly courage, I could think of nothing else but that any manner of death, however frightful, was preferable to so degrading an end.[48a]

Whether such a sexual conflict is true of all or even many male paranoid psychotics is currently unknown. A study of 150 hospitalized schizophrenic patients from the early 1960s that reflected the contemporary vogue for Freudian interpretation nevertheless concluded that "paranoid development and homosexuality as found in schizophrenia are not specifically related to each other."[49] However, a later review of a large sample of psychiatric reports found more overt homosexual pre-occupations and behaviour in paranoid as compared to non-paranoid psychotics. As the author remarks, "This suggests some kind of association between homosexuality and paranoid delusions," but it does not confirm Freud's expectation that paranoid schizophrenics are characterized by strong *unconscious* rather than conscious homosexual impulses.[50] On the contrary, there is overwhelming evidence for conscious homosexual pre-occupations in Schreber's *Memoirs*, most notably in the following passage:

> I could see beyond doubt that the Order of the World imperiously

demanded my unmanning, whether I personally liked it or not, and that therefore it was *common sense* that nothing was left to me but to reconcile myself to the thought of being transformed into a woman. Nothing of course could be envisaged as a further consequence of unmanning than fertilization by divine rays for the purpose of creating new human beings...

Since then I have wholeheartedly inscribed the cultivation of femininity on my banner... I have yet to meet the man who, faced with the choice of either becoming a demented human being in male habitus or a spirited woman, would not prefer the latter. Such and *only such* is the issue for me.[48b]

Indeed, Schreber also claimed that:

Something like the conception of Jesus Christ by an Immaculate Virgin—i.e. one who never had intercourse with a man—happened in my own body. Twice at different times (while I was in Fleschig's asylum) I had a female genital organ, although a poorly developed one, and in my body felt quickening like the first signs of life of a human embryo: by a divine miracle God's nerves corresponding to male seed had been thrown into my body; in other words, fertilization had occurred.[48c]

Freud maintains that the idea of being transformed into a woman was the salient feature and the earliest germ of his delusional system. It also proved to be the one part of it that persisted after his cure, and the only part that was able to retain a place in his behaviour in real life after he had recovered. Freud concludes: "He took up a feminine attitude towards God; he felt that he was God's wife."[51]

Quite apart from its role in explaining Schreber's hyper-mentalism and its contribution to his psychosis, the X chromosome may also hold the key to these transparent bisexual fantasies and rationalizations—not to mention many other paranoiacs' apparent pre-occupation with homosexuality. To see how this comes about, we need to consider sex chromosome inheritance a little further.

From an evolutionary point of view, X chromosome genes spend two-thirds of their time in female bodies thanks to females having two X chromosomes and males having one. As a result, they are regularly subjected to twice as much selection for female, as opposed to male, reproductive interests.[52] Essentially, this is why we found that X chromosome genes are comparable to maternally active imprinted ones elsewhere in the genome: they have a naturally selected female bias. Consequently, if women are normally more mentalistic than men, X chromosome genes can be expected to show the same tendency, explaining the role of the X in psychosis described earlier.

People sometimes balk at such so-called *intragenomic conflict*, and treat it very much as a metaphor (in other words, mentalistically) rather than a reality (that is, as something mechanistic). But sex chromosome gene conflict is very real, and can sometimes have far-reaching consequences for the whole organism. For example, a gene on the X chromosome called *DAX1* acts as an antagonist to the gene on the Y that initiates male development. Normally, this gene, *SRY* (for *sex-determining region of the Y*, but alias *TDF* for *testis-determining factor*) transforms what would otherwise develop as ovaries into testes, with subsequent masculinization of the whole body (largely thanks to the male sex hormones produced by the testes). However, otherwise normal XY males with a duplication of part of the short arm of the X chromosome that contains *DAX1* show male-to-female sex reversal. Although the exact mechanism by which this comes about had not been determined at the time of writing, protein products of the two genes probably compete with each other for control of sexual development. It seems likely that the dose of *DAX1* carried on a normal male's single X chromosome is not enough to reverse male development, but a double dose provided by duplication of the *DAX1* region of the X chromosome is sufficient, and so sex reversal occurs. At the very least, this finding shows that particular genes on sex chromosomes can be in conflict with one another. Indeed, *DAX1* has been described as more of an "anti-testis gene" than a "pro-ovary" gene.[53]

Of course, genetic conflict need not only antagonize male development. Examples are now known which can cause ostensibly female individuals with two X chromosomes and no *SRY* gene at all nevertheless to develop as males.[54] But whichever way they work, such examples as these show that conflicts involving individual sex chromosome genes can have a critical bearing on sexual development in humans. For example, genes for male homosexuality could act like *DAX1*, and may simply have an effect depending on the dosage: too much, and partial feminization of behaviour occurs, showing itself as a homosexual tendency in the men affected.

A case in point is the finding that homosexual males are more often later-born than first-born, and that they have more older brothers than older sisters. Boys with an average of 2.5 older brothers are twice as likely to be homosexual as those with none, and boys with four older brothers are three times as likely to be homosexual. However, older sisters make no difference to the incidence of homosexuality in their younger brothers. Nor can the finding be explained by the increased age of the mother, and there is no similar effect on later-born females. Regardless of culture, demography, or psychological state, having more older brothers predisposes a man to being homosexual.[55] Furthermore, the effect appears to be genetic rather than environmental: a study of 944 men found the older brother effect only in those who shared the same mother, not in those with different mothers, and irrespective of whether they shared the same home.[56]

The most likely explanation is that the mother's immune system progressively reacts to male foetuses in a way that increasingly predisposes them to homosexuality. For example, maternal antibodies to an antigen produced by male foetuses may be capable of affecting foetal brain development without affecting gross anatomy. The so-called *Y-linked minor histo-compatibility antigen*—or *H-Y antigen*—is present only in males and highly conserved in evolution. It is strongly presented on the surface of brain cells, and male mice whose mothers were given the H-Y antigen prior to pregnancy were much less likely to mate successfully when they matured.[57]

Although this might look at first like an almost random

environmental factor, further reflection shows it to be yet another case of genetic conflict, albeit this time one between a mother and her male foetus. This is because it is the XX mother's immune system's reaction to the presence of the Y chromosome-linked antigen that appears to be the operative factor. Essentially, the mother is treating the H-Y antigen as if it were alien genetic material, such as that in a virus or other infecting pathogen. And far from being exceptional or pathological, genetic conflict of many different kinds between mother and foetus of either sex is now a firmly established fact of human development. As I briefly mentioned in the previous chapter, both diabetes and hypertension in pregnant women are attributable to paternally active genes in the foetus which produce effects that benefit the baby at a cost to the mother. Furthermore, there is evidence that the mother's immune system actively counters the aggressive implantation of the placenta.[58]

The inheritance of sex chromosomes as a whole is also the occasion for a major problem where sex-determination is concerned. To see why, suppose for a moment that all the genes needed to make a male rather than a female were on the Y chromosome. Because females never normally inherit any part of this chromosome, there could be no danger of a female being affected by male genes, and being masculinized as a result. You could not have bearded ladies if the genes for beards were exclusively found on the Y chromosome! But if, as is in fact the case, very few genes indeed relating to being male are found on the Y chromosome, it follows that most of them must be on other chromosomes that females do inherit: 22 non-sex chromosomes and the X. If this is so, then any such genes could be accidentally expressed, resulting perhaps in masculinized females (not to mention bearded ladies!). Furthermore, the problem is not confined to the Y. The fact that the X chromosome is also inherited by males but that, as we have already seen, its genes find themselves in female bodies twice as often as they do in male ones, means that female-benefiting X chromosome genes can all too easily be expressed in males. A still-controversial example is the claim that at least some cases of male homosexuality have a genetic basis, probably to be found on the X chromosome.[59,60]

At first sight, it might seem very strange that there could ever be "gay genes." You might wonder why natural selection could have been so foolish as to place genes that usually reduce male reproductive success in the male genome. Surely, those without such genes would do better in competition for mates and offspring, and so genes for male homosexuality would soon be selected out (at least if they feminized males, or reduced a male's reproductive success in any other significant way). Nevertheless, it is perfectly possible that the genes concerned with male homosexuality on the X chromosome may ultimately turn out to be "for" much more basic physiological processes, such as enzymes involved in female reproductive physiology. It may simply be that these genes benefit female reproductive success at a cost to males who carry them and perhaps lack other genes that might otherwise protect them, or compensate in some way. So most males might escape, but a proportion would pay the price for genes whose benefit accrued to their near female relatives. The point is that, as Hamilton was the first to fully realize, natural selection is not ultimately concerned with individuals, but with their genes. If particular genes benefit the reproductive success of female relatives of males who carry them more than they harm that of males concerned, natural selection cannot correct the situation.

Certainly, there is now good evidence that male homosexuality is more heritable through the female line and that male homosexuals are found to have female relatives with above average fertility. In a sample of 98 homosexual and 100 heterosexual men and their relatives (a total of over 4600 individuals), female maternal relatives of homosexuals were found to have higher fecundity than female maternal relatives of heterosexuals, but this difference was not found in female paternal relatives. In the view of the authors there might be some hitherto unsuspected reproductive advantages associated with male homosexuality, and the study confirmed previous reports that homosexuals have more maternal than paternal male homosexual relatives.[61]

Furthermore, there is evidence from several studies of increased fertility of non-affected first-degree relatives (brothers, sisters, or parents) of schizophrenics comparable to that which we have just seen in relation to homosexuality. Although schizophrenia like homosexuality definitely reduces male fertility, some studies show that the mothers of schizophrenics have significantly more siblings than do controls, but that this difference does not hold for schizophrenics' fathers. There have also been reports of higher numbers of children born to parents of schizophrenics compared to the general population, and of a significantly higher number to siblings of schizophrenics compared to a community sample (after controlling for demographic and socio-economic factors). A few studies show no difference in fecundity of siblings, but others find significantly more children being born to sisters—but not to the brothers—of schizophrenics. And reminiscent of the birth-order finding in relation to male homosexuality we noticed just now, one study reported a higher risk of schizophrenia in male first-degree relatives of schizophrenics with more than seven siblings compared to those with fewer than seven (along with a significantly higher number of siblings for male schizophrenics with a family history of the disorder compared to such males without such a history). Finally, a recent study with large samples showed that fertility in parents of individuals with schizophrenia and bipolar disorder was "substantially and significantly" increased.[9]*

ASD, PSD, and normality

A mentalistic continuum stretching all the way from autism to psychosis could provide a completely new basis for psychiatric diagnosis and classification (so-called *nosology*). Throughout this book I have used the

---

* Admittedly, some of this may represent not increased fertility in first-order relatives of schizophrenics, but instead might be an effect of family size on the risk of developing schizophrenia. If psychotic tendencies are part of a pattern of reduced growth during development, then coming from a large family might in itself be a predisposing factor, and there is some evidence that this is so. These findings suggest that in some populations, larger families and shorter inter-birth intervals engender stresses on mothers and offspring that increase schizophrenia risk. This mechanism cannot, however, explain reports of higher fitness in siblings of schizophrenics compared to controls.[9]

term ASD as an acronym for *autism spectrum disorder,* but the symmetry implied by hyper-mentalism as opposed to hypo-mentalism suggests that we might also begin to think in terms of *psychotic spectrum disorder,* or PSD. Just as the autistic spectrum can be seen running from classical, Kanner-type autism via Asperger's syndrome to normal male mentality, so you might imagine a psychotic spectrum ranging from extreme forms of psychosis to normal female mentality via so-called schizotypy and perhaps other syndromes on the hyper-mentalistic side of normality. Although today there seem to be more of these disorders than are found on the autistic spectrum, it remains a possibility that most or even all psychiatric syndromes could be allocated to one or the other extreme of mentalism. In a previous chapter, I drew attention to the fact that catatonic paralysis might be the end result of hyper-mentalizing about each and every move, and that hyper-activity was linked to a mentalistic deficit in attention deficit hyper-activity disorder (see pp. 113–114). If so, catatonia and ADHD could be seen as sister syndromes on the autistic and psychotic sides of the spectrum respectively. But as we have also seen, such sister syndromes would be the outcome of opposite expression of the same complexes of genes, with more paternal/less maternal and/or X chromosome gene expression producing the autistic spectrum disorders and the converse the psychotic ones.

A natural criticism of autistic/psychotic spectrum classification might be that it seems far too one-dimensional to capture the full complexity of psychiatric disorders such as schizophrenia, and this chapter has implicitly underlined the point by introducing a new factor: sex, and the sex chromosome gene expression on which it relies. Consequently, we might remedy the one-dimensional deficiency of the scheme suggested earlier in this chapter by introducing a second, sexual dimension as illustrated in the diagram opposite. Effectively, this gives a visual representation to my argument in this chapter: namely that the expression of sex chromosome genes interacts with that of imprinted ones to produce four fundamental outcomes. Where the imbalance lies in the direction of paternal genes in a male, the outcome is more likely to be Asperger's syndrome: what we have already seen as the equivalent of the "extreme male brain." However, where paternal genes are over-expressed in a female, classical Kanner-type autism is more likely, explaining why there are more female cases (as in Rett syndrome) and perhaps also why retardation is more severe, as we saw in the previous chapter (see p. 160). Where psychosis is concerned, excess expression of maternal genes in a male might explain the trans-sexual fantasies seen in cases such as Schreber's, and the resulting internal conflict might explain the greater severity of the symptoms. However, an imbalance in favour of maternal gene expression in a woman might result in an extreme female brain equivalent of Asperger's syndrome perhaps comparable to the milder symptoms seen in so-called schizotypy. So far, little research has been done into the latter, probably because the relative mildness of the symptoms means that many cases escape psychiatric attention.

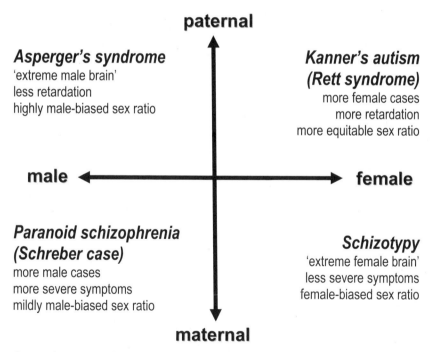

The two dimensions of genetic conflict and the four principal psychiatric outcomes Arrows represent axes of gene expression: maternal-paternal refers to imprinted gene expression, and male-female to sex chromosome gene expression. (Redrawn and modified from Crespi & Badcock, 2008).

In conclusion, both psychosis and homosexuality in men could turn out to have a genetic basis very similar to that proposed earlier for autism. If psychosis is indeed an extreme maternal brain disorder in the same way that autism might be seen as an extreme paternal one, then conflicted homosexuality in male psychotics such as Schreber would make sense. Indeed, a role for imprinted genes in male trans-sexuals has also been proposed, making the parallel with autism and psychosis even more exact.[62] And of course, because the number of genes involved in both psychosis and homosexuality may be considerable, a variable outcome is likely, with perhaps only some male psychotics showing the homosexual complication.

With the benefit of hindsight like this, what is so instructive about the case of Schreber is not the fact that both male and female sexual mentalities were present in his psychological make-up, but the degree of the conflict to which these opposing tendencies gave rise. According to this way of looking at things, the only thing that truly distinguished Schreber from the rest of us was the degree to which his mind was distorted by genetic conflict, not the existence of the conflict as such. Comparable, if less intense, conflicts probably take place in all of us, even if most of us are lucky enough to escape their worst effects. Writing with characteristic autistic candour, Hamilton himself came to realize that "My own conscious and seemingly indivisible self was turning out far from what I had imagined… I was an ambassador ordered abroad by some fragile coalition, a bearer of conflicting orders from the uneasy masters of a divided empire"—or, in other words, his own genome. He goes on:

> As I write these words, evenso as to be able to write them, I am pretending to a unity that, deep inside myself, I now know does not exist. I am fundamentally mixed, male with female, parent with offspring, warring segments of chromosomes that interlocked in strife millions of years before…[63]

Here surely lies a secure foundation for a humane and constructive attitude to mental health and illness alike. Normality, according to this view, would be the happy outcome of a more or less balanced expression of oppositely imprinted and sex chromosome genes built into a brain which could walk the tight-rope between the hypo-mentalism of ASD and the hyper-mentalism of PSD while avoiding internal conflicts of the kind that completely unbalanced Schreber.

Beyond
the Balanced Brain

New scientific theories often have major impacts on thinking far beyond their immediate field of application. Copernicus's sun-centred solar system, for example, was not just an innovation in astronomy, it implied a new cosmology: one that not only contradicted the old Earth-centred one, but had implications so radical and far-reaching for religion and philosophy that it remained bitterly controversial for centuries. Exactly the same was true of Darwin's theory of evolution. Indeed, in his case the reverberations continue today, 200 years after his birth. Whether the same will be true of the new theory of mental evolution and development set out here remains to be seen, but in this concluding chapter I would like to consider one or two of its more obvious implications for wider issues.

Specifically, I want to focus on one of the most striking characteristics of the new theory: its remarkable symmetry, which is immediately and visually apparent from the diagrams on pp. 185 and 190. Fundamental symmetries are a feature of mathematics and natural science that have often been commented on. In chemistry, they can be seen in the periodic table of the elements, and in physics there are numerous examples, principally in relativity and quantum mechanics, where according to the latter for example, every particle has an equal and opposite anti-particle. Up to now, fundamental symmetries of nature have not been a characteristic of theories in psychiatry or behavioural science, but readers who have persevered this far will now understand

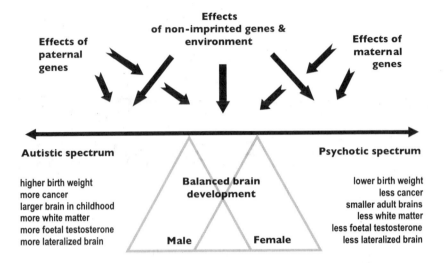

The imprinted brain theory (Redrawn and modified from Crespi & Badcock 2008).

why this may be about to change. In this final chapter let me set a precedent by beginning to consider just some of the most obvious and immediate implications of the striking symmetry between autistic and psychotic spectrum disorders that has emerged in the course of this book. Later I shall suggest that there is a symmetrical psychotic equivalent of autistic savantism and illustrate it with the case of Freud and psychoanalysis. But first we need to consider another aspect of the theory's symmetry, one that goes beyond the balanced brain in a different sense and opens up a surprising new insight into one of the greatest mysteries of human cognition: genius.

The cognitive configuration of genius

A mentalistic spectrum stretching from autism at one extreme to psychosis at the other with normally balanced sanity in between would make you suppose that a person could not be psychotic and autistic at the same time—or that, if they were, they would be normal! But if measures of mentalism were analogous to those of temperature or blood pressure a person could have a high reading at one time, and a low one at another. Higher or lower than normal readings of blood pressure or temperature need not be pathological in themselves because such measures fluctuate naturally over a certain range depending on circumstances, many of which might be completely normal, such as the heightened blood pressure and temperature that accompany vigorous exercise. Clearly, the same could be true of mentalism, and although the fluctuations in most people might be expected to be quite mild and only over a narrow range of variation, there is no reason in principle why you should not find quite wide fluctuations in exceptional instances. Furthermore, there are well-known cases where evidence of both autistic and paranoid tendencies can be found in the same persons. Beethoven, for example, has been posthumously diagnosed as meeting the criteria for both Asperger's syndrome and schizoid personality disorder.[1a]

As we have already seen, Newton has been described as autistic, and his supreme achievements in mathematics and physics certainly fit the typical picture of Asperger savantism (see pp. 25–34). But Newton's biographers speak of a "paranoid episode" during which he accused acquaintances such as Pepys and Locke of being atheists or Catholics involved in a Jesuitical conspiracy to embroil him with women.[2,3] And reminiscent of Schreber, a recent account concludes that "Newton believed that he had been chosen by God to discover the truth about the decline of Christianity, and he believed it to be by far the most important work he would ever undertake."[4]

An analysis of what were believed to be locks of Newton's hair in 1979 claimed to have detected toxic levels of mercury, one of whose effects in adults can be paranoid delusions, and another of which is cited as "pronounced mental hyper-activity."[5] Clearly, if mercury poisoning is the explanation of Newton's paranoid tendencies, there is no contradiction with the theory proposed here: imbalances in gene expression and/or environmental factors predisposed him to autistic savantism early on, but mercury poisoning caused paranoid tendencies much later.

Nevertheless, the mercury-poisoning theory has been seriously questioned,[6] and it is an indisputable fact that Newton devoted more time in his life to activities that would fit the label of religion, magic, and superstition much better than that of science, mathematics, or philosophy. What I have in mind here are his lengthy ruminations on biblical numerology and prophecy—not to mention the alchemical experiments that purportedly gave rise to the poisoning. Indeed, John Maynard Keynes (1883–1946), who acquired many of Newton's unpublished manuscripts and spent a life-time studying them, concluded that it was "utterly impossible to deny" that all this was "wholly magical and wholly devoid of scientific value," and that "it is impossible not to admit that Newton devoted years of work to it." He concluded that "Newton was not the first of the age of reason. He was the last of the magicians."[7] Nor was this the superstition of pigeons and autistics. Newton's biblical and historical researches were truly hyper-mentalistic: the product of a true—if characteristically quirky—religious faith (Newton was a closet Unitarian) and the exercise of a mighty mind.

Could geniuses such as Newton be paranoid and autistic at one and the same time? For example, could this be the explanation of the astonishingly dangerous experiments he carried out on his own eyes? These involved staring at the sun as paranoiacs such as Schreber are known to do for so long that he could summon up perceptible after-images years later just by recalling the incident (see p. 78). But he also inserted "a bodkin" (or stiletto-like blade soliloquized about by Hamlet as a means of suicide) "betwixt my eye & the bone as near to the Backside of my eye as I could" to see what effect the resulting deformation of his vision would have![8] Such a feat could only perhaps be fully explained by autistic insensitivity to pain (box, p. 18) combined with the astonishing single-mindedness in the pursuit of knowledge that is typical of Asperger savants. Could it be that what we perceive as transcendent genius in people such as Newton is a supreme form of savantism in which mechanistic and mentalistic cognitive skills unite to widen, deepen, and elevate mental powers to encompass a vastly greater range of insight than that achieved by more normal minds? After all, if mentalism is indeed a completely different mode of thought from mechanistic cognition, the fact that Newton could have made remarkable discoveries in the latter is in no way necessarily compromised by his forays into the former, however absurd they may seem to us today (and however much they may embarrass his biographers). Certainly, the extent to which mentalistic and mechanistic cognition could be seen as parallel but independent axes of insight into different universes would not rule out the possibility that someone could achieve extreme feats in one, the other, or both—and perhaps some people do.

A much more recent case that might argue the same conclusion is that of the mathematician, game-theorist, and winner of the 1994 Nobel Prize for Economics, John Forbes Nash. True to the classic profile of someone with autistic tendencies, Nash's father was an engineer. Of Nash himself as a child, his biographer says that his great passion was experimenting, and that, by the time he was 12 or so, he had turned his room into a laboratory. He tinkered with radios, fooled around with electrical gadgets, and did chemistry experiments.[9a] Others described him as "a singular little boy, solitary and introverted," who his aunts considered "bookish and slightly odd," while his teachers complained of his "atrocious writing and out-of-turn talking."[10a]

Nash himself intended to follow in his father's footsteps and become an electrical engineer. Indeed, he published an article in an electrical journal describing an improved method for calculating the proper tensions of electric cables which won the young Nash a George Westinghouse Engineering Scholarship. His professors noticed his outstanding mathematical gifts—one of them calling him "a young Gauss"—and it was not long before he was studying maths at Carnegie and later at Princeton. Recalling my earlier observation about the visual, spatial mode of thinking characteristic of autistics, those who knew him commented that "he would see a mathematical situation as a picture in his mind," and that "visual insight was the strongest part of his talent." However, Nash's peers found him "weird and socially inept," a person who avoided eye-contact and was impossible to engage in a normal conversation without walking off in the middle or simply not responding. As a result, he got a reputation for being eccentric and aloof, and certainly behaved oddly. He is reported playing a single chord on the piano over and over, leaving an ice cream cone melting on top of his cast-off clothing in the lounge, or walking on his room-mate's sleeping body to turn off a light. His biographer recounts that fellow students believed that Nash felt nothing remotely resembling love, friendship, or real sympathy, but existed instead in an "arid state of emotional isolation" and at times he certainly referred to other people as "humanoids." As another of his fellow students put it, "Here was a guy who was socially underdeveloped and acting much younger... We sensed he had a mental problem." Others described him as "spiteful," "absurdly childish," and having the social IQ of a 12-year old.[9b]

All this seems distinctly autistic, and when taken into consideration with his outstanding mathematical and engineering abilities, it is not hard to see that Nash might be yet another candidate for inclusion in the list of autistic geniuses cited earlier. Arshad and Fitzgerald certainly think so, concluding that he had been "fulfilling the criteria of Asperger's syndrome since childhood." They add that "John was involved more with mathematical mysteries than with people" while possessing a genius that was of the "mysterious variety more often associated with music and art than with...mathematics."[10b]

Perhaps the last comment gives some hint as to why Nash was subject to paranoid delusions and consequently hospitalized later in his life, and despite their diagnosis of Asperger's syndrome in his early years, Arshad and Fitzgerald conclude that schizophrenia eventually supervened. Although these authorities rightly remark that the co-occurrence of Asperger's syndrome and schizophrenia "will be decided by molecular genetic studies,"[10c] the possibility of both states of mind co-existing—or perhaps alternating—definitely has to be considered. Indeed, you could imagine that this might be the basis of genius, whether in the arts or sciences. Could it be that true genius in any field of endeavour relies on having a mind that is not merely more or less normally balanced between autistic and psychotic, but actually represents something of an over-development of both? (In Nash's case it would certainly give a whole new meaning to *Nash equilibrium!*) Would greatly extended mechanistic and mentalistic abilities underlie every case of exceptional achievement, but could it be that mentalistic skill might predominate in those on the arts-and-literature side of the divide, and mechanistic talent predominate in science and technology? We have already seen Asperger remarking that a dash of autism is essential for success in science or art (see p. 25), but perhaps a dose of psychosis can help too—particularly in the arts and literature (not to mention psychology, religion, or politics). At the very least, these considerations suggest that we cannot rule out the possibility that a person could have something of an extreme paternal *and* an extreme maternal brain at one and the same time. Genius, in short, might lie in extending the limits of both of our fundamental cognitive systems, and the extent to which a person of genius exhibited autistic and/or psychotic symptoms might simply depend on which tendency was most pronounced.

Again, we should not overlook the fact that autism and psychosis are developmental disorders, and unfold over a person's lifetime. We saw that this way of looking at things makes the early onset of autism and the normally late onset of schizophrenia in particular easy to understand simply because, while autistics never fully develop mentalism, potential psychotics would have to do so before they could surpass it in the hyper-mentalism that characterizes PSD (see pp. 117–118). If this is so, it suggests a possible resolution of the apparent paradox, and a specific prediction that future research could confirm or refute. This is the contention that if genius is typified by some combined measure of hypo- and hyper-mentalism, then the hypo-mentalistic, autistic element should normally be developed first—typically in childhood—and the hyper-mentalistic over-compensation might usually be expected to come later—probably in adolescence or adulthood. We must also presume that the earlier autistic under-development leaves permanent features in place (such as the single-mindedness mentioned by Asperger, or the savant skills seen in geniuses such as Nash and Newton). The later, psychotic phase would then be seen as adding further enduring features to a mind that had already taken on an autistic cast. Whether the developmental trajectories and cognitive architecture of geniuses would typically fit this picture remains to be seen, but the cases of Nash and Newton do seem to do so, suggesting that, at the very least, there are good reasons for keeping an open mind on the issue.

A number of other cases of famous artists and writers who we saw in an earlier chapter have been placed on the autistic spectrum by some authorities, such as van Gogh, Michelangelo, Hans Christian Andersen, and Herman Melville, have also been proposed as manic-depressives.[11] Earlier I pointed out that manic-depression (bipolar disorder) and schizophrenia are now not thought to be very different illnesses (see pp. 116–117), and according to the view proposed here would certainly be seen as close together on the psychotic spectrum of hyper-mentalistic disorders. The fact that the high-achieving social background (though not the mechanistic occupations) and pattern of inheritance of manic-depression seem strikingly similar to that of autism suggests that, in some cases at least, both tendencies might be found in the same person, perhaps explaining their genius in the way that I have just speculated might be true of Newton and Nash.

Cases can certainly be found which exhibit both autistic and manic-depressive tendencies in the same person. Indeed, I quoted one at the end of an earlier chapter, where a correspondent reports cycling from autistic gaze-aversion to megalomania and back again, with a predictable improvement in social skills during the hyper-mentalistic, manic phase (see p. 96). However, despite testing poorly for executive function, he also reports doing well in school thanks to "an ability to grasp the technical aspects of subjects and memorize which led to virtually perfect grades"—or in other words mechanistic skills bordering on savantism.[12] At least one other case is known to me personally where bipolar disorder and autism appear to co-exist in a successful engineer, suggesting that this situation is by no means unique.[13] And as we shall see later in this chapter, manic-depression is definitely linked to outstanding mentalistic talents in poets, writers, and artists of many different kinds.

The genius of detective fiction

Sir Arthur Conan Doyle's most famous creation, Sherlock Holmes, has been widely seen as one of the most notable fictional portrayals of an Asperger's savant.* As described in the stories and novels, Holmes is a lonely, compulsive, mechanistic thinker with a "photographical" memory, who his chronicler, Dr. Watson, describes in *A Scandal in Bohemia* as "the most perfect reasoning and observing machine the world has seen." As such, Holmes agonizes over the meaning of tiny details whose significance eludes more mentalistic minds:

> What interests Holmes is not status but the problems he is asked to solve. It is puzzles that fascinate Holmes—the intellectual aspects of cases. These satisfy his curiosity. He is clearly bored by social gatherings of affluent people, parties, etc. His interests are narrow: he reads only criminal news and the agony column. This is a perfect example of autistic narrowness of interests.[1b]

Indeed, according to Rennison's "unauthorized biography" of Holmes, there are certainly notable parallels between what we know of Holmes and modern case histories of autistics:

> The odd detachment from the everyday world, the peculiar fixations on particular objects and the careful classification of them (his monographs on the 140 different varieties of pipe, cigar and cigarette tobacco ash, for example), the inability to understand or empathize fully with other people's emotions and the heightened acuity of some senses—these all mirror ways in which the autistic interact with the world.[14]

Of course, most other famous fictional detectives also show evidence of a genius for detail and for getting at the truth of the case they are

---

* But he may not be the only one. Where comic fiction is concerned, P. G. Wodehouse's Jeeves seems very much a caricature of an Asperger's savant. His combination of self-effacement and sense of superiority, pedantic manner of speaking, encyclopaedic knowledge and universal reading, punctilious insistence on following proper form (and fashion), and well-meaning if often disastrous forays into psychology and other people's personal affairs all portray aspects of Asperger's syndrome with wonderful comic effect in the Jeeves novels.

investigating. And even if better adjusted socially than Holmes, a good fictional detective needs to be sceptical about the seemingly obvious, taken-for-granted, conventional interpretation of events, and needs to be able to think the unthinkable—often to the initial dismay or disgust of others. And inevitably—and particularly in murder mysteries—a distinctly paranoid element of suspicion is wholly appropriate, not to mention an ability to read the mind of a suspect, to understand a murderer's *modus operandi,* and to intuit a criminal's motivation. Indeed, it has been pointed out that Miss Marple, another of the immortals of detective fiction, "is in every way the opposite" of Holmes or Agatha Christie's other famous creation, Hercule Poirot, "and has no autistic traits at all: she solves crimes by intuition, immersing herself in the context without analytic deduction."[15]

Could this be because Miss Marple is female, and therefore likely to be of a more mentalistic turn of mind as we have seen women in general to be? Authorities on detective fiction have pointed out that "detection was understood as a distinctly feminine talent—women had the opportunities for 'intimate watching'…and an instinct for deciphering what they saw," while also noting that "The perfect detective…was not so much a scientist as a machine."[16a] If so, then once again, both mentalistic—and even hyper-mentalistic—aspects can be found fused with autistic ones in what is perhaps the most distinctive literary genre of modern times: the detective story. Indeed, this may explain why thrillers are so endlessly fascinating and why detective fiction has emerged as such a major factor in modern literature. Could it be that, rather than adopt a safe, central, normal mix of mentalistic and mechanistic cognition comparable to that found in most people, detective stories balance hyper-mentalistic paranoid suspicion against hypo-mentalistic, autistic obsession with conflicting detail to get the best of both? Could this explain the "atmosphere of mysterious greatness" which Dickens attributed to Inspector Bucket in *Bleak House,* a character who has been described as "the supreme fictional detective of his era?"[16b] At the very least, this would explain why autistic characters such as Sherlock Holmes and highly mentalistic ones such as Miss Marple could both make convincing fictional detectives—not to mention why so many female writers have made a success of their detective fiction.

Psychotic savants

Characters such as Miss Marple throw up another possibility that is suggested by the symmetry of the mentalistic continuum graphically set out in diagram on p. 190. This is that, if there are autistic savants as we have seen there indeed are, then there also might be *psychotic savants*. As we saw, autistic savantism is characterized by outstanding, if isolated, mechanistic skills or expertise set against a background of cognitive deficits, particularly where mentalism is concerned (see pp. 25–38). Accordingly, we might predict that psychotic savantism might show the opposite cognitive configuration: remarkable, if perhaps highly circumscribed, mentalistic talents co-existing with more specific mechanistic deficits. Indeed, in a previous chapter I quoted leading psychiatric authorities such as Bleuler commenting on the exceptional mental sensitivities of many psychotics—a trait you could regard as savant-like in a mentalistic sense (see p. 107). Furthermore, if there are indeed high-functioning, Asperger savants who exhibit the savantism without notable deficits in intelligence as we saw there certainly are (see p. 26), then there might also be high-functioning psychotic savants, with a similar mental configuration, but with exceptional mentalistic gifts in place of the mechanistic ones seen in the autistic case.

But of course, the symmetry cannot be exact. For a start, deficits in mechanistic cognition are unlikely to be detected as readily by standard IQ tests for the reasons explained in an earlier chapter: sex-specific sub-tests, such as those for mechanical ability, are routinely excluded (see p. 142). Again, the normally sad plight of autistics reminds us that mentalistic deficits are typically much more significant socially and have an enormous impact on people's personal relationships in a way in which mechanistic deficits seldom if ever do. Not being able to programme the video, change a plug, or read a map is one thing, but failing to understand other people's motives, actions, and intentions is quite another—and much more damaging from a social point of view. Hyper-mentalistic tendencies of the kind predicted in high-functioning psychotic savants might normally promote a person's social adjustment because of the skill these consummate mentalists have in manipulating others and exploiting them thanks to their natural empathic understanding. Consequently, high-functioning psychotic savants are likely to be identified at worst as cranks or charlatans rather than psychopaths— at least as long as their hyper-mentalism stops short of Schreberian lunacy and their behaviour remains within acceptable bounds. So at best we should not expect such psychotic savants to be anything like as noticeable as autistic ones usually are, or as readily diagnosed as such. On the contrary, we can expect them to be deeply embedded in critical social networks that may have far-reaching social, political, and historical consequences.

Again, the areas of expertise involved in psychotic savantism might not be so obviously striking as are calendar-calculation, photographic memory, or computer-like maths skills. By contrast, hyper-mentalistic savantism might be predicted to be reflected in skills and areas of expertise that are far less alien and much closer to normal social life and everyday concerns. Examples might be outstanding achievement in religious and ideological evangelism; literary and theatrical culture; litigation and the law; hypnosis, faith-healing, and psychotherapy; fashion and advertising; politics, public-relations, and the media; commerce, confidence-trickery, and fraud of all kinds. Indeed, this might also explain why studies have found that artistic and literary gifts— mentalistic ones, in other words—make men attractive to women in a way in which mechanistic ones like those seen in autistic savantism seldom if ever do. Hyper-mentalizing individuals may make better partners, because, being what Hamilton called "people people" rather than "things people" (see pp. 34–38), they take into account the needs and desires of others.[17]

Furthermore, the fact that such psychotic savantism is quintessentially mentalistic might explain why savantism in the past has seemed to be mainly a male attribute. As we have already seen, there is a strong male bias in the incidence of autism, particularly in the milder range, so it is not surprising that if we are considering autistic and Asperger's savants, they should be male by about 5-to-1.[18] Another factor might be that male development generally goes to extremes much more than does female: for example, 20 per cent more males than females have IQs above 140 and even more have IQs below 70[19] (something probably explained by the fact that males have only a single X chromosome, which is known to carry many genes implicated in IQ). But an additional consideration may be that mechanistic genius stands out much more obviously than genius in more mentalistic areas of expertise and that, as we have seen, women are generally more mentalistic than men. If so, female savantism might be expected to be much less eccentric, and much more centrally coherent with social norms in areas such as religion and politics, literature and the theatre, law and psychotherapy—not to mention fashion and public relations in all their aspects. Here true female psychotic savants might be found, but without the alien weirdness often seen in male autistic savants. Nevertheless, to the extent that an early autistic tendency forms the cognitive foundation of genius in later life, the greater vulnerability of males to autism—and particularly to high-functioning forms such as Asperger's syndrome—may be enough in itself to explain why true genius is so often seen in males.

Of course, the term *psychotic savant* should not be interpreted to imply that all such savants are suffering from PSD, merely that their peculiar form of savantism belongs on the psychotic, rather than the autistic, side of the mentalistic continuum. Nevertheless, a study of over a thousand Americans who made outstanding contributions to the arts, sciences, public office, the military, business, and social activism during the twentieth century revealed that the life-time rate of suffering from any form of mental disorder was 87 per cent for poets, 77 per cent for writers, 74 per cent for those employed in the theatre, 73 per cent for artists, 68 per cent for musicians, and 60 per cent for composers. By contrast, the corresponding figure for scientists was 28 per cent—below the background rate for the whole population, which was 32 per cent. Overall, the findings suggest that members of those creative arts professions that rely more on precision, reason, and logic—or what I would call mechanistic cognition (for example, architects, designers, journalists, essayists, and literary critics)—are less prone to mental disturbances. However, those who tend more to mentalism in relying more on emotive expression, personal experiences, and vivid imagery as sources of inspiration (such as poets, novelists, actors, and musical entertainers) are more prone to a psychotic illness. Indeed, the same author concludes that writing poetry is the occupation most associated with the highest life-time risk of depression, psychosis, and suicide.[20a]

There certainly is good evidence that many of the world's leading poets have shown unmistakeable signs of PSD, most notably bipolar/manic-depressive illnesses (and quite apart from those I mentioned earlier in whom autistic tendencies had also been suspected). Examples from literature in English include William Blake (1757–1827), Robert Burns (1759–96), Lord Byron (1788–1824), Samuel Taylor Coleridge (1875–1912), Emily Dickinson (1830–86), Gerard Manley Hopkins (1844–89), John Keats (1795–1821), Sylvia Plath (1932–63), Ezra Pound (1885–1972), Percy Bysshe Shelley (1792–1822), Alfred Lord Tennyson (1809–92), Dylan Thomas (1914–53), and Walt Whitman (1819–92). A study of all major British and Irish poets born between 1705 and 1805 found a strikingly high rate of mood disorders, suicide, and institutionalization within this group of writers and their families. By comparison with the rate of manic-depressive illness in the general population, these British poets were 30 times more likely to suffer from manic-depression, 10 to 20 times more likely to suffer from milder forms of manic-depressive illness, more than five times more likely to commit suicide, and at least 20 times more likely to have been committed to an asylum or madhouse. Other large-scale studies have found rates of psychiatric abnormality in 50 per cent of poets (compared to 38 per cent of musicians, 20 per cent of painters, 18 per cent of sculptors, and 17 per cent of architects). An analysis of biographies of individuals that had been reviewed in *The New York Times Book Review* between 1960 and 1990 found much the same, along with the fact that 18 per cent of poets included had committed suicide. Compared to people in other professions, the rate of forced psychiatric hospitalization of artists, writers, and composers was six to seven times higher.[11] Nor is this effect limited to successful, established writers: of 30 people attending the University of Iowa Writers' Workshop, 80 per cent reported a mood disorder (compared to 30 per cent in a control group), and half of those had a manic-depressive illness (four times the rate of the controls).[20b]

Nevertheless, it is important to point out that:

> Manic-depressive illness, unlike schizophrenia or Alzheimer's disease, is not a dementing illness. It may on occasion result in episodes of acute psychosis and flagrant irrationality, but these bouts of madness are almost always temporary and seldom progress to chronic insanity.[11a]

Consequently, as in the perhaps parallel but mentalistically opposite case of Asperger's savants, psychotic savants with a manic-depressive cognitive configuration may be sufficiently normal most of the time to be able to realize the advantages of their extended mentalism without being too disabled by it. On the contrary:

> Overall peak creativity may be enhanced, on average, in sub- jects showing milder and, perhaps, sub-clinical expressions of potential bipolar liability... There may be a positive compensa- tory advantage (...) to genes associated with great liability for bipolar disorder. The possibility that normal relatives of manic- depressives...have heightened creativity may have been over- looked because of a medical-model orientation that focused on dysfunction rather than positive characteristics of such indi- viduals. Such a compensatory advantage among the relatives of a disorder affecting at least 1% of the population could affect a relatively large group of people.[21]

In other words, some features associated with the manic side of bipolar disorder, such as outgoingness, increased energy, intensified sexuality, increased risk-taking, persuasiveness, self-confidence, and heightened productivity might contribute to success in many walks of life as long as they were not taken to extremes.[11b] Indeed, even depressive episodes may contribute in view of the finding that mildly depressed people tend to be more realistic and objective than non-depressed ones.[22] Taken together, all this might explain why three-quarters of studies report a link between manic-depressive illness and the professional or upper classes across several cultures and in different historical periods.[11c] In terms of the cognitive model proposed here, this would be the mentalistic equivalent of the point I made earlier about the mechanistic benefits of autism (see pp. 136–138). If autistic tendencies have contributed to mathematics, science, and technology, mentalistic ones have also clearly done so where literature, art, religion, politics, and society are concerned. Indeed, to the extent that there is an important cultural dimension to mentalism reflected in social conventions and political, religious, and ethnic beliefs, values, and ideals, mentalistic savantism has clearly played a major role in history. And just as we have seen many major contributors to human scientific and technological culture diagnosed as autistic savants, so you could imagine that a large number of literary, artistic, religious, and political luminaries might be their hyper-mentalistic equivalents—as many poets evidently were.

The case of Freud

Another cultural activity intimately associated with mentalism where high-functioning psychotic savantism might be expected to be found is psychotherapy. I pointed out earlier that women might be predicted to be much more prominently associated with psychotic savantism, and so it is not surprising that today psychotherapy features a large number of women practitioners and that women analysts were prominent in psychoanalysis from the very beginning. Notable examples are Lou Andreas-Salomé (1861–1937), Marie Bonaparte (1882–1962), Anna Freud (1895–1982), Karen Horney (1885–1952), Melanie Klein (1882–1960), Margaret Mahler (1897–1985), and Sabina Spielrein (1885–1941/2).

As for the founder of psychoanalysis, you could make a good case for diagnosing Sigmund Freud as a compulsive systemizer (see p. 38). He also showed distinct mechanistic talents, at least in his youth (and I have already explained why my theory predicts that if autistic and psychotic excesses co-exist in the same individual, the autistic phase must come first). In this respect you could cite the younger Freud's discovery of an original method for staining cell sections with gold-chloride for microscopic analysis and his discovery of the testes of eels and the origin of the posterior nerve roots of the lamprey—all feats of remarkably close and detailed scientific observation. This was at the very beginning of his career, when his aspirations certainly seem to have been principally scientific and his allegiance firmly with the anti-vitalist, mechanistic world-view of the Helmholtz school. And even much later in his life he could still be found consoling himself with the thought that "all our provisional ideas in psychology will presumably some day be based on an organic substructure."[23a]

We saw earlier that although deficient in mind-reading abilities, autistics could be described as "desire psychologists," and can understand basic needs such as hunger and basic emotions such as fear (see p. 55). Freud's daughter and successor in psychoanalysis, Anna Freud, once remarked to me that the libido theory was and remained for true Freudians the "heart and lungs of psychoanalysis."[24] *Libido* means "desire," and with the comment about autistic desire psychology in mind, you could see the libido theory as distinctly hypo-mentalistic in this sense. By contrast, most psychoanalytic theorizing went to the opposite extreme, and perhaps this explains why the libido theory fell so rapidly out of fashion with post-Freudians and remains to this day one of its most controversial aspects. The libido theory, in other words, could be seen as "autistic" desire psychology epitomized as a formal theory of mind. Indeed, we saw in the previous chapter that it provided Freud with a striking insight into the Schreber case that agrees surprisingly well with the latest findings from neuroscience and evolutionary genetics. And Freud certainly seems to have anticipated Hamilton's selfish-gene view of evolution in his comment that:

The individual himself regards sexuality as one of his own ends; whereas from another point of view he is an appendage to his germ-plasm, at whose disposal he puts his energies in return for a bonus of pleasure. He is the mortal vehicle of a (possibly) immortal substance—like the inheritor of an entailed property, who is only the temporary holder of an estate that survives him.[23b]

At a time when DNA was unknown, and August Weismann's (1834–1914) germ-line theory of inheritance was still highly controversial, this was a remarkably prescient insight—and a quintessentially mechanistic one. Indeed, Freud uses the German equivalent of the very term that we saw Richard Dawkins was to use 60-odd years later to epitomize Hamilton's view of the organism as the *vehicle* of its genes[25,26] (see p. 144). Although psychoanalysis quickly forgot its scientific roots and rapidly degenerated into the rampant hyper-mentalistic savantism of Melanie Klein, Jacques Lacan (1901–81) and others, Freud's premonitory remark quoted here suggests that his "autistic" libido theory could be seen as providing a mechanistic grounding for psychoanalysis which would complement it in much the same way that mentalistic insights complemented our modern view of autism.[27]

Nevertheless, and despite protests from less credulous colleagues such as Ernest Jones (1879–1958),[28] Freud revealed his mentalistic feet of clay in his belief in Lamarckian evolution-by-will, and the inheritance of mentally-acquired characteristics—not to mention telepathy and the death instinct.[29,30]* Worse still—and perhaps significantly in view of my earlier remarks about literature and psychotic savantism—at the very end of his life Freud wrote what he himself called a "historical novel" about Moses. According to this remarkable work, Moses was murdered by the Jews, whose inheritance of guilt about the murder

---

* A biographical detail that fits with such hyper-mentalistic tendencies is Freud's life-long addiction to cigars. Smoking has been interpreted as a form of self-medication to remedy a deficit in natural nicotinoids found in people with schizophrenic tendencies, and perhaps this was also true of Freud.[31–33] (along with their habit of circumcision according to Freud acquired in Egypt) was in his opinion the root cause of anti-Semitism![34,35]

As Kate Summerscale points out in her fascinating study of a classic Victorian murder case, Freud explicitly compared detection to psychoanalysis, observing that "In both we are concerned with a secret, with something hidden"—in one case by the criminal, in the other by the patient. She adds that "Like a sensation novelist or a super-detective, Freud fancied that people's secrets would flood up to the surface, in blushes and blanches, or worm their way out to the world in the fingers' twitches."[16c] Reading her account, you are left wondering to what extent the then-new genre of detective fiction might not have been Freud's true, original inspiration, overlaid by more plausible, pseudoscientific rationalizations later on, but returning from the repressed on his death-bed like the confession to a murder.*

Freud's book on Moses certainly reads very much like a work of detective fiction, and, true to the pattern I suggested just now, combines both "autistic" or mechanistic cognitive style with a "paranoid" or hyper-mentalistic one. The former is revealed in the obsessive devil-in-the-detail forensic de-construction to which the biblical text and myths about Moses are subjected—not to mention thinking the unthinkable where the founder of both the Jewish nation and religion is concerned: that Moses was in fact born an Egyptian and that Judaism began as the monotheism of the Pharaoh Akhenaten! As for paranoia, the whole thesis centres round Freud's belief that Moses was murdered by the people he chose and that attempts were then made to hide any

---

* Not long before her death, I remarked to Anna Freud on the large collection of detective fiction in the house Freud occupied in London at the end of his life. She informed me that it belonged to her father and that he had been an avid reader of thrillers. Perhaps appropriately then, Freud is now to be found playing a minor role in the Viennese detective stories of Frank Tallis. The hero, Dr. Max Liebermann, is described as a "disciple of Freud" who consults the great sleuth of the unconscious in connection with his cases—and inevitably becomes idealized in the process. Although Tallis has Freud claiming to be "usually a very perceptive judge of character,"[36] the man himself thought the exact opposite and in conversations with me Anna Freud confirmed that her father was, as she put it, "not much of a *menschkenner!*"

evidence of the fact by editing and doctoring the biblical text and re-writing traditional history and mythology—a clear case of cultural conspiracy, if not a criminal one. Again, Schlomo Freud (to cite his given Jewish name[28a]) came to see the Jews as persecuted because of their inherited guilt, and an element of mass megalomania is implied in his comment that they "have a particularly high opinion of themselves, that they regard themselves as more distinguished, of higher standing, as superior to other peoples...as God's chosen people."[35a]

Perhaps worst of all, Freud was not above using psychoanalysis as a means of character-assassination where his political enemies were concerned. During the 1930s he collaborated with an American ex-diplomat, William C. Bullitt, to produce "a psychological study" of his exact contemporary, Woodrow Wilson (1856–1924), 28th President of the USA, 1913–21. The result portrays Wilson ultimately as "a pathetic invalid, a querulous old man full of rage and tears, hatred and self-pity" who had been unable to stand up to the other statesmen who drafted the Treaty of Versailles to ensure the justice that Freud believed had been denied to the defeated powers after World War 1.[37] This is the mentalistic skill of naming, blaming, and shaming at its most vicious, vindictive, and vituperative, and perhaps not surprisingly, this work was omitted from *The Standard Edition of the Complete Psychological Works of Sigmund Freud* despite being published elsewhere before it was complete. But to the extent that it is indeed mightier than the sword, those who live by the pen can die by it just as surely. So perhaps there is some poetic justice in the fact that Freud himself was to prove prone to such psychoanalytic character-assassination at the hands of his more belligerent biographers! Little wonder then that recent works with titles such as *Killing Freud* come to the conclusion that "Psychoanalysis is a serious menace based on a top-heavy theoretical edifice, faulty premises, circular and self-validating arguments, methodological laxity, motivated self-deception, bad faith and lies piled upon lies for more than a century."[38a]

Whereas behaviourism denied the mind altogether and banished all consideration of mentalistic content as "unscientific," Freudian psychoanalysis increasingly and progressively banned any recognition of the physical, biological, or genetic basis of the mind as "un-psychological." As a result, psychoanalysis developed into an institutionalized form of mentalistic—and even hyper-mentalistic—savantism in which the parallels with paranoid, delusional cognition became all too clear in some cases (most notably in child-abuse witch-hunts). Indeed, with the examples of Wilhelm Reich (1897–1957) or Karl Jung (1875–1961) in mind, it is hard not to notice the parallel with many aspects of Schreber's delusions—particularly in Reich's delusional belief in "orgone energy" or Jung's mystical and religious writings. As an authority on the Schreber case has noted, "One might thus wonder which of the two, Schreber or Jung, had a greater identification with the occult or who was more delusional."[39] But unlike Schreber, Jung succeeded in becoming something of a prophet who spoke confidently of his knowledge about God, and certainly attracted a cult-like following which invested his writings with biblical authority. Paradoxically, this psychiatrist became the founder of a quasi-religious cult, and the man who hoped to be a prophet became the most famous psychiatric case of all time!

Jung and Reich—not to mention Freud himself—illustrate an important difference between autistic and psychotic savantism in this respect.* Autistic savants are often very young when first discovered and usually need some devoted care-giver (such as Kim Peek's father or Leslie Lemke's step-mother) to nurture and promote their remarkable talent to the point of gaining public appreciation. But the talent itself, being mechanistic in quality, is easy to validate simply by consulting an almanac, encyclopaedia, or phone-book—or in the case of a musical savant such as Lemke, simply by listening to what he is playing! High-functioning psychotic savants such as Freud, Jung, and Reich, on the other hand, take many years to develop their talents and are often much older by comparison before they are fully recognized. Thanks to their consummate mentalistic skills in the art of making friends and influencing people, such savants often surround themselves with

---

* As in the parallel case of autistic savantism, the ratio of savantism to the disorder can vary widely. My personal judgement would be that Reich was by far the most psychotic of the three, with Freud the least, and Jung somewhere in between.

devotees, disciples, and admirers vying for their attention, affection, and endorsement. However, because their expertise is mentalistic and therefore beyond the scope of factual, objective refutation, psychotic savants tend to find appreciation in the like-minded and corroboration in the eyes of those who see things as they do. Inevitably, they become confirmed in their beliefs and increasingly dogmatic in their assertions. Criticism of, or disputes with, successful psychotic savants such as these typically lead to schisms, defections, or purges within the ranks of the followers like those seen in psychoanalysis, which became a byword for such doctrinal sectarianism. Seldom if ever will criticism or controversy lead to the correction of the psychotic savant's errors. On the contrary, the anathematization of the heretics who dare to question the prophet's vision and the excommunication of the infidels who fail to keep the faith only serves to reinforce the dogmatism of the movement and to insulate it from criticism. Hamilton made essentially the same point when he remarked that "Human Groups which lack things people may be uncreative, and, even on the social side, may be too Machiavellian for their own good."[40a] He might have been writing the epitaph of psychoanalysis.*

At its best, so-called psychoanalytic "insight" was wholly mentalistic: in other words, inherently subjective rather than objective, qualitative rather than quantitative, particular rather than universal, and—like placebos, faith-healing, or hypnosis—entirely dependent on the belief of the subject for its efficacy. As a therapy, psychoanalysis began with hypnotism and, being a purely mental means of intervention, could never get far beyond it, prompting the commonplace but correct objection that it was essentially suggestion masquerading as insight (see the table opposite).

---

* He might certainly have had the so-called social sciences in mind, and I can corroborate from my own experience that a close parallel to psychoanalysis in these respects can be found in sociology. Here, too, psychotic savants abound, and here even more than in psychoanalysis, feminism (a mentalistic faith with a distinctly paranoid flavour) has predictably become the dominant and definitive ideology, and dogmatic sectarianism the underlying social structure.

Contrasting characteristics of mentalistic and mechanistic cognition

Mentalistic cognition	Mechanistic cognition
psychological interaction with self and others	physical interaction with nature and objects
uses social, psychological, and political skills	uses mechanical, spatial, and engineering skills
deficits in autism, augmented in women	accentuated in autism, augmented in men
voluntaristic, subjective, particularistic	deterministic, objective, universal
abstract, general, ambivalent	concrete, specific, single-minded
verbal, metaphoric, conformist	visual, literal, eccentric
top-down, holistic, centrally coherent	bottom-up, reductionistic, field-independent
epitomized in literature, politics, and religion	epitomized in science, engineering, and technology
'pseudo-science': astrology, alchemy, creationism	'hard science': astronomy, chemistry, Darwinism
nurtured: culturally and personally determined	natural: factually and genetically determined
belief-based therapies: placebos, faith-healing, psychotherapy	physical effect-based therapies: drugs, surgery, physiotherapy

Therapeutic implications of the imprinted brain theory

With the benefit of hindsight, traditional psychoanalysis—the so-called *talking cure*—seems to be the very worst possible kind of therapy that anyone on the psychotic side of the spectrum could receive. By encouraging the patient to mentalize randomly—in other words, to free-associate, fantasize, and report their dreams—therapists would be encouraging the very factor that is the root cause of most (and possibly all) psychotic symptoms: hyper-mentalism. A schizophrenic remarks that "In psychosis, nothing is what it seems. Everything exists to be understood beneath the surface"[41] and the same was true of psychoanalysis. At best this could hardly help patients with psychotic tendencies, and at worst might be expected to do real harm. Indeed, something very like the "hyper-reflexive" self-observation that Sass[42] describes in schizophrenics was institutionalized in psychoanalytic therapy (see above p. 114). What good—if any—psychoanalysis ever achieved could probably be attributed to placebo effects stemming from the patient's belief in the therapy. A sympathetic view might see psychoanalysis as a modern, secular version of faith-healing—and a recent book argues that philosophically all counselling and psychotherapy can be regarded as prayer.[43] But from a less forgiving point of view—and particularly with the examples of Reich and Jung in mind—psychoanalysis begins to look like a modern madness whose hyper-mentalism embraced not just the traditional arena of religious and magical belief, but extended it into psychology and psychotherapy. In the case of Reich and other more demented psychoanalysts, analytic therapy almost amounted to Shared Psychotic Disorder, or *Folie à Deux*, described by *DSM IV* as "a delusion that develops in an individual who is involved in a close relationship with another person...who already has a Psychotic Disorder with Prominent Delusions"—the latter, of course, being the analyst![44]

Where disorders at the opposite pole of the mentalistic continuum were concerned, even the very best of Freudian child-analysts such as Anna Freud completely failed to understand autism and how it could be treated. Thanks to their tendency to over-attribute mentalism to children and to sexualize it by calling it *auto-erotism*,[45] Freudians never realized that autism was a disorder featuring serious mentalistic deficits and consequently failed to appreciate the significance of Asperger's and Kanner's discovery.* Contrary to Freudian belief, autism suggests that, if the mind normally takes considerable time to emerge in childhood (and never does completely in autistics) then the origin it emerges from is not an unconscious mental one, but a *pre-mental* or *non-mental* one. This has particular importance for schools of psychoanalysis such as the Kleinian one that credit the child with an unconscious mind from the moment of birth (or even before), and interpret very early behaviour in terms of adult depth-psychology.[46] Indeed, and in stark contradiction to the view of paranoia proposed here, Klein even attributed a "paranoid schizoid position" to the child! But even the more cautious classical Freudians used the term *infantile amnesia* to describe the more or less complete forgetting of the first four or five years of life.[47]

However, no mentalistic memories could be laid down if there were as yet little in the way of a mind which could record them as such and even less of a sense of self to which they could be related. To use an archaeological analogy like those so often used by Freud himself, the situation is a bit like discovering that a culture did not have a written, recorded history and then concluding that the reason must be that its history had been suppressed, or erased in some way. But the fact that such a culture might have been pre-literate would immediately explain why written history did not exist without the need for any conspiracy theories. In other words, the mind of the child need not necessarily develop from a pre-existing unconscious one otherwise comparable to an adult mind. Moreover, to believe that it does so is to indulge the hyper-mentalistic illusion that the child's mind is the same as the adult's. A much more reasonable view is to conclude that infants resemble autistics and simply do not have much of a mind—at least to begin with.

---

* For the best part of three years at the very end of her life I had a private didactic analysis with Anna Freud. With the benefit of hindsight, I can report that the insights from autism research summarized in this book gave me an immeasurably greater and more real understanding of myself and my childhood than anything I ever got from psychoanalysis.

Admittedly, there is evidence that a small number of high-functioning autistics preserve memories from as early as one year of age. Several different explanations have been proposed, but most of them suggest that this exceptional outcome is an unusual manifestation of the strikingly uneven cognitive development that is typical of such cases, and could even be seen as a form of savantism.[48] Nevertheless, the subjects themselves report that—contrary to what Freudians might expect—such "memories consist of objects rather than personal stuff."[49a] For example, William Hamilton's reminiscences of his autistic tendencies as a child (see pp. 34–35) include the report that "fewer of my earliest memories than with most children are of people...and more are of dramatic physical and especially visual experiences."[40b] Autistics' childhood memories certainly do not reveal repressed traumas, such as that of birth, which psychoanalytic writers such as Otto Rank (1884–1939) raised to the status of dogma.[50] On the contrary, autistic savantism is perhaps the greatest of all refutations of the Freudian view of the mind of the child. If the mind of the child really was as Freudians believed, autistic children would have had no hesitation in revealing it thanks to their incorrigible truthfulness, immunity to convention, and insistence on being themselves. But what autism actually revealed was a whole new world of mechanistic cognition much closer to thinking machines than to the medieval mentalistic inferno of demonic drives, lurid lusts, and sleazy sexuality portrayed by Freud and his followers.

Of course, adults are a different matter. Nevertheless, the Freudian unconscious is in part infantile—or at least laid down on an infantile foundation according to the so-called *topographic* view of the mind, which sees it layered like geological strata, grading from the most recent on the surface to the most ancient at the bottom.[51] To this extent, infancy remains the imputed foundation of the Freudian unconscious, even in adult life. But if the remarks immediately above are correct, there is in reality no such infantile foundation to the adult, repressed unconscious. Perhaps this partly explains why Temple Grandin believes that "autistic people don't seem to have repression. Or if they do, they have it only to a weak degree," adding that "We *can't* forget bad stuff on purpose."[52a] Indeed, Grandin denies that she has any of Freud's defence mechanisms, and is "always amazed when normal people do." On the contrary, she claims not to have an unconscious at all![52b]★

You could dismiss such denials as symptomatic of the character-istic mind-blindness of autistics—at least where insight into their own minds is concerned. In other words, if autistics cannot read other people's minds, why should we expect them to be able to read their own? And if most of what goes on in the brain is unconscious, is it any wonder that an autistic ends up knowing even less about their own unconscious than many less mentalistically deficient people do? Nevertheless, the most compelling case for the Freudian, repressed un-conscious has been made in relation to self-deception,[53] and in particu-lar to its role in deceiving others. Here the idea is that the best liars are those who lie with total sincerity, unconscious of their lies and therefore much less likely to reveal them, even inadvertently.[26,54,55] But we have already seen that autistics are typically poor deceivers because they lack the mentalistic skills that successful deception demands (see pp. 105–110). If this is so, then it is also likely that autistics are even more deficient where lying to themselves is concerned, and so claims by autistics such as Temple Grandin that they lack much of a repressed, Freudian unconscious may well be true. As an Asperger's case quoted by Tony Attwood remarked, "You wouldn't need a Theory of Mind if everyone spoke their mind,"[49b] and the same is even more true of the Freudian theory of the unconscious: you wouldn't need it if people were honest with themselves!

★   There are reports that Freud once terminated the analysis of an American, claim-ing that he had no unconscious![38b] If the man was autistic as this comment by Grandin suggests he may have been, Freud also terminated what might have been his best hope of making the most important discovery in twentieth-century psy-chiatry: that of Asperger and Kanner. Anna Freud also complained to me that some candidates for analytic training seemed to lack much of an unconscious on which the training analyst could work. But she even more than her father had no excuse for failing to recognize autism, given that her speciality was child-analysis and that, as a native German-speaker, Asperger's work was not inaccessible to her in the way it was to others before it was translated into English around the time of her death. Indeed, I know for a fact that she had a chance to analyse at least one transparent case of an adult with many characteristics of Asperger's syndrome but, like her father, completely failed to understand or even notice the condition.

Another of Temple Grandin's comments suggests that, far from providing access to the unconscious, primitive, animalistic parts of the mind, the fundamental method of Freudian psychotherapy, *free association*, in fact draws on the most recent, mentalistic, and centrally coherent aspects of it. Professor Grandin is an acknowledged authority on animal behaviour, and to the extent that it is indeed the instinctual, feral foundation of the human mind, ought to know something about the Freudian unconscious thanks to her undisputed expertise where animal psychology is concerned. But she remarks regarding the neo-cortex (what I called the *maternal brain* in the previous chapter) that:

> What the neo-cortex does better than the dog brain or lizard brain is tie everything together. The whole neo-cortex is one big *association cortex*, making connections between all kinds of things that stay more separate for animals. For instance, take the fact that humans have *mixed emotions*. A human can love and hate the same person. Animals don't do that. Their emotions are simpler and cleaner, because categories like love and hate stay separate in their brains...

—as they also tend to do in her view in the brains of autistics such as herself.[52c]

What Grandin is talking about here is *ambivalence*, which, like *autism*, was originally coined by Bleuler to describe one of the major characteristics of schizophrenia. The term designates the simultaneous presence of conflicting thoughts, beliefs, or feelings about the same thing. Freud saw ambivalence as the epitome of the unconscious, and as one of the most primitive aspects of the mind,[56] but it need not necessarily be understood this way. On the contrary, we could follow Temple Grandin's suggestion and see it as an epitome of central-coherence. Ambivalence, in other words, means not just love *or* hate, yes *or* no, but both love *and* hate, yes *and* no as part of a larger, top-down, mentalistic, centrally coherent picture. As such, ambivalence may much more likely be an outcome of the most recently evolved capacity of the human mind: the maternal brain's ability to impose holistic coherence by associating discrepant ideas and contradictory emotions. This is particularly so in view of the fact that nothing is more likely to inhibit or compromise an outcome than feeling ambivalent about it (and we saw earlier why the mother has a vested genetic self-interest in inhibiting her offspring in the interest of sharing and conserving her resources: see pp. 155–156.) If this is so, the emotional and instinctual inferno portrayed by Freud as the repressed unconscious is likely to be the most recent, most mentalistically-elaborated and contingent aspect of the mind, not the primitive foundation of it that he imagined. And although Bleuler's term *autism* now seems wrong when associated with schizophrenia, *ambivalence* is certainly correct as the psychotic alternative to autistic *single-mindedness* (see table on p. 151). Indeed you could see it as central-coherence in over-drive, and as such yet another manifestation of hyper-mentalism.

Some success can be obtained with autistic children by teaching them to *mind-read:* in other words, to compensate for their mind-blindness by learning explicit mentalistic skills,[57] and we have already noted that some high-functioning adult autistics such as Temple Grandin apply comparable consciously learnt rules to help them function socially (see p. 58).[58] If it is indeed true that psychotics are the exact opposite of this, and implicitly over-mentalize where autistics under-mentalize, it follows that it might be worth trying the exact opposite of psychoanalysis: to teach psychotics the contrary skills to those prescribed for autistics. There is evidence that even in normal individuals who have suffered bereavement, avoidance of mentalizing their loss reduced grief symptoms after 14 months—and most certainly did not increase them, as conventional Freudian wisdom would have suggested. Avoiding unpleasant thoughts and emotions, in other words, might not be such a bad thing after all.[59] Indeed, according to a recent summary of the literature, despite assertions that lack of observable grief is pathological and frequent endorsement among clinicians of the existence of so-called "delayed grief reactions," there is little evidence that expression of emotions has any beneficial effect following bereavement. On the contrary, there is evidence that it may impede successful coping.[60]

The same could apply to other kinds of traumatic experience. In an online survey of a large national sample of Americans, researchers tested people's responses to the terrorist attacks of the 11th of September 2001, beginning immediately after the event and continuing for the following two years. The study did not support the common assumption that choosing *not* to express one's thoughts and feelings in the immediate aftermath of a collective trauma is harmful and indicative of vulnerability to future negative consequences. Instead, the opposite pattern emerged. The researchers found that people who chose not to express their feelings about the event had fewer negative physical and mental health symptoms than people who did choose to do so. Indeed, when the researchers tested the length of the responses of those who chose to express their thoughts and feelings they found a similar pattern: those who did had worse mental and physical health than those who expressed less, and no other factor could explain the effect. They conclude that:

> Contrary to common assumption, this study demonstrates that individuals who choose not to express their thoughts and feelings in the immediate aftermath of a collective trauma are capable of coping successfully and in fact are more likely to do so than individuals who do express.[60a]

Findings such as these suggest that an obvious therapeutic strategy would be to try to induce hyper-mentalizing psychotics to be less mentalistic—or more autistic, if you like, and certainly less hyper-reflexive—and consciously to try to avoid reading too much into each and every thing. So paranoid schizophrenics might be encouraged to reduce their sensitivity to gaze or to avoid over-interpreting other people's words, expressions, and behaviour; to avoid ruminating about other people's intentions; to distrust magical and megalomanic thinking, and so on. Furthermore, the recovered schizophrenic I quoted in an earlier chapter on why asking *how?* is better than always asking *why?* (see p. 80) advocates that delusions can be countered by cultivating doubt and scepticism and becoming something of a "detective" where such beliefs are concerned. Indeed, he comments that "Doubting can be the gateway to truth. Without doubt, one's delusions are pre-served. With doubt, one discovers."[61] Essentially this is the same as the mechanistic, bottom-up, devil-in-the-detail way of thinking enshrined in the "autistic" aspects of detection and epitomized in science—and certainly is the exact contrary of the mentalistic, top-down, holistic style of self-deception found in psychosis and in religions both sacred and secular.

Of course, a very similar strategy is already used in Cognitive Behavioural Therapy (CBT), and many psychotherapists using CBT or similar methods already routinely follow something like this ap-proach—indeed, as we have just seen, some patients discover it for themselves. But psychoanalysis has one huge advantage that CBT lacks, and that is the provocative persuasiveness of its seemingly pro-found view of the mind and of mental development. Modern therapies such as CBT seem *ad hoc* and eclectic by comparison, and lacking in a unified theoretical foundation. But should the imprinted brain theory be fully—or even partially—vindicated by the facts, things would be very different, and CBT could be re-built on a theory with even deeper foundations and much greater credibility than psychoanalysis. As an article in *The New York Times* remarked recently, "the new idea provides psychiatry with perhaps its grandest working theory since Freud, and one that is founded in work at the forefront of science."[62] Specific genes and their measured effects could be substituted for metaphysical life and death instincts; Hamilton's insight into the psychological con-sequences of genetic conflicts would replace Freudian family psycho-drama and Oedipal mythology; and imaged maternal and paternal brain regions could be substituted for the imagined id, ego, and superego of psychoanalysis. Indeed, popular books are already appearing which use *Who's Who*/Facebook-style symbolism to represent parts of the brain and their associated functions in a way which makes Freudian—or any other kind of—meta-psychology completely redundant.[63]

To this extent, the new theory outlined here could also be seen as supplanting behaviourism, which, as we saw at the beginning, was characterized by its doctrine of *anti-mentalism*, or denial of the mind (see pp. 56–57). The imprinted brain theory, by contrast, does not deny the mind, but does distinguish between normal mentalism and pathological hyper-mentalism in a way that takes mental factors seriously. To this extent the new theory is not so much anti-mentalistic as a radical new critique of mentalism, which can see both its virtues and its vices. This is important, because up to now there has been a tendency in human cultures to idolize and idealize anything and everything mental as representing some higher, spiritual, metaphysical, or transcendent reality. In recent Western culture in particular, this tendency—especially when cast in religious terms—has certainly not gone unchallenged, but the theory set out here provides a much more radical, scientific basis for such critiques, and suggests that it is not religion, superstition, or irrationality that are the problem, but hyper-mentalism in all its forms—which we have just seen also embraces pseudo-sciences such as psychoanalysis. In this concluding chapter I have only touched on some of the most obvious aspects of this: for example in my comments about psychotic savants and their role in culture. But clearly, this is just a start, and the wider implications of the imprinted brain theory for society and civilization as a whole remain to be explored. Insights into autism and psychosis as mentalistic disorders ought to have far-reaching implications for the social sciences and for our understanding of society and history because mentalism is primarily an adaptation for social life. Indeed, you could claim that autism is essentially a social disorder and that to a perhaps surprisingly large extent normality in any given society represents a somewhat arbitrary point of balance on the mentalistic continuum. If so, then entire societies and whole civilizations might be compared mentalistically, and sociology like psychology and psychiatry could be transformed by the newly discovered symmetries of the mind.[64]

But however that may be, one thing is clear. If the imprinted brain theory as set out here were to be widely accepted, a remarkable advance would have been made in our understanding of the relation between genes, brains, and behaviour. We would have discovered the genetic basis of ASD and PSD, and would begin to understand how the genes in question affect normal brain development and give rise to symptoms. Thanks to the symmetry implied by the way these genes work, the contrasts between autism and psychosis that I describe in this book would be explained and placed on a sound genetic and neurological foundation. What is set out here as an arresting series of antithetical symptoms would be revealed as not simply clinical, but physically based realities, rooted in genetics, and built into the brain before birth. And as I have already pointed out, psychiatric diagnosis and classification could be re-established on the basis of these findings, ultimately founded on genetic tests for patterns of gene-expression as indicated by the theory.

More important still, the discovery of the specific genes and associated expression products linked with disorders such as autism and psychosis would create exciting new possibilities for both drug therapies and genetic testing—and ultimately perhaps even genetic engineering. The new theory could provide conceptual links between genes, drugs, and symptoms, along with explanations and predictions of their effects which few other approaches could offer. Indeed, as this book went to press, reports came to my attention suggesting that the symmetry between ASD and PSD proposed here reaches right down to the level of cell chemistry and could be exploited in pharmacology. Drugs which act as antagonists to cell-surface receptors critically involved in neurotransmission (the mGlur5 glutamate receptor and the nicotinic cholinergic CHRNA7 receptor) have been proposed as treatments for autism spectrum disorders. Other drugs are also being experimented with as agonists to these receptors in the treatment of schizophrenia (in other words, they enhance the same receptors in treating psychosis which are blocked in treating autism). If findings like these are confirmed, the symmetry discussed in this chapter could truly claim to be both natural and fundamental, and would certainly have found its ultimate therapeutic application.[65]

Notes

Introduction

1. Happé, 2006.
2. Aitken, 2008a, p. 29.
3. Gooddale & Milner, 2004.

Chapter 1 Autism and Its Compensations

1. Bleuler, 1912.
2. Bleuler, 1950, p. 63.
3. Asperger, 1938.
4. Asperger, 1944.
5. Kanner, 1943. a) p. 250. b) p. 247, Kanner's emphasis. c) p. 222.
6. Lyons & Fitzgerald, 2007a.
7. Rimland, 1964. a) pp. 31–34. b) p. 204.
8. Ssucharewa, 1926.
9. Ssucharewa & Wolff, 1996.
10. Grinker, 2007, p. 103.
11. Vaillant, 1962.
12. Bottomer, 2007.
13. Bleuler in Rapaport, 1959.
14. Monto, 2003.
15. Frith, 2003, p. 14.
16. Trevarthen, Aitken, et al., 1998, pp. 14–27.
17. Moore, 2004b.
18. Fitzgerald, 2005. a) p. 228. b) p. 39. c) p. 20. d) p. 236. e) p. 236. f) p. 226.
19. Silva, Ferrari, et al., 2003.
20. Kanner, 1946.
21. Attwood, 2008, a) p. 130. b) p. 14. c) p. 241.
22. Attwood in Simmons, 2006, p. 6.
23. American Psychiatric Association, 2000, p. 80.
24. Knapp, Romeo & Beecham, 2007.
25. Kaplan in Simmons, 2006, p. 44.
26. Skuse, 2007.
27. Dawson, Soulières, et al., 2007.
28. Hayashi, Kato, et al., 2008.
29. Kana, Keller, et al., 2006.
30. Mottron, Belleville, et al., 1999.
31. Ashwin, Ashwin, et al., 2008.
32. Bonnel, Mottron, et al., 2003.
33. O'Riordan & Passetti, 2006.
34. Blakemore, Sarfati, et al., 2006.
35. Tavassoli, Ashwin, et al., in press.
36. Ashwin, Ashwin, et al., in press.
37. Rimland, 1978, p. 77.
38. Mottron & Burack in Burack, Charman, et al., 2001, p. 138.
39. Happé, 1999a, p. 216.
40. Sanders, 2004, p. 69.
41. Asperger in Frith, 1991, pp. 89, 74.
42. Lyons & Fitzgerald, 2007b.
43. James, 2006.
44. O'Connell & Fitzgerald, 2003.
45. Hough, 2007.
46. Baron-Cohen, 2003. a) p. 3.
47. Arshad & Fitzgerald, 2004.

48. Fitzgerald, 2004.
49. Ledgin, 1998.
50. Sacks, 2004, p. 241.
51. Treffert, 2006. a) p. 10.
52. Treffert, 2001.
53. Sacks, 1995.
54. Treffert, 2000. a) pp. 180–182. b) p. 33.
55. Treffert & Christensen, 2005.
56. Tammet, 2006, p. 226.
57. Miller, Cummings, *et al.*, 1998.
58. Hermelin, 2001. a) p. 120. b) p. 50. c) p. 71.
59. Snyder, Mulcahy, *et al.*, 2003. a. p. 154.
60. Flagg, Cardy, *et al.*, 2005.
61. Koshino, Carpenter, *et al.*, 2005.
62. Tréhin, 2006b, p. 10.
63. Zatorre, 2005.
64. Hamilton, 1996, p. 26.
65. Hamilton, 2001. a) p. xxvii. c) p. 369. c) pp. xxviii–xxix.
66. Hamilton, 2005. a) p. 205. b) p. 210. c) p. 206.
67. Bliss, 2001.
68. Mitchell, 1997, p. 89.
69. Baron-Cohen, Wheelwright, *et al.*, 2001.
70. Baron-Cohen & Else, 2001.
71. Baron-Cohen, Wheelwright, *et al.*, 1999, pp. 475–483.
72. Hippler & Klicpera in Frith & Hill, 2004.
73. Grandin & Scariano, 1996. a) pp. 108–109. b) pp. 175, 91. c) p. 136. d) pp. 106–107. e) p. 34.
74. Grandin, 1995, pp. 20–21.
75. Kanner, 1949, p. 423.
76. Darr & Worden, 1951, pp. 569, 570.
77. Vermeulen, 2001. a) p. 28. b) pp. 45, 39.
78. Grandin & Johnson, 2005, pp. 30, 27, author's emphasis.
79. Jones, 1953, p. 55.
80. Shore, 2001, pp. 114, 122.

Musical savants

1. Treffert, 2000. a) pp. 37, 39. b) p. 140.
2. Hermelin, 2001, pp. 156–166.
3. Fitzgerald, 2005.

Savant artists

1. Grandin & Johnson, 2005, p. 300, author's emphasis.
2. Tréhin, 2006b.
3. Humphrey, 1998.
4. Humphrey, 2002.
5. Steadman, 2001.
6. Tréhin, 2006a.

Chapter 2 Deficits in Mind

1. Hermelin, 2001, p. 103.
2. Grandin in Ledgin, 1998, p. 199.
3. Grandin in Simmons, 2006, p. 180.
4. Koenig, Tsatsanis, *et al.* in Burack, Charman, *et al.*, 2001.
5. Caron, Mottron, *et al.*, 2006.
6. Frith, 2003. a) pp. 152–155. b) p. 154. c) pp. 153–154. d. p. 105.
7. Grossberg & Seidman, 2006.
8. Vladusich, 2008.
9. Just, Cherkassky, *et al.*, 2004.
10. Kana, Keller, *et al.*, 2006.
11. Baron-Cohen & Belmonte, 2005.
12. Baron-Cohen, Knickmeyer, *et al.*, 2005.
13. Ramachandran & Rogers-Ramachandran, 1996.
14. Mattingley, Rich, *et al.*, 2001.
15. Happé in Baron-Cohen, Tager-Flusberg, *et al.*, 1999b, p. 215.
16. Snowling & Frith, 1986.
17. Rimland, 1964, p. 83.
18. Trevarthen, Aitken, *et al.*, 1998. a) p. 24, author's emphasis. b) p. 25.
19. Frith, 1989.
20. Rutter, 1983.

21. Fitzgerald, 2005, p. 141.
22. Wimmer & Perner, 1983.
23. Baron-Cohen, Leslie, *et al.*, 1985.
24. Zaitchik, 1990.
25. Leslie & Thaiss, 1992.
26. Premack & Woodruff, 1978.
27. Baron-Cohen, 1989.
28. Baron-Cohen, Tager-Flusberg, *et al.*, 2000.
29. Castelli, Frith, *et al.*, 2002, p. 1844.
30. Grandin, 1995. a) p. 43. b) pp. 103, 104. c) p. 92.
31. Sacks, 1995, p. 258.
32. Dawkins, 2005.
33. Grandin & Johnson, 2005, pp. 1, 6–7, 57, author's emphasis.
34. O'Neill, 1999, p. 28.
35. Tager-Flusberg in Baron-Cohen, Tager-Flusberg, *et al.*, 1993, p. 150.
36. Johnson, 2008, p. 128.
37. Sheldrake, 2003, p. 203.
38. Williams in Dawkins & Ridley, 1985. a) pp. 21–22. b) p. 21.
39. Williams, 1996, p. 169.
40. Dawkins, 1995, p. 221.
41. Donaldson, 1978.
42. Llinás, 2001.
43. Eisenberg & Kanner, 1956, p. 559.
44. Gillberg, 1992.
45. Baron-Cohen in Ellis & Bjorklund, 2005b, p. 468.
46. Shore, 2001. a) p. 53. b) p. 38. c) p. 53.
47. Sainsbury, 2006, p. 21.
48. Rogers, Dziobek, *et al.*, 2007.
49. Abu-Akel & Abushua'leh, 2004, p. 50.
50. Nettle, 2007.
51. Troisi, 2008.
52. Emery, 2000.
53. Allman, 1999.
54. Ricciardelli, 2001.
55. LeDoux, 1996.
56. Whalen, Kagan, *et al.*, 2004.
57. Adolphs, Gosselin, *et al.*, 2005.
58. Povinelli, 2000, p. 20.
59. Langdon, Corner, *et al.*, 2006.
60. Baron-Cohen, 1995, pp. 38–58.
61. Robinson, 2007.
62. Asperger in Frith, 1991, pp. 68–69.
63. Grandin & Scariano, 1996, p. 145.
64. Swettenham, Condie, *et al.*, 2004.
65. Senju, Tojo, *et al.*, 2004.
66. Howlin, 2003, p. 33.
67. Houston & Frith, 2000, p. 113.
68. Cheng, Tzeng, *et al.*, 2006.
69. Ramani & Miall, 2004.
70. Crespi & Badcock, 2008.
71. Gooddale & Milner, 2004.
72. Badcock in Crawford & Salmon, 2004b.

Do chimps interpret gaze as we do?

1. Povinelli, 2000.

Chapter 3 From Gaze to Grandeur

1. Sheldrake, 2003, a) p. 9. b) pp. 126, 138–45, 183–97. c) p. 136. d) p. 202. e) p. 206. f) p. 10. g) p. 151. h) p. 136. i) p. 120. j) p. 1.
2. Philips, 2004, p. 14.
3. Morgan, 2003.
4. Israëls, 1989, p. xi.
5. Dinnage, 2000, p. xi.
6. Schreber, 2000, a) p. 53. b) p. 330. c) pp. 207–209. d) p. 235. e) pp. 107–108. f) pp. 124, 152, 201. g) p. 202, n: 96. h) pp. 47–48. i) pp. 63, 99. j) pp. 66, 96. k) p. 139, 258. l) p. 218. m) p. 205. n) pp. 81, 110. o) pp. 57, 58. p) p. 114, n: 57. q) p. 149, n: 73. r) pp. 22, 233. s) p. 264. t) p. 233. u) pp. 258, 17n, 252.

7. Jaspers, 1962, a) p. 101. b) p. 101. c) pp. 296, 101–2. d) 296, quoting Hilfiker.
8. Sass, 1992, a) p. 235. b) p. 286. c) p. 295.
9. Thompson, 2001.
10. Langdon, Corner, et al., 2006.
11. Galaiena, 1976.
12. Gerbaldo & Thaker, 1991.
13. Gerbaldo, Thaker, et al., 1992.
14. Grinker, 2007 p. 111.
15. Custance, 1951, a) p. 18. b) p. 51.
16. Sass & Parnas, 2001.
17. Chapman, 2002, p. 549.
18. Moore, 2004. a) p. 41. b) pp. 237–238. c) pp. 53, 113.
19. Shore, 2001, p. 87.
20. Williams, 1994, a) p. 207, b) pp. 8–9, c) p. 207
21. de Clérambault, 1942.
22. American Psychiatric Association, 2000, pp. 324–325.
23. Dalí, 1968, pp. 265–6.
24. Leekam & Moore, 2001.
25. Grandin, 1995, pp. 91–92.
26. Eckblad & Chapman, 1983.
27. Chapman, Chapman, et al., 1994.
28. Møller & Husby, 2000.
29. Sass & Parnas, 2003.
30. Claridge, Pryor, et al., 1990, p. 219.
31. Taylor & Brown, 1988.
32. Baron-Cohen, 1989.
33. Frith & Happé, 1999b, pp. 49, 78.
34. Fitzgerald, 2005. a) p. 84. c) p. 133. d) p. 141.
35. Houston & Frith, 2000, p. 165.
36. Lawson, 1998, p. i.
37. Grandin & Scariano, 1996, p. 137.
38. Gerland, 1997, pp. 99, 101.
39. Frith, 2003.
40. Attwood, 2008, p. 26.
41. MacLane, 1917, p. 31.
42. Kaplan, 2008.

The Schreber case

1. Schreber, 1903.
2. Freud, 1911.
3. Lothane, 1992.
4. Israëls, 1989.

Chapter 4 Cancers of the Mind

1. Tulving, 1985.
2. Baddeley, 2002.
3. Conway, 2002.
4. Conway, 2005, p. 595–6.
5. Bowler, 2003.
6. Schacter & Dodson, 2002, p. 81.
7. Gardiner, 2002, p. 26.
8. Salazar-Fraile et al., 2004.
9. Schreber, 2000. a) p. 77. b) pp. 34–5. c) pp. 16, 39. d) pp. 69, 83, 221. e) p. 20. f) p. 340. g) p. 82.
10. Jaspers, 1962. a) p. 102. b) p. 102.
11. Sass, 1992. a) p. 48. b) p. 102. c) p. 415. d) p. 53. e) p. 236. f) p. 8. g) p. 241. h) p. 102. i) p. 518.
12. Suddendorf & Corballis, 1997.
13. Lothane, 1992, p. 7.
14. Sontag, 1988, p. 293.
15. Cameron, 1939.
16. Payne, 1966.
17. Crespi & Badcock, 2008.
18. Rimland, 1964, p. 167.
19. Fitzgerald, 2005, p. 135.
20. Laing, 1960. a) p. 176. b) p. 71. c) p. 73. d) p. 116.
21. Sacks, 1995, p. 14.
22. Grandin, 1995. a) p. 135. b) p. 201. c) p. 200. d) pp. 200–201.
23. Slotnick, 2002.
24. Hadcroft, 2005. a) p. 79. b) p. 67.
25. Houston & Frith, 2000. a) p. 169. b) pp. 164–165.
26. Moore, 2004. a) pp. 247–248. b) pp. 217–8.

27. Nesse, 2004, p. 862.
28. Claridge, Pryor, *et al.*, 1990. a) p. 221.
29. Claridge, 1987, p. 40, author's emphasis.
30. Shapiro, 1965, p. 61.
31. Weiner, 2003, p. 877.
32. BGW, 2002, pp. 748–749.
33. MacDonald, 1960, p. 218.
34. LaRusso, 1978.
35. Pilowsky, Yirmiya *et al.*, 2000.
36. Rim, 1994.
37. Dinn, Harris *et al.*, 2002.
38. Folley & Park, 2005.
39. Nettle, 2001.
40. Seiferth, Pauly, *et al.*, 2008.
41. Blakemore, Sarfati *et al.*, 2003, p. 1439.
42. Russell, Reynaud, *et al.*, 2006, p. 110.
43. Badcock, 2004b.
44. Abu-Akel & Bailey, 2000, p. 735.
45. Craig, Hatton, *et al.*, 2004.
46. Blackshaw, Kinderman *et al.*, 2001, p. 158.
47. Attwood, 2008. a) p. 141. b) p. 321. c) p. 181 .
48. Harrington, Langdon, *et al.*, 2005.
49. Drury, Birchwood, *et al.*, 1998.
50. Bowler, 1992, p. 888.
51. Pickup, 2006, p. 178.
52. Sprong, Schothorst, *et al.*, 2007.
53. Libet, 2004, p. 136.
54. Sass & Parnas, 2003, p. 432, author's emphasis.
55. Jaynes, 1979, p. 419.
56. Sass, 2001, p. 261.
57. Hill & Frith, 2003.
58. Taylor, Welsh *et al.*, 2007.
59. Tanaka, 2008.
60. Baethge, Baldessiorini, *et al.*, 2005.
61. Goodwin & Jamison, 1990, pp. 31–35.
62. Dunayevich & Keck, 2000.
63. Jacobsen & Rapoport, 1998.
64. Frith, 1992.

65. Langdon, 2005.
66. Sheldrake, 2003, pp. 9, ix–x, 213–222.
67. Chapman, 2002, p. 547.
68. Boyer, 2008.
69. Guthrie, 1993. a) p. 69. b) p. 70. c) p. 5, 6. d) p. 5.
70. Bering, 2002.
71. Moore, 2004a.
72. Peek, 1996, pp. 48, 75, 59, 49.
73. Isanon, 2001, p. 75.
74. Dawkins, 2006. a) p. 15.
75. George, 2005.
76. Grandin & Johnson, 2005, p. 57.
77. Skinner, 1948. a) p. 171.
78. Vyse, 1997, p. 71.
79. Frith, 2003, p. 214.
80. Viertiö, *et al.*, 2007.
81. Lang, 1940.
82. Spitzer, 1990, p. 391, author's emphasis.
83. Walter, Ciaramidaro, *et al.*, 2009.
84. Cutting & Murphy, 1988.
85. Toulopoulou, Mapua-Filbey, *et al.*, 2006.
86. Kravariti, Toulopoulou, *et al.*, 2006.
87. New Scientist, 2007.

Chapter 5 The Battle of the Sexes in the Brain

1. Autism Society of America, 2000, p. 3.
2. Kanner, 1943, a) p. 248, Kanner's emphasis. b) p. 250.
3. Kanner, 1949, p. 421.
4. Kanner, 1944, p. 217.
5. Constantino & Todd, 2005.
6. Silberman, 2001.
7. Baron-Cohen, 2005a.
8. Szatmari & Jones, 1998, p. 109.
9. Happé, Ronald, *et al.*, 2006.
10. Volkmar, Klin & Pauls, 1998.

11. Dyches & Wilder, et al., 2004.
12. Gottesman, 1991.
13. Crow, 1997.
14. Horrobin, 1998.
15. Crespi & Summers, 2007.
16. Baron-Cohen, Wheelwright, et al., 1997, pp. 106–107.
17. Grandin & Barron, 2005, pp. 90–91.
18. Wing, 1991
19. American Psychiatric Association, 2000, pp. 73, 82.
20. Gillberg, 1980.
21. Wing, 1988.
22. Ehlers et al., 1997.
23. Asperger, 1991, pp. 84–85.
24. Lutchmaya, Baron-Cohen, et al., 2002a.
25. Lutchmaya, Baron-Cohen, et al., 2002b.
26. Knickmeyer, Baron-Cohen, et al., 2004.
27. Baron-Cohen, 2005b.
28. Pierce, Muller, et al., 2001.
29. Schultz, Gauthier, et al., 2000.
30. Harasty, Double, et al., 1997.
31. Gur, Gunning-Dixon, et al., 2002.
32. Davatzikos & Resmick, 1998.
33. Shaywitz, Shaywitz, et al., 1995.
34. Kimura, 2000. a) p. 69.
35. Baron-Cohen, 2002.
36. van Goozen, Cohen-Ketennis, et al., 1995.
37. Dabbs & Dabbs, 2000. a) pp. 41–42.
38. Vanston & Watson, 2005.
39. Salminen, 2005.
40. Charles, 2001.
41. Grön, Wunderlich, et al., 2000.
42. Liben, 1995.
43. Cross, 1987.
44. Motluk, 2002.
45. Silverman & Eals, 1992.
46. Rimland, 1978.
47. Bradley, 2006, p. 54.
48. Lynn, 1998.
49. Browne, 2002, p. 31.

50. Browne, 2001, p. 92.
51. Browne, 2006, p. 146.
52. Hamilton, 2001, p. xxi.
53. Badcock, 2000. a) pp. 69–71. b) pp. 192–226. c) pp. 262–268. d) pp. 263–264.
54. Crespi, Summers, et al., In press.
55. Barker, 1998.
56. Pawlowski, Dunbar, et al., 2000.
57. Potts & Short, 1999, p. 134.
58. Newton, 2001.
59. Haig, 1999.
60. Nicholls, Saitoh, et al., 1998.
61. Franke, Kerns, et al., 1995.
62. Angelman, 1965.
63. Cook, Lindgren, et al., 1997.
64. Haig & Wharton, 2003.
65. Attwood, 2008, p. 18.
66. Crespi & Badcock, 2008.
67. Schroer, 1998.
68. Nurmi, Dowd, et al., 2003.
69. Aitken, 2008b.
70. Reichenberg, Gross, et al., 2006.
71. Crow, 2000.
72. Malaspina, Harlap, et al., 2001.
73. Keverne, Fundele, et al., 1996.
74. Hannah, Hayward, Sheridan, & Bonthron, 2002.
75. MacLean, 1996, a) p. 455.
76. Allen, Logan, et al., 1995.
77. Thomson, 1985.
78. Goldstone, 2004.
79. Deacon, 1990.
80. Jones, 2008.
81. Goldstein, Seidman, et al., 2001.
82. Badcock, 2004a.
83. Trivers, 1974.
84. Lathe, 2006.
85. Maestro, Muratori, et al., 2002.
86. Zwaigenbaum, Bryson, et al., 2005.
87. McNamara, McLaren, et al., 2005.

88. Anderson, Jacobs-Stannard, *et al.*, 2007.
89. Mills, Hediger, *et al.*, 2007.
90. Sugie, Sugie, *et al.*, 2005.
91. MacLean, 1990.
92. Grandin, 1995.
93. LeDoux, 1996.
94. Mendrek, 2007.

Chapter 6 Sex and Psychosis

1. Crespi, 2008b.
2. Skuse, 2000.
3. Badcock, 2000, a) pp. 253–260, b) 208–212.
4. Bainbridge, 2003.
5. Talebizadeh, Bittel, *et al.*, 2005.
6. Badcock & Crespi, 2006.
7. Crespi, Summers, *et al.*, In press.
8. Crespi, 2008c.
9. Crespi & Badcock, 2008.
10. Troisi, 2008.
11. Whittington, Holland, *et al.*, 2001.
12. Boer, Holland, *et al.*, 2002.
13. Whittington & Holland, 2004.
14. Veltman, Thompson, *et al.*, 2004.
15. Whittington, Holland, *et al.*, 2004.
16. Kent, Bowdin, *et al.*, 2008.
17. Bejerot & Nylander, 2003.
18. Crespi & Summers, 2005.
19. St Clair, 2005.
20. Susser, St Clair, *et al.*, 2008.
21. Wicks, 2005.
22. Heijmansa, Tobia, *et al.*, 2008.
23. Ward, 1993, p. 56.
24. Gillberg, 1992, p. 815.
25. Der, Gupta, *et al.*, 1990.
26. Woogh, 2001.
27. Webster, Lamberton, *et al.*, 2006.
28. Randerson, 2002.
29. Ginsburg, 2004.
30. Taylor, Welsh, *et al.*, 2007.

31. Yolken & Torrey, 2008.
32. Bennett, 2000.
33. Motluk, 2000.
34. Williams, Pepitore, *et al.*, 2000.
35. Arato, Frecska, *et al.*, 2004.
36. Voracek, 2008.
37. Frecska & Kiss, 2004.
38. American Psychiatric Association, 2000, pp. 307–308.
39. Irwin, 1993.
40. Hamer, 2004, p. 36.
41. Humphrey, 1996, p. 51.
42. Stark, 2002.
43. Miller & Stark, 2002.
44. Ingudomnukul, Baron-Cohen, *et al.*, 2007.
45. Grandin & Johnson, 2005.
46. Mendrek, 2007.
47. Gur, Kohler, *et al.*, 2004.
48. Schreber, 2000. a) pp. 240, 64. b) pp. 164–165. c) pp. 17–18 n.
49. Planansky & Johnston, 1962.
50. Lester, 1975, p. 292.
51. Freud, 1911, pp. 21, 32.
52. Haig, 2006.
53. Swain, Narvaez, *et al.*, 1998.
54. Parma, Radi, *et al.*, 2006.
55. Motluk, 2003, p. 45.
56. Bogaert, 2006.
57. Blanchard, 1999.
58. Haig, 1993.
59. Hamer, Hu, *et al.*, 1993.
60. Hamer & Copeland, 1994.
61. Camperio-Ciani, Corna, *et al.*, 2004.
62. Green & Keverne, 2000.
63. Hamilton, 1996, pp. 133–134.

Side-effects of genetic conflict

1. Crespi, 2008a.
2. Crespi & Badcock, 2008.
3. Crespi, Summers, *et al.*, In press.

4. Kanazawa & Vandermassen, 2005.
5. James, 2000.

Chapter 7 Beyond the Balanced Brain

1. Fitzgerald, 2005. a) p. 167. b) p. 85.
2. Claridge, Pryor & Watkins, 1990.
3. Storr, 1976.
4. Iliffe, 2007, p. 72.
5. Spargo & Pounds, 1979, p. 26.
6. Ditchburn, 1980.
7. Keynes, 1972, p. 370, 363–364.
8. Johnson, 2008, p. 38.
9. Nasar, 1998. a) p. 32. b) pp. 129, 99, 42, 115, 101.
10. Arshad & Fitzgerald, 2002. a) p. 90. b) p. 92. c) p. 93.
11. Jamison, 1993. a) p. 96. b) p. 87. c) p. 86.
12. Kaplan, 2008.
13. Uht, 2008.
14. Rennison, 2005, p. 10.
15. Frith, 2003, p. 24.
16. Summerscale, 2008, a) pp. 187–8, 199. b) p. 53. c) pp. 259, 103.
17. Nettle, 2008.
18. Treffert, 2006.
19. Browne, 2002, p. 31.
20. Ludwig, 1995. a) pp. 5, 148–50. b) p.2.
21. Richards, Kinney, et al., 1988, p. 287.
22. Taylor & Brown, 1988.
23. Freud, 1914, a) p. 78, b) p. 91.
24. Badcock, 2002.
25. Dawkins, 1978.
26. Badcock, 2000.
27. Badcock, 1994.
28. Jones, 1953, a) p. 2.
29. Freud, 1920.
30. Freud, 1922.
31. Crespi, Summers, et al., 2007.
32. Freedman, 1997.
33. Xu, Pato, et al., 2001.
34. Freud, 1938.
35. Freud, 1939, a) p. 105–6.
36. Tallis, 2006, p. 163.
37. Freud & Bullitt, 1967, p. 253.
38. Dufresne, 2005. a) p. 37. b) p. 66.
39. Lothane, 1992, p. 321.
40. Hamilton, 2005, a) p. 206, b) p. 205.
41. Weiner, 2003, p. 877.
42. Sass, 2001.
43. Gubi, 2007.
44. American Psychiatric Association, 2000, p. 332.
45. Bleuler, 1950, p. 63 n. 19.
46. Piontelli, 1992.
47. Freud, 1905, pp. 174–6.
48. Lyons & Fitzgerald, 2005.
49. Attwood, 2008, a) p. 244, b) p. 126.
50. Rank, 1924.
51. Freud, 1923.
52. Grandin & Johnson, 2005. a) p. 191, author's emphasis. b) p. 92. c) p. 55.
53. Sackheim, 1983.
54. Trivers, 1981.
55. Trivers, 1997.
56. Laplanche & Pontalis, 1973, pp. 26–8.
57. Howlin, Baron-Cohen, et al., 1999.
58. Grandin & Barron, 2005.
59. Bonanno, Holen, et al., 1990.
60. Seery, Cohen Silver, et al., 2008. a) p. 666.
61. Chapman, 2002, p. 550.
62. Carey, 2008.
63. Nunn, Hanstock, et al., 2008.
64. Badcock, in preparation.
65. Crespi, 2009.

References

Abu-Akel, A. and K. Abushua'leh (2004). "Theory of mind" in violent and nonviolent patients with paranoid schizophrenia. *Schizophrenia Research* **69**(1): 45–53.

Abu-Akel, A. and A. L. Bailey (2000). Letter to the Editor. *Psychological Medicine* **30**: 735–738.

Adolphs, R., F. Gosselin, *et al.* (2005). A mechanism for impaired fear recognition after amygdala damage. *Nature* **433**: 68–72.

Aitken, K. J. (2008a). *Dietary Interventions in Autism Spectrum Disorders: Why They Work When They Do, Why They Don't When They Don't.* London and Philadelphia, PA, Jessica Kingsley Publishers.

Aitken, K. J. (2008b). Intersubjectivity, affective neuroscience, and the neurobiology of autistic spectrum disorders: A systematic review. *Keio Journal of Medicine* **57**(1): 15–36.

Allen, N. D., K. Logan, *et al.* (1995). Distribution of parthenogenetic cells in the mouse brain and their influence on brain development and behavior. *Proceedings of the National Academy of Sciences, USA* **92**(11/95): 10782–10786.

Allman, J. (1999). *Evolving Brains.* New York, Scientific American Library.

American Psychiatric Association (2000). *Diagnostic and Statistical Manual of Mental Disorders.* Washington, DC, American Psychiatric Association.

Anderson, G. M., A. Jacobs-Stannard, *et al.* (2007). Placental trophoblast inclusions in autism spectrum disorder. *Biological Psychiatry* **6**: 487–491.

Angelman, H. (1965). "Puppet" children: A report on three cases. *Developmental Medicine and Child Neurology* **7**: 681–688.

Arato, M., E. Frecska, *et al.* (2004). Digit length pattern in schizophrenia suggests disturbed prenatal hemispheric lateralization. *Progress in Neuropsychopharmacological and Biological Psychiatry* **28**: 191–194.

Arshad, M. and M. Fitzgerald (2002). Did Nobel Prize winner John Nash have Asperger's syndrome and schiz[o]phrenia? *Irish Psychiatrist* **3**(3): 90–94.

Arshad, M. and M. Fitzgerald (2004). Did Michaelangelo (1475–1564) have high-functioning autism? *Journal of Medical Biography* **12**: 115–120.

Ashwin, C., E. Ashwin, *et al.* (in press). Olfactory hypersensitivity in autism spectrum conditions.

Ashwin, E., C. Ashwin, *et al.* (2008). Eagle-eyed visual acuity: An experimental investigation of enhanced perception in autism. *Biological Psychiatry* **65**(1): 17–21.

Asperger, H. (1938). Das psychich abnorme Kind. *Wiener klinische Wochenschrift* **49**: 1–12.

Asperger, H. (1944). Die "Autistichen Psychopathen" im Kindesalter. *Archiv für Psychiatrie und Nervenkrankheiten* **117**: 76–136.

Asperger, H. (1991). "Autistic psychopathy" in childhood. *Autism and Asperger Syndrome*. U. Frith. Cambridge, Cambridge University Press: 37–92.

Attwood, T. (2006). What is Asperger's Syndrome? *The Official Autism 101 Manual: Autism Today*. K. L. Simmons. Alberta, Canada, Autism Today: 6–7.

Attwood, T. (2008). *The Complete Guide to Asperger's Syndrome*. London and Philadelphia, Jessica Kingsley Publishers.

Autism Society of America (2000). What is autism? *Advocate: The Newsletter of the Autism Society of America* **33**: 3.

Badcock, C. R. (1994). *PsychoDarwinism: The New Synthesis of Darwin and Freud*. London, Harper-Collins.

Badcock, C. R. (2000). *Evolutionary Psychology: A Critical Introduction*. Cambridge, Polity Press.

Badcock, C. R. (2002). The libido theory. *The Freud Encyclopedia*. E. Erwin. New York and London, Routledge: 321–324.

Badcock, C. R. (2004a). Emotion versus reason as a genetic conflict. *Emotion, Evolution, and Rationality*. D. Evans and P. Cruse. Oxford, Oxford University Press: 207–222.

Badcock, C. R. (2004b). Mentalism and mechanism: the twin modes of human cognition. *Human Nature and Social Values: Implications of Evolutionary Psychology for Public Policy*. C. Crawford and C. Salmon. Mahwah, NJ, Lawrence Erlbaum Associates: 99–116.

Badcock, C. R. (in preparation). *The Age of Asperger: Autism, Society and History*.

Badcock, C. R. and B. Crespi (2006). Imbalanced genomic imprinting in brain development: an evolutionary basis for the etiology of autism. *Journal of Evolutionary Biology* **19**(4): 1007–3102.

Baddeley, A. (2002). The concept of episodic memory. *Episodic Memory: New Directions in Research*. A. Baddeley, J. P. Aggleton, *et al*. Oxford, Oxford University Press: 1–10.

Baethge, C., R. J. Baldessarini, *et al*. (2005). Hallucinations in bipolar disorder: Characteristics and comparison to unipolar depression and schizophrenia. *Bipolar Disorders* **7**(2): 136–145.

Bainbridge, D. (2003). The double life of women. *New Scientist* 10 May: 42–45.

Barker, D. J. P. (1998). *Mothers, Babies and Health in Later Life*. Edinburgh, Churchill Livingstone.

Baron-Cohen, S. (1989). Are autistic children "behaviourists"? An examination of their mental-physical and appearance-reality distinctions. *Journal of Autism and Developmental Disorders* **19**(4): 579–600.

Baron-Cohen, S. (1995). *Mindblindness: An Essay on Autism and Theory of Mind*. Cambridge, MA, MIT Press.

Baron-Cohen, S. (2002). The extreme male brain theory of autism. *Trends in Cognitive Science* **6**(6): 248–254.

Baron-Cohen, S. (2003). *The Essential Difference: Men, Women, and the Extreme Male Brain*. London, Allen Lane.

Baron-Cohen, S. (2005a). "The assortative mating theory." *Edge 158*. Retrieved 6 April, 2005, from www.edge.org/documents/archive/edge158.html.

Baron-Cohen, S. (2005b). The empathizing system. *Origins of the Social Mind*. B. J. Ellis and D. F. Bjorklund. New York and London, The Guilford Press: 468–492.

Baron-Cohen, S. and M. K. Belmonte (2005). Autism: A window onto the development of the social and the analytic brain. *Annual Review of Neuroscience* **28**: 109–126.

Baron-Cohen, S. and L. Else (2001). In a different world. *New Scientist* 14 April.

Baron-Cohen, S., R. C. Knickmeyer, *et al.* (2005). Sex differences in the brain: Implications for explaining autism. *Science* **310**: 819–823.

Baron-Cohen, S., A. M. Leslie, *et al.* (1985). Does the autistic child have a "theory of mind"? *Cognition* **21**: 37–46.

Baron-Cohen, S., H. Tager-Flusberg, *et al.*, Eds. (2000). *Understanding Other Minds*. Oxford, Oxford University Press.

Baron-Cohen, S., S. Wheelwright, *et al.* (2001). Are intuitive physics and intuitive psychology independent? A test with children with Asperger Syndrome. *Journal of Developmental and Learning Disorders* **5**: 47–78.

Baron-Cohen, S., S. Wheelwright, *et al.* (1999). A mathematician, a physicist and a computer scientist with Asperger syndrome: Performance on folk psychology and folk physics tests. *Neurocase* **5**: 475–483.

Baron-Cohen, S., S. Wheelwright, *et al.* (1997). Is there a link between engineering and autism? *Autism* **1**(1): 101–109.

Bejerot, S. and L. Nylander (2003). Low prevalence of smoking in patients with autism spectrum disorders. *Psychiatry Research* **119**: 177–182.

Bennett, R. (2000). Sexual orientation linked to handedness. *Science News* **158** 22 July: 53.

Bering, J. M. (2002). The existential theory of mind. *Review of General Psychology* **6**(1): 3–24.

BGW (2002). Graduate student in peril: A first person account of schizophrenia. *Schizophrenia Bulletin* **28**(4): 745–755.

Blackshaw, A. J., P. Kinderman, *et al.* (2001). Theory of mind, causal attribution and paranoia in Asperger syndrome. *Autism* **5**(2): 147–163.

Blakemore, S.-J., Y. Sarfati, *et al.* (2003). The detection of intentional contingencies in simple animations in patients with delusions of persecution. *Psychological Medicine* **33**: 1433–1441.

Blakemore, S.-J., T. Tavassoli, *et al.* (2006). Tactile sensitivity in Asperger syndrome. *Brain and Cognition* **61**: 5–13.

Blanchard, R. (1999). *Conference Presentation: Theory and Research on Birth Order and Sexual Orientation*. Human Behavior and Evolution Society, Salt Lake City, UT.

Bleuler, E. (1912). Das autistiche Denken. *Jahrbuch für psychoanalytische und psychopathologische Forschungen* **4**(1).

Bleuler, E. (1950). *Dementia Praecox or The Group of Schizophrenias*. New York, International Universities Press.

Bleuler, E. (1959). Autistic thinking. *Organization and Pathology of Thought*. D. Rapaport. New York, Columbia University Press: 399–437.

Bliss, M. R. (2001). *In Memory of Bill Hamilton: Hazards of Modern Medicine*. Origin of HIV and Emerging Persistent Viruses, Accademia Nazionale dei Lincei, Rome.

Boer, H., A. J. Holland, *et al.* (2002). Psychotic illness in people with Prader Willi syndrome due to chromosome 15 maternal uniparental disomy. *Lancet* **359**: 135–136.

Bogaert, A. (2006). Biological versus nonbiological older brothers and men's sexual orientation. *Proceedings of the National Academy of Sciences of the USA* **103**(28): 10771–10774.

Bonanno, G., A. Holen, *et al.* (1990). When avoiding unpleasant emotions might not be such a bad thing. *Journal of Personality and Social Psychology* **69**(5): 975–989.

Bonnel, A., L. Mottron, *et al.* (2003). Enhanced pitch sensitivity in individuals with autism: A signal detection analysis. *Journal of Cognitive Neuroscience* **15**: 226–235.

Bottomer, P. F. (2007). *So Odd a Mixture: Along the Autistic Spectrum in "Pride and Prejudice".* London and Philadelphia, Jessica Kingsley Publishers.

Bowler, D. M. (1992). "Theory of Mind" in Asperger's Syndrome. *Journal of Child Psychology and Psychiatry* **33**(5): 877–893.

Bowler, D. M. (2003). *Self-awareness and Memory in Adults with Autism.* Cognitive Sciences Seminars, University College, London.

Boyer, P. (2008). Religion: Bound to believe? *Nature* **455**: 1038–1039.

Bradley, B. (2006). Art of stone. *New Scientist* 24 June: 54–55.

Browne, K. R. (2001). Women at war: An evolutionary perspective. *Buffalo Law Review* **49**(1): 51–247.

Browne, K. R. (2002). *Biology At Work: Rethinking Sexual Equality.* New Brunswick, NJ, Rutgers University Press.

Browne, K. R. (2006). Evolved sex differences and occupational segregation. *Journal of Organizational Behavior* **27**: 143–162.

Cameron, N. (1939). Schizophrenic thinking in a problem-solving situation. *Journal of Mental Science* **85**: 1012–1035.

Camperio-Ciani, A., F. Corna, *et al.* (2004). Evidence for maternally inherited factors favouring male homosexuality and promoting female fecundity. *Proceedings of the Royal Society of London B* **271**: 2217–2221.

Camus, A. (2000). *The Outsider.* London, Penguin Books.

Carey, B. (2008). In a novel theory of mental disorders, parents' genes are in competition. *The New York Times* 11 November: D4 and 10.

Caron, M.-J., L. Mottron, *et al.* (2006). Cognitive mechanisms, specificity and neural underpinnings of visuospatial peaks in autism. *Brain* **129**: 1789–1802.

Castelli, F., C. Frith, *et al.* (2002). Autism, Asperger syndrome and brain mechanisms for the attribution of mental states to animated shapes. *Brain* **125**(8): 1839–1849.

Chapman, L. J., J. P. Chapman, *et al.* (1994). Putatively psychosis prone subjects ten years later. *Journal of Abnormal Psychology* **103**: 171–183.

Chapman, R. K. (2002). First person account: Eliminating delusions. *Schizophrenia Bulletin* **28**: 545–553.

Charles, J. (2001). In a virtual maze, men are smart rats. *New York Times* 28 June.

Cheng, Y.-W., O. J. L. Tzeng, *et al.* (2006). Gender divergences in the human mirror system: a magnetoencephalography study. *Neuroreport* **7** (11): 1115–1119.

Claridge, G. (1987). Schizophrenia and human individuality. *Mindwaves: Thoughts on Intelligence, Identity, and Consciousness.* C. Blakemore and S. Greenfield. Oxford, Blackwell.

Claridge, G., R. Pryor, *et al.* (1990). *Sounds from the Bell Jar: Ten Psychotic Authors.* London, Macmillan Press.

Constantino, J. N. and R. D. Todd (2005). Intergenerational transmission of subthreshold autistic traits in the general population. *Biological Psychiatry* **57**: 655–660.

Conway, M. A. (2002). Sensory-perceptual episodic memory and its context: Autobiographical memory. *Episodic Memory: New Directions in Research.* A. Baddeley, J. P. Aggleton, *et al.* Oxford, Oxford University Press: 53–70.

Conway, M. A. (2005). Memory and the self. *Journal of Memory and Language* **53**: 594–628.

Cook, E. H. J., V. Lindgren, *et al.* (1997). Autism or atypical autism in maternally but not paternally derived proximal 15q duplication. *American Journal of Human Genetics* **60**(4): 928–934.

Craig, J. S., C. Hatton, *et al.* (2004). Persecutory beliefs, attributions and theory of mind: comparison of patients with paranoid delusions, Asperger's syndrome and healthy controls. *Schizophrenia Research* **69**: 29–33.

Crespi, B. (2008a). Cancer risk in autism. *Unpublished manuscript.*

Crespi, B. (2008b). Genomic imprinting in the development and evolution of psychotic spectrum conditions. *Biological Reviews* **83**: 441–493.

Crespi, B. (2008c). Turner syndrome and the evolution of human sexual dimorphism. *Evolutionary Applications* **1**: 449–461.

Crespi, B. J. (2009). Darwin and Your Brain: Lecture video, http://www.sfu.ca/lidcvan/clients/continuing_studies/science/darwin_series_2009/darwin-series_4_feb16-09.mov

Crespi, B. and C. Badcock (2008). Psychosis and autism as diametrical disorders of the social brain. *Behavioral and Brain Sciences* **31**(3): 241–320.

Crespi, B. and K. Summers (2005). Evolutionary biology of cancer. *TRENDS in Ecology and Evolution* **20**(10): 545–552.

Crespi, B., K. Summers, *et al.* (2007). Adaptive evolution of genes underlying schizophrenia. *Proceedings of the Royal Society B: Biological Sciences* **274**: 2801–2810.

Crespi, B. J., K. Summers, *et al.* (In press). Genomic sister-disorders of neurodevelopment: an evolutionary approach. *Evolutionary Applications.*

Cross, J. A. (1987). Factors associated with students' place location knowledge. *Journal of Geography* **86**: 59–63.

Crow, J. F. (2000). The origins, patterns and implications of human spontaneous mutation. *Nature Reviews Genetics* **1**(1): 40–47.

Crow, T. J. (1997). Is schizophrenia the price that *Homo sapiens* pays for language? *Schizophrenia Research* **28**: 127–141.

Custance, J. (1951). *Wisdom, Madness and Folly: The Philosophy of a Lunatic.* London, Victor Gollancz Ltd.

Cutting, J. and D. Murphy (1988). Schizophrenic thought disorder: A psychological and organic interpretation. *British Journal of Psychiatry* **152**: 310–319.

Dabbs, J. M. and M. G. Dabbs (2000). *Heroes, Rogues and Lovers: Testosterone and Behavior.* New York, McGraw-Hill.

Dalí, S. (1968). *The Secret Life of Salvador Dalí.* London, Vision.

Darr, G. C. and F. G. Worden (1951). Case report twenty-eight years after an infantile autistic disorder. *American Journal of Orthopsychiatry* **21**: 559–569.

Davatzikos, C. and S. M. Resmick (1998). Sex differences in anatomic measures of interhemispheric connectivity: Correlations with cognition in women but not men. *Cerebral Cortex* **8**: 634–640.

Dawkins, M. S. (2005). An autistic look at animals. *Nature* **435**: 147–148.

Dawkins, R. (1978). *The Selfish Gene.* Oxford, Oxford University Press.

Dawkins, R. (1995). Reply to Lucy Sullivan. *Philosophical Transactions of the Royal Society B* **349**: 212–224.

Dawkins, R. (2006). *The God Delusion.* London, Bantam Press.

Dawson, M., I. Soulières, *et al.* (2007). The level and nature of autistic intelligence. *Psychological Science* **18**(8): 657–662.

de Clérambault, G. G. (1942). Les psychoses passionelles. *Œuvre Psychiatrique.* J. Fretet. Paris, Presses Universitaires de France. **1**: 323–443.

Deacon, T. W. (1990). Problems of ontogeny and phylogeny in brain-size evolution. *International Journal of Primatology* **11**(3): 237–282.

Der, G., S. Gupta, *et al.* (1990). Is schizophrenia disappearing? *The Lancet* **335**: 513–516.

Dinn, W. M., C. L. Harris, *et al.* (2002). Positive and negative schizotypy in a student sample: Neurocognitive and clinical correlates. *Schizophrenia Research* **56**: 171–185.

Dinnage, R. (2000). Introduction. *Schreber, D. P. (2000) Memoirs of My Nervous Illness.* New York, New York Review Books: xi–xxiv.

Ditchburn, R. W. (1980). Newton's illness of 1692–3. *Notes and Records of the Royal Society* **35**: 1–16.

Donaldson, M. (1978). *Children's Minds.* London, Fontana/Collins.

Drury, V. M., M. Birchwood, *et al.* (1998). Theory of mind skills during an acute episode of psychosis and following recovery. *Psychological Medicine* **28**: 1101–1112.

Dufresne, T. (2005). *Killing Freud: Twentieth Century Culture and the Death of Psychoanalysis.* London, Continuum.

Dunayevich, E. and P. E. Keck (2000). Prevalence and description of psychotic features in bipolar mania. *Current Psychiatry Reports* **2**: 286–290.

Dyches, T. T., L. K. Wilder, *et al.* (2004). Multicultural issues in autism. *Journal of Autism and Developmental Disorders* **34**(2): 211–222.

Eckblad, M. and L. J. Chapman (1983). Magical ideation as an indicator of schizotypy. *Journal of Consulting and Clinical Psychology* **51**: 215–225.

Ehlers, S., A. Nyden, *et al.* (1997). Asperger syndrome, autism, and attention disorders: A comparative study of the cognitive profiles of 120 children. *Journal of Child Psychology and Psychiatry* **38**: 207–218.

Eisenberg, L. and L. Kanner (1956). Early infantile autism, 1943–1945. *American Journal of Orthopsychiatry* **26**: 556–566.

Emery, N. J. (2000). The eyes have it: The neuroethology, function and evolution of social gaze. *Neuroscience and Biobehavioral Reviews* **24**: 581–604.

Fitzgerald, M. (2004). *Autism and Creativity.* Hove and New York, Brunner-Routledge.

Fitzgerald, M. (2005). *The Genesis of Artistic Creativity: Asperger's Syndrome and the Arts.* London and Philadelphia, Jessica Kingsley Publishers.

Flagg, E. J., J. E. Cardy, *et al.* (2005). Language lateralization development in children with autism: Insights from the late field magnetoencephalogram. *Neuroscience Letters* **386**(2): 82–87.

Folley, B. S. and S. Park (2005). Verbal creativity and schizotypal personality in relation to prefrontal hemispheric laterality: A behavioral and near-infra-red optical imaging study. *Schizophrenia Research* **80**(2–3): 271–282.

Franke, U., J. A. Kerns, *et al.* (1995). The SNRPN gene Prader-Willi syndrome. *Genomic*

Imprinting: Causes and Consequences. R. Ohlsson, K. Hall, *et al.* Cambridge, Cambridge University Press: 309–321.

Frecska, E. and H. Kiss (2004). Digit length pattern in schizophrenia suggests disturbed prenatal hemispheric lateralization. *Progress in Neuro-Psychopharmacology & Biological Psychiatry* **28**(1): 191–194.

Freedman, R. (1997). Linkage of a neurophysiological deficit in schizophrenia to a chromosome 15 locus. *Proceedings of the National Academy of Sciences of the USA* **94**: 587–592.

Freud, S. (1905). Three essays on the theory of sexuality. *The Complete Psychological Works of Sigmund Freud*. J. Strachey, A. Freud, *et al.* London, The Hogarth Press and the Institute of Psychoanalysis. **7**: 123–231.

Freud, S. (1911). Psycho-analytic notes on an autobiographical account of a case of paranoia. *The Standard Edition of the Complete Psychological Works of Sigmund Freud*. J. Strachey, A. Freud, *et al.* London, The Hogarth Press and the Institute of Psychoanalysis. **12**: 1–82.

Freud, S. (1914). On narcissism: An introduction. *The Standard Edition of the Complete Psychological Works of Sigmund Freud*. J. Strachey, A. Freud, *et al.* London, The Hogarth Press and the Institute of Psychoanalysis. **14**: 69–102.

Freud, S. (1920). Beyond the pleasure principle. *The Standard Edition of the Complete Psychological Works of Sigmund Freud*. J. Strachey, A. Freud, *et al.* London, The Hogarth Press and the Institute of Psychoanalysis. **18**: 1–64.

Freud, S. (1922). Dreams and telepathy. *The Complete Psychological Works of Sigmund Freud*. J. Strachey, A. Freud, *et al.* London, The Hogarth Press and the Institute of Psychoanalysis. **18**: 197–220.

Freud, S. (1923). The ego and the id. *The Standard Edition of the Complete Psychological Works of Sigmund Freud*. J. Strachey, A. Freud, *et al.* London, The Hogarth Press and the Institute of Psychoanalysis. **19**: 1–66.

Freud, S. (1938). A comment on anti-Semitism. *The Standard Edition of the Complete Psychological Works of Sigmund Freud*. J. Strachey, A. Freud, *et al.* London, The Hogarth Press and the Institute of Psychoanalysis. **23**: 291–293.

Freud, S. (1939). Moses and monotheism. *The Complete Psychological Works of Sigmund Freud*. J. Strachey, A. Freud, *et al.* London, The Hogarth Press and the Institute of Psychoanalysis. **23**: 1–138.

Freud, S. and W. C. Bullitt (1967). *Thomas Woodrow Wilson, Twenty-eighth President of the United States: A Psychological Study*. London, Weidenfeld and Nicolson.

Frith, C. D. (1992). *The Cognitive Neuropsychology of Schizophrenia*. Hove and Hillsdale, Lawrence Erlbaum.

Frith, U. (1989). *Autism: Explaining the Enigma*. Oxford, Blackwell.

Frith, U. (2003). *Autism: Explaining the Enigma*. Oxford, Blackwell.

Frith, U. and F. Happé (1999). Theory of mind and self-consciousness: What is it like to be autistic? *Mind and Language* **14**: 23–32.

Galaiena, M. L. (1976). Solar retinopathy. *American Journal of Ophthalmology* **8**(3): 304–306.

Gardiner, J. M. (2002). Episodic memory and autonoetic consciousness: A first-person approach. *Episodic Memory: New Directions in Research*. A. Baddeley, J. P. Aggleton, *et al.* Oxford, Oxford University Press: 11–30.

George, A. (2005). Practical passions. *New Scientist* 4 June: 50–51.

Gerbaldo, H. and G. Thaker (1991). Photophilic and photophobic behaviour in patients with schizophrenia and depression. *Canadian Journal of Psychiatry* **36**(9): 677–679.

Gerbaldo, H., G. Thaker, *et al.* (1992). Abnormal electroretinography in schizophrenic patients with a history of sun gazing. *Neuropsychobiology* **25**(2): 99–101.

Gerland, G. (1997). *A Real Person: Life on the Outside.* London, Souvenir Press.

Gillberg, C. (1980). Maternal age and infantile autism. *Autism and Development Disorders* **10**: 293–297.

Gillberg, C. L. (1992). Autism and autistic-like conditions: Subclasses among disorders of empathy (The Emanuel Miller Memorial Lecture 1991). *Journal of Child Psychology and Psychiatry* **33**(5): 813–842.

Ginsburg, J. (2004). Coughs and sneezes spread mind diseases. *New Scientist* 6 November: 40.

Goldstein, J. M., L. J. Seidman, *et al.* (2001). Normal sexual dimorphism of the adult human brain assessed by in vivo magnetic resonance imaging. *Cerebral Cortex* **11**: 490–497.

Goldstone, A. P. (2004). Prader-Willi syndrome: Advances in genetics, pathophysiology and treatment. *Trends in Endocrinology and Metabolism* **15**: 12–20.

Gooddale, M. and D. Milner (2004). *Sight Unseen: The Exploration of Conscious and Unconscious Vision.* Oxford, Oxford University Press.

Goodwin, F. K. and K. R. Jamison (1990). *Manic-Depressive Illness.* New York, Oxford University Press.

Gottesman, I. (1991). *Schizophrenia Genesis: The Origins of Madness.* New York, W. H. Freeman.

Grandin, T. (1995). *Thinking in Pictures and Other Reports from My Life with Autism.* New York, Vintage Books.

Grandin, T. (1998). Comments. *Diagnosing Jefferson: Evidence of a Condition that Guided His Beliefs, Behavior, and Personal Associations.* N. Ledgin. Arlington, TX, Future Horizons: 197–207.

Grandin, T. (2006). Genius may be an abnormality: Educating students with Asperger's Syndrome or high functioning autism. *The Official Autism 101 Manual: Autism Today.* K. L. Simmons. Alberta, Canada, Autism Today: 178–182.

Grandin, T. and S. Barron (2005). *The Unwritten Rules of Social Relationships.* Arlington, TX, Future Horizons Inc.

Grandin, T. and C. Johnson (2005). *Animals in Translation: Using the Mysteries of Autism to Decode Animal Behavior.* New York, Scribner.

Grandin, T. and M. M. Scariano (1996). *Emergence: Labelled Autistic.* New York, Warner Books.

Green, R. and E. B. Keverne (2000). The disparate maternal aunt-uncle ratio in male transsexuals: An explanation invoking genomic imprinting. *Journal of Theoretical Biology* **202**: 55–63.

Grinker, R. (2007). *Unstrange Minds: Remapping the World of Autism.* New York, Basic Books.

Grön, G., A. P. Wunderlich, *et al.* (2000). Brain activation during human navigation: Gender-different neural networks as substrate of performance. *Nature Neuroscience* **3**: 404–408.

Grossberg, S. and D. Seidman (2006). Neural dynamics of autistic behaviors: Cognitive, emotional, and timing substrates. *Psychological Review* **113**(3): 483–525.

Gubi, P. M. (2007). *Prayer in Counselling and Psychotherapy: Exploring a Hidden Meaningful Dimension.* London, Jessica Kingsley Publishers.

Gur, R. C., F. Gunning-Dixon, *et al.* (2002). Sex difference in temporo-limbic and frontal brain volumes of healthy adults. *Journal of the Cerebral Cortex* **12**: 998.

Gur, R. E., C. Kohler, *et al.* (2004). A sexually dimorphic ratio of orbitofrontal to amygdala volume is altered in schizophrenia. *Biological Psychiatry* **55**: 512–517.

Guthrie, S. (1993). *Faces in the Clouds: A New Theory of Religion.* Oxford, Oxford University Press.

Hadcroft, W. (2005). *The Feeling's Unmutual: Growing Up with Asperger Syndrome (Undiagnosed).* London, Jessica Kingsley Publishers.

Haddon, M. (2003). *The Curious Incident of the Dog in the Night-time.* London, Jonathan Cape.

Haig, D. (1993). Genetic conflicts in human pregnancy. *Quarterly Review of Biology* **68**(4): 495–532.

Haig, D. (1999). Genetic conflicts of pregnancy and childhood. *Evolution in Health and Disease.* S. C. Stearns. Oxford, Oxford University Press: 77–90.

Haig, D. (2006). Intragenomic politics. *Cytogenetic and Genome Research* **113**: 68–74.

Haig, D. and R. Wharton (2003). Prader-Willi syndrome and the evolution of human childhood. *American Journal of Human Biology* **15**: 320–329.

Hamer, D. (2004). *The God Gene: How Faith Is Hardwired into Our Genes.* New York, Anchor Books.

Hamer, D. and P. Copeland (1994). *The Science of Desire: The Search for the Gay Gene and the Biology of Behavior.* New York, Simon & Schuster.

Hamer, D., S. Hu, *et al.* (1993). A linkage between DNA markers on the X chromosome and male sexual orientation. *Science* **261**(16/7): 321–326.

Hamilton, W. D. (1996). *Narrow Roads of Gene Land: Evolution of Social Behaviour.* Oxford, W. H. Freeman/Spektrum.

Hamilton, W. D. (2001). *Narrow Roads of Gene Land: The Evolution of Sex.* Oxford, W. H. Freeman/Spektrum.

Hamilton, W. D. (2005). *Narrow Roads of Gene Land: Last Words.* Oxford, W. H. Freeman/ Spektrum.

Hannah, J., B. E. Hayward, *et al.* (2002). A global disorder of imprinting in the human female germ line. *Nature* **416**: 539–542.

Happé, F. (1999a). Autism: Cognitive deficit or cognitive style? *Trends in Cognitive Sciences* **3**(6): 216–222.

Happé, F. (1999b). Parts and wholes, meaning and minds: Central coherence and its relation to theory of mind. *Understanding Other Minds.* S. Baron-Cohen, H. Tager-Flusberg, *et al.* Oxford, Oxford University Press: 203–221.

Happé, F., A. Ronald, *et al.* (2006). Time to give up on a single explanation of autism. *Nature Neuroscience* **9**(10): 1218–1220.

Harasty, J., K. L. Double, *et al.* (1997). Language-associated cortical regions are proportionally larger in the female brain. *Archives of Neurology and Psychiatry* **54**: 171–176.

Harrington, L., R. Langdon, *et al.* (2005). Schizophrenia, theory of mind, and persecutory delusions. *Cognitive Neuropsychiatry* **10**(2): 87–104.

Hayashi, M., M. Kato, *et al.* (2008). Superior fluid intelligence in children with Asperger's disorder. *Brain and Cognition* **66**: 306–310.

Heijmansa, B. T., E. W. Tobia, *et al.* (2008). Persistent epigenetic differences associated with prenatal exposure to famine in humans. *Proceedings of the National Academy of Sciences* **105**(44): 17046–17049.

Hermelin, B. (2001). *Bright Splinters of the Mind: A Personal Story of Research with Autistic Savants.* London and Philadelphia, Jessica Kingsley Publishers.

Hill, E. L. and U. Frith (2003). Understanding autism: insight from mind and brain. *Autism: Explaining the Enigma.* U. Frith and E. L. Hill. Oxford, Blackwell: 1–19.

Hippler, K. and C. Klicpera (2004). A retrospective analysis of the clinical case records of "autistic psychopaths" diagnosed by Hans Asperger and his teaching at the University Children's Hospital, Vienna. *Autism: Mind and Brain.* U. Frith and E. Hill. Oxford, Oxford University Press: 21–42.

Horrobin, D. F. (1998). Schizophrenia: the illness that made us human. *Medical Hypotheses* **50**: 269–288.

Hough, S. E. (2007). *Richter's Scale: Measure of an Earthquake, Measure of a Man.* Princeton, NJ, Princeton University Press.

Houston, R. and U. Frith (2000). *Autism in History: The Case of Hugh Blair of Borgue.* Oxford, Blackwell.

Howlin, P. (2003). *Autism: Preparing for Adulthood.* London, Routledge.

Howlin, P., S. Baron-Cohen, *et al.* (1999). *Teaching Children with Autism to Mind-Read: A Practical Guide.* Chester, John Wiley & Sons.

Humphrey, N. (1996). *Leaps of Faith: Science, Miracles, and the Search for Supernatural Consolation.* New York, Springer-Verlag.

Humphrey, N. (1998). Cave art, autism, and the evolution of the human mind. *Cambridge Archaeological Journal* **8**(2): 165–191.

Humphrey, N. (2002). Commentary on Michael Winkelman, "Shamanism and cognitive evolution". *Cambridge Archaeological Journal* **12**: 91–93.

Iliffe, R. (2007). *Newton: A Very Short Introduction.* Oxford, Oxford University Press.

Ingudomnukul, E., S. Baron-Cohen, *et al.* (2007). Elevated rates of testosterone-related disorders in women with autism spectrum conditions. *Hormones and Behavior* **51**(5): 597–604.

Irwin, H. J. (1993). Belief in the paranormal: A review of the empirical literature. *Journal of the American Society for Psychical Research* **87**(1): 1–37.

Isanon, A. (2001). *Spirituality and the Autism Spectrum.* London, Jessica Kingsley Publishers.

Israëls, H. (1989). *Schreber: Father and Son.* Madison, CT, International Universities Press Inc.

Jacobsen, L. K. and J. L. Rapoport (1998). Research update: Childhood-onset schizophrenia: Implications of clinical and neuro-biological research. *Journal of Child Psychology and Psychiatry* **39**: 101–113.

James, I. (2006). *Asperger's Syndrome and High Achievement: Some Very Remarkable People.* London and Philadelphia, Jessica Kingsley Publishers.

James, W. H. (2000). The hypothesized hormonal control of offspring sex ratio: Evidence from families ascertained by schizophrenia and epilepsy. *Journal of Theoretical Biology* **206**: 445–447.

Jamison, K. R. (1993). *Touched with Fire: Manic-depressive Illness and Artistic Temperament.* New York, Free Press.

Jaspers, K. (1962). *General Psychopathology.* Manchester, Manchester University Press.

Jaynes, J. (1979). *The Origin of Consciousness in the Breakdown of the Bicameral Mind.* London, Allen Lane.

Johnson, G. (2008). *The Ten Most Beautiful Experiments.* London, The Bodley Head.

Jones, D. (2008). Killer instincts. *Nature* **451**: 512–515.

Jones, E. (1953). *The Life and Work of Sigmund Freud.* New York, Basic Books.

Just, M. A., V. L. Cherkassky, *et al.* (2004). Cortical activation and synchronization during sentence comprehension in high-functioning autism: Evidence of underconnectivity. *Brain* **127**(8): 1811–1821.

Kana, R. K., T. A. Keller, *et al.* (2006). Sentence comprehension in autism: Thinking in pictures with decreased functional connectivity. *Brain* **129**: 2484–2493.

Kanazawa, S. and G. Vandermassen (2005). Engineers have more sons, nurses have more daughters: an evolutionary psychological extension of Baron-Cohen's extreme male brain theory of autism. *Journal of Theoretical Biology* **233**: 589–599.

Kanner, L. (1943). Autistic disturbances of affective contact. *Nervous Child* **2**: 217–250.

Kanner, L. (1944). Early infantile autism. *Journal of Pediatrics* **25**: 211–217.

Kanner, L. (1946). Irrelevant and metaphorical language in early infantile autism. *American Journal of Psychiatry* **103**: 242–246.

Kanner, L. (1949). Problems of nosology and psychodynamics of early infantile autism. *American Journal of Orthopsychiatry* **19**: 416–426.

Kaplan, B. (2008). Personal communication.

Kaplan, L. P. (2006). How autism has been understood. *The Official Autism 101 Manual: Autism Today.* K. L. Simmons. Alberta, Canada, Autism Today: 44–45.

Kent, L., S. Bowdin, *et al.* (2008). Beckwith-Wiedemann syndrome: A behavioral phenotype-genotype study. *American Journal of Medical Genetics, Part B: Neuropsychiatric Genetics* **147B**(7): 1295–1297.

Keverne, E. B., R. Fundele, *et al.* (1996). Genomic imprinting and the differential roles of parental genomes in brain development. *Developmental Brain Research* **92**: 91–100.

Keynes, J. M. (1972). Newton, the man. *Essays in Biography.* London, MacMillan St Martin's Press. **10**: 363–374.

Kimura, D. (2000). *Sex and Cognition.* Cambridge, MA, MIT Press.

Knapp, M., R. Romeo, *et al.* (2007). *The Economic Consequences of Autism in the UK*, Foundation for People with Learning Disabilities.

Knickmeyer, R., S. Baron-Cohen, *et al.* (2004). Foetal testosterone, social relationships, and restricted interests in children. *Journal of Child Psychology and Psychiatry* **45**: 1–13.

Koenig, K., K. D. Tsatsanis, *et al.* (2001). Neurobiology and genetics of autism: A developmental perspective. *The Development of Autism: Perspectives from Theory and Research.* J. A. Burack, C. Charman, *et al.* Mahwah, NJ, Erlbaum: 81–101.

Koshino, H., P. A. Carpenter, *et al.* (2005). Functional connectivity in an fMRI working memory task in high-functioning autism. *NeuroImage* **24**(3): 810–821.

Kravariti, E., T. Toulopoulou, *et al.* (2006). Intellectual asymmetry and genetic liability in first-degree relatives of probands with schizophrenia. *British Journal of Psychiatry* **188**: 186–187.

Laing, R. D. (1960). *The Divided Self: An Existential Study in Sanity and Madness.* London, Tavistock Publications.

Lang, J. (1940). The other side of the ideological aspects of schizophrenia. *Psychiatry and Clinical Neurosciences* **3**: 389–392.

Langdon, R. (2005). Theory of mind in schizophrenia. *Other Minds: How Humans Bridge the Divide between Self and Others*. B. F. Malle and S. D. Hodges. New York, Guilford Press: 323–342.

Langdon, R., T. Corner, *et al.* (2006). Attentional orienting triggered by gaze in schizophrenia. *Neuropsychologia* **44**: 417–429.

Laplanche, J. and J.-B. Pontalis (1973). *The Language of Psychoanalysis*. London, The Hogarth Press and the Institute of Psychoanalysis.

LaRusso, L. (1978). Sensitivity of paranoid patients to nonverbal cues. *Journal of Abnormal Psychology* **87**(5): 463–471.

Lathe, R. (2006). *Autism, Brain, and Environment*. London and Philadelphia, Jessica Kingsley Publishers.

Lawson, W. (1998). *Life Behind Glass: A Personal Account of Autism Spectrum Disorder*. London, Jessica Kingsley Publishers.

Ledgin, N. (1998). *Diagnosing Jefferson: Evidence of a Condition that Guided His Beliefs, Behavior, and Personal Associations*. Arlington, TX, Future Horizons.

LeDoux, J. (1996). *The Emotional Brain: The Mysterious Underpinnings of Emotional Life*. New York, Simon & Schuster.

Leekam, S. and C. Moore (2001). The development of attention and joint attention in children with autism. *The Development of Autism: Perspectives from Theory and Research*. J. A. Burack, C. Charman, *et al.* Mahwah, NJ, Erlbaum: 105–129.

Leslie, A. M. and L. Thaiss (1992). Domain specificity in conceptual development: Evidence from autism. *Cognition* **43**: 225–251.

Lester, D. (1975). The relationship between paranoid delusions and homosexuality. *Archives of Sexual Behavior* **4**(3): 285–294.

Liben, L. (1995). Psychology meets geography: Exploring the gender gap on the National Geography Bee. *Psychological Science Agenda* **8**: 8–9.

Libet, B. (2004). *Mind Time: The Temporal Factor in Consciousness*. Cambridge, MA, Harvard University Press.

Llinás, R. R. (2001). *I of the Vortex*. Cambridge, MA, MIT Press.

Lothane, Z. (1992). *In Defense of Schreber: Soul Murder and Psychiatry*. Hillsdale, NJ, The Analytic Press.

Ludwig, A. M. (1995). *The Price of Greatness: Resolving the Creativity and Madness Controversy*. New York, Guilford Press.

Lutchmaya, S., S. Baron-Cohen, *et al.* (2002a). Foetal testosterone and eye contact at 12 months. *Infant Behaviour and Development* **25**(3): 327–335.

Lutchmaya, S., S. Baron-Cohen, *et al.* (2002b). Foetal testosterone and vocabulary size in 18- and 24-month-old infants. *Infant Behaviour and Development* **24**(4): 418–424.

Lynn, R. (1998). Sex differences in intelligence: Some comments on Mackintosh and Flynn. *Journal of Biosocial Science* **30**: 555–559.

Lyons, V. and M. Fitzgerald (2005). Early memory and autism. *Journal of Autism & Developmental Disorders* **35**(5): 683.

Lyons, V. and M. Fitzgerald (2007a). Asperger (1906–1980) and Kanner (1894–1981), the two pioneers of autism. *Journal of Autism and Developmental Disorders* **37**(10): 2022–2023.

Lyons, V. and M. Fitzgerald (2007b). Did Hans Asperger (1906–1980) have Asperger Syndrome? *Journal of Autism and Developmental Disorders* **37**(10): 2020–2021.

MacDonald, N. (1960). Living with schizophrenia. *Canadian Medical Association Journal* **82**: 218–221.

MacLane, M. (1917). *I, Mary MacLane: A Diary of Human Days*. New York, Stokes.

MacLean, P. D. (1990). *The Triune Brain in Evolution*. New York, Plenum Press.

MacLean, P. D. (1996). Limbic system. *The Blackwell Dictionary of Neuropsychology*. J. G. Beaumont, P. Kenealy, *et al.* Rogers. Oxford, Blackwell.

Maestro, S., F., M. C. Muratori, *et al.* (2002). Attentional skills during the first 6 months of age in autism spectrum disorder. *Journal of the American Academy of Child and Adolescent Psychiatry* **41**: 1239–1245.

Malaspina, D., S. Harlap, *et al.* (2001). Advancing paternal age and the risk of schizophrenia. *Archives of General Psychiatry* **58**: 361–367.

Mattingley, J., A. N. Rich, *et al.* (2001). Unconscious priming eliminates automatic binding of colour and alphanumeric form in synaesthesia. *Nature* **410**: 580–583.

McEwan, I. (1997). *Enduring Love*. London, Jonathan Cape.

McNamara, P., D. McLaren, *et al.* (2005). A '"Jekyll and Hyde'" within: Aggressive versus friendly interactions in REM and non-REM dreams. *Psychological Science* **16**(2): 130–136.

Mendrek, A. (2007). Reversal of normal cerebral sexual dimorphism in schizophrenia: Evidence and speculations. *Medical Hypotheses* **69**(4): 896–902.

Miller, A. S. and R. Stark (2002). Gender and religiousness: Can socialization explanations be saved? *American Journal of Sociology* **107**(6): 1399–1423.

Miller, L., J. Cummings, *et al.* (1998). Emergence of artistic talents in frontotemporal dementia. *Neurology* **51**(4): 978–982.

Mills, J. L., M. L. Hediger, *et al.* (2007). Elevated levels of growth-related hormones in autism and autism spectrum disorder. *Clinical Endocrinology* **67**: 230–237.

Mitchell, P. (1997). *Introduction to Theory of Mind: Children, Autism and Apes*. London, Arnold.

Møller, A. P. and R. Husby (2000). The initial prodrome in schizophrenia: Searching for naturalistic core dimensions of experience and behavior. *Schizophrenia Bulletin* **26**(1): 217–232.

Monto, A. (2003). Private communication.

Moore, C. (2004a). Different connections. *Sunday Times* 10 October.

Moore, C. (2004b). *George and Sam*. London, Viking.

Morgan, M. (2003). *The Space between Our Ears: How the Brain Represents Visual Space*. London, Weidenfeld & Nicolson.

Motluk, A. (2000). Handy guide: Do a person's fingers reveal their sexual orientation? *New Scientist* 1 April: 5.

Motluk, A. (2002). You're holding the map upside-down. *New Scientist* 24 August: 21.

Motluk, A. (2003). The big brother effect. *New Scientist* 29 March: 44–45.

Mottron, L., S. Belleville, *et al.* (1999). Local bias in autistic subjects as evidenced by graphic tasks: Perceptual hierarchization or working memory deficit? *Journal of Child Psychology and Psychiatry* **40**: 743–755.

Mottron, L. and J. A. Burack (2001). Enhanced perceptual functioning in the development of autism. *The Development of Autism: Perspectives from Theory and Research.* J. A. Burack, T. Charman, *et al.* Mahwah, NJ, Lawrence Erlbaum Associates: 131–193.

Nasar, S. (1998). *A Beautiful Mind.* London, Faber and Faber.

Nesse, R. M. (2004). Cliff-edged fitness functions and the persistence of schizophrenia. *Behavioral and Brain Sciences* **27**: 862–863.

Nettle, D. (2001). *Strong Imagination: Madness, Creativity and Human Nature.* Oxford, Oxford University Press.

Nettle, D. (2007). Empathizing and systemizing: What are they, and what do they contribute to our understanding of psychological sex differences? *British Journal of Psychology* **98**: 237–255.

Nettle, D. (2008). Why is creativity attractive in a potential mate? *Behavioral and Brain Sciences* **31**(3): 275–276.

New Scientist (2007). Video game helps detect depression. *New Scientist* 10 March: 18.

Newton, G. (2001). The case of the biparental mole. *Wellcome News* **27**: 18–19.

Nicholls, R. D., S. Saitoh, *et al.* (1998). Imprinting in Prader-Willi and Angelman syndromes. *Trends in Genetics* **14**(5): 194–200.

Nunn, K., T. Hanstock, *et al.* (2008). *Who's Who of the Brain: A Guide to Its Inhabitants, Where They Live and What They Do.* London and Philadelphia, Jessica Kingsley Publishers.

Nurmi, E. L., M. Dowd, *et al.* (2003). Exploratory subsetting of autism families based on savant skills improves evidence of genetic linkage to 15q11–q13. *Journal of the American Academy of Child and Adolescent Psychiatry* **42**(7): 856–863.

O'Connell, H. and M. Fitzgerald (2003). Did Alan Turing have Asperger's Syndrome? *Irish Journal of Psychological Medicine* **20**: 28–31.

O'Neill, J. L. (1999). *Through the Eyes of Aliens: A Book about Autistic People.* London, Jessica Kingsley Publishers.

O'Riordan, M. and F. Passetti (2006). Discrimination in autism within different sensory modalities. *Journal of Autism and Developmental Disorders* **36**: 665–675.

Parma, P., O. Radi, *et al.* (2006). R-spondin 1 is essential in sex determination, skin differentiation and malignancy. *Nature Genetics* **38**(11): 1304–1309.

Pawlowski, B., R. Dunbar, *et al.* (2000). Tall men have more reproductive success. *Nature* **403**: 156.

Payne, R. W. (1966). The measurement and significance of overinclusive thinking and retardation in schizophrenic patients. *Psychopathology of Schizophrenia.* P. H. Hoch and J. Zubin. New York, Grune & Stratton.

Peek, F. (1996). *The Real Rain Man, Kim Peek.* Salt Lake City, UT, Harkness Publishing Consultants.

Philips, H. (2004). Do we perceive using "mindsight"? *New Scientist* 7 February: 14.

Pickup, G. J. (2006). Theory of mind and its relation to schizotypy. *Cognitive Neuropsychiatry* **11**(2): 177–192.

Pierce, K., R. A. Muller, *et al.* (2001). Face processing occurs outside the fusiform "face area" in autism: Evidence from function MRI. *Brain* **124**: 1337–1353.

Pilowsky, T., N. Yirmiya, *et al.* (2000). Theory of mind abilities of children with schizophrenia, children with autism, and normally developing children. *Schizophrenia Research* **42**: 145–155.

Piontelli, A. (1992). *From Fetus to Child: An Observational and Psychoanalytic Study.* London, Tavistock/Routledge.

Planansky, K. and R. Johnston (1962). The incidence and relationship of homosexual and paranoid features in schizophrenia. *Journal of Medical Science* **108**: 604–615.

Potts, M. and R. Short (1999). *Ever Since Eve: The Evolution of Human Sexuality.* Cambridge, Cambridge University Press.

Povinelli, D. J. (2000). *Folk Physics for Apes: The Chimpanzee's Theory of How the World Works.* Oxford, Oxford University Press.

Premack, D. and G. Woodruff (1978). Does the chimpanzee have a theory of mind? *Behavioral and Brain Sciences* **1**(4): 515–526.

Ramachandran, V. S. and D. Rogers-Ramachandran (1996). Synaesthesia in phantom limbs induced with mirrors. *Proceedings of the Royal Society of London, B* **263**: 377–386.

Ramani, N. and R. C. Miall (2004). A system in the human brain for predicting the actions of others. *Nature Neuroscience* **7**(1): 85–90.

Randerson, J. (2002). All in the mind? Suspicion is growing that one of the most common human parasites in the world is messing with our minds. *New Scientist* 26 October: 10.

Rank, O. (1924). *Das Trauma der Geburt und seine Bedeutung für die Psychoanalyse.* Wien, Internationaler Psychoanalytischer Verlag.

Reichenberg, A., R. Gross, *et al.* (2006). Advancing paternal age and autism. *Archives of General Psychiatry* **63**(9): 1026–1032.

Rennison, N. (2005). *Sherlock Holmes: The Unauthorized Biography.* London, Atlantic Books.

Ricciardelli, P. (2001). Look at me! Studies of gaze perception and joint attention. *Institute of Cognitive Neuroscience Research Seminar* Tuesday 6 November 2001.

Richards, R. L., D. K. Kinney, *et al.* (1988). Creativity in manic-depressives, cyclothymes, and their normal first-degree relatives: A preliminary report. *Journal of Abnormal Psychology* **97**: 281–288.

Rim, Y. (1994). Impulsivity, venturesomeness, empathy and schizotypy. *Personality and Individual Differences* **17**: 853–854.

Rimland, B. (1964). *Infantile Autism: The Syndrome and Its Implications for a Neural Theory of Behavior.* New York, Appleton-Century-Crofts.

Rimland, B. (1978). Inside the mind of the autistic savant. *Psychology Today* **12**(3): 68–80.

Robinson, J. E. (2007). *Look Me in the Eye: My Life with Asperger's.* London, Ebury Press.

Rogers, K., I. Dziobek, *et al.* (2007). Who cares? Revisiting empathy in Asperger syndrome. *Journal of Autism and Developmental Disorders* **37**(4): 709–715.

Russell, T. A., E. Reynaud, *et al.* (2006). Do you see what I see? Interpretations of intentional movement in schizophrenia. *Schizophrenia Research* **81**: 101–111.

Rutter, M. (1983). Cognitive deficits in the pathogenesis of autism. *Journal of Child Psychology and Psychiatry* **24**: 526.

Sackheim, H. A. (1983). Self-deception, self-esteem, and depression: The adaptive value of lying to oneself. *Empirical Studies of Psychoanalytic Theories.* J. Masling. Hillsdale, NJ, Analytic Press. **1**: 101–157.

Sacks, O. (1995). *An Anthropologist on Mars: Seven Paradoxical Tales.* London, Picador.

Sacks, O. (2004). Autistic geniuses? We're too ready to pathologize. *Nature* **429**: 241.

Sainsbury, C. (2006). *Martian in the Playground: Understanding the Schoolchild with Asperger's Syndrome.* London, Paul Chapman Publishing.

Salazar-Fraile, J., R. Tabarés-Seisdedos, et al. (2004). Recall and recognition confabulation in psychotic and bipolar disorders: Evidence for two different types without unitary mechanisms. Comprehensive Psychiatry 45(4): 281–282.

Salminen, E. (2005). Men's trouble. New Scientist 5 March: 20.

Sanders Jnr., R. S. (2004). Overcoming Asperger's: Personal Experience and Insight. Murfreesboro, TN, Armonstrong Valley Publishing Company.

Sass, L. A. (1992). Madness and Modernism. New York, Basic Books.

Sass, L. A. (2001). Self and world in schizophrenia: Three classic approaches. Philosophy, Psychiatry and Psychology 8(4): 252–270.

Sass, L. A. and J. Parnas (2001). Phenomenology of self-disturbance in schizophrenia: Some research findings and directions. Philosophy, Psychiatry and Psychology 8(4): 348–356.

Sass, L. A. and J. Parnas (2003). Schizophrenia, consciousness, and the self. Schizophrenia Bulletin 29(3): 427–444.

Schacter, D. L. and C. S. Dodson (2002). Misattribution, false recognition and the sins of memory. Episodic Memory: New Directions in Research. A. Baddeley, J. P. Aggleton, et al. Oxford, Oxford University Press: 71–85.

Schreber, D. P. (1903). Denkwürdigkeiten eines Nervenkranken. Leipzig, Oswald Wusse.

Schreber, D. P. (2000). Memoirs of My Nervous Illness. New York, New York Review Books.

Schroer, R. J. (1998). Autism and maternally derived aberrations of chromosome 15q. American Journal of Medical Genetics 76: 327–336.

Schultz, R. T., I. Gauthier, et al. (2000). Abnormal ventral temporal cortical activity during face discrimination among individuals with autism and Asperger syndrome. Archives of General Psychiatry 57(4): 331–340.

Seery, M., R. Cohen Silver, et al. (2008). Expressing thoughts and feelings following a collective trauma: Immediate responses to 9/11 predict negative outcomes in a national sample. Journal of Consulting and Clinical Psychology 76(4): 657–667.

Seiferth, N. Y., K. Pauly, et al. (2008). Increased neural response related to neutral faces in individuals at risk for psychosis. NeuroImage 40(1): 289–297.

Senju, A., Y. Tojo, et al. (2004). Reflexive orienting in response to eye gaze and an arrow in children with and without autism. Journal of Child Psychology and Psychiatry 45(3): 445–458.

Shapiro, D. (1965). Neurotic Styles. New York, Basic Books.

Shaywitz, B. A. and S. E. Shaywitz, et al. (1995). Sex differences in the functional organization of the brain for language. Nature 373: 607–609.

Sheldrake, R. (1999). Dogs that Know when Their Owners Are Coming Home, and Other Unexplained Powers of Animals. London, Hutchinson.

Sheldrake, R. (2003). The Sense of Being Stared At and Other Aspects of the Extended Mind. London, Hutchinson.

Shore, S. (2001). Beyond the Wall: Personal Experiences with Autism and Asperger Syndrome. Shawnee Mission, KS, Autism Asperger Publishing Co.

Silberman, S. (2001). The geek syndrome. Wired 9(12): December.

Silva, J. A., M. M. Ferrari, et al. (2003). Asperger's disorder and the origins of the Unabomber. American Journal of Forensic Psychiatry 24(2): 5–43.

Silverman, I. and M. Eals (1992). Sex differences in spatial abilities: Evolutionary theory and data. *The Adapted Mind: Evolutionary Psychology and the Generation of Culture.* J. Barkow, L. Cosmides, *et al.* Oxford, Oxford University Press: 533–549.

Skinner, B. F. (1948). "Superstition" in the pigeon. *Journal of Experimental Psychology* **38**: 168–172.

Skuse, D. H. (2000). Imprinting, the X-chromosome, and the male brain: Explaining sex differences in the liability to autism. *Pediatric Research* **47**(1): 9–16.

Skuse, D. H. (2007). Rethinking the nature of genetic vulnerability to autistic spectrum disorders. *TRENDS in Genetics* **23**(8): 387–395.

Slotnick, R. S. (2002). Diogenes' new lamp. *American Scientist* **90**: 127–128.

Snowling, M. and U. Frith (1986). Comprehension of "hyperlexic" readers. *Journal of Experimental Child Psychology* **42**: 392–415.

Snyder, A. W., E. Mulcahy, *et al.* (2003). Savant-like skills exposed in normal people by suppressing the left frontotemporal lobe. *Journal of Integrative Neuroscience* **2**(2): 149–158.

Sontag, S., Ed. (1988). *Antonin Artaud: Selected Writings.* Berkeley, CA, University of California Press.

Spargo, P. E. and C. A. Pounds (1979). Newton's "Derangement of the Intellect": New light on an old problem. *Notes and Records of the Royal Society* **34**: 11–32.

Spitzer, M. (1990). On defining delusions. *Comprehensive Psychiatry* **31**: 377–397.

Sprong, M., P. Schothorst, *et al.* (2007). Theory of mind in schizophrenia: Meta-analysis. *British Journal of Psychiatry* **191**: 5–13.

Ssucharewa, G. E. (1926). Die Schizoiden Psychopathien im Kindesalter. *Monatschriftfuer Psychiatrie und Neurologie* **60**: 235–261.

Ssucharewa, G. E. and S. Wolff (1996). The first account of the syndrome Asperger described? *European Child and Adolescent Psychiatry* **5**: 119–132.

St Clair, D. (2005). Rates of adult schizophrenia following prenatal exposure to the Chinese famine of 1959–1961. *Journal of the American Medical Association* **294**(5): 557–562.

Stark, R. (2002). Physiology and faith: Addressing the universal gender difference in religious commitment. *Journal for the Scientific Study of Religion* **41**(3): 495–507.

Steadman, P. (2001). *Vermeer's Camera: Uncovering the Truth behind the Masterpieces.* Oxford, Oxford University Press.

Storr, A. (1976). *The Dynamics of Creation.* Harmondsworth, Penguin.

Suddendorf, T. and M. C. Corballis (1997). Mental time travel and the evolution of the human mind. *Genetic, Social, and General Psychology Monographs* **123**(2): 133–167.

Sugie, Y., H. Sugie, *et al.* (2005). Neonatal factors in infants with Autistic Disorder and typically developing infants. *Autism* **9**(5): 487–494.

Summerscale, K. (2008). *The Suspicions of Mr Whicher or The Murder at Road Hill House.* London, Bloomsbury.

Susser, E., D. St Clair, *et al.* (2008). latent effects of prenatal malnutrition on adult health: The example of schizophrenia. *Annals of the New York Academy of Sciences* **1136**: 185–192.

Swain, A., V. Narvaez, *et al.* (1998). *Dax1* antagonizes *Sry* action in mammalian sex differentiation. *Nature* **391**: 761–767.

Swettenham, J., S. Condie, *et al.* (2004). Does the perception of moving eyes trigger reflexive visual orienting in autism? *Autism: Mind and Brain.* U. Frith and E. Hill. Oxford, Oxford University Press: 89–107.

Szatmari, P. and M. B. Jones (1998). Genetic epidemiology of autism and other pervasive developmental disorders. *Autism and Pervasive Developmental Disorders*. F. R. Volkmar. Cambridge, Cambridge University Press: 109–129.

Tager-Flusberg, H. (1993). What language reveals about the understanding of mind in children with autism. *Understanding Other Minds*. S. Baron-Cohen, H. Tager-Flusber, *et al.* Oxford, Oxford University Press: 138–157.

Talebizadeh, Z., D. C. Bittel, *et al.* (2005). Brief report: Non-random X chromosome inactivation in females with autism. *Journal of Autism and Developmental Disorders* **35**(5): 675–681.

Tallis, F. (2006). *Vienna Blood*. London, Century.

Tammet, D. (2006). *Born on a Blue Day: A Memoir of Asperger's and an Extraordinary Mind*. London, Hodder & Stoughton.

Tanaka, S. (2008). Dysfunctional GABAergic inhibition in the prefrontal cortex leading to "psychotic" hyperactivation. *BMC Neuroscience* **9**: 41.

Tavassoli, T., E. Ashwin, *et al.* (In press). Tactile and auditory hypersensitivity in autism spectrum conditions.

Taylor, S. E. and J. D. Brown (1988). Illusion and well-being: A social psychological perspective on mental health. *Psychological Bulletin* **103**: 193–210.

Taylor, S. F., R. C. Welsh, *et al.* (2007). Medial frontal hyperactivity in reality distortion. *Biological Psychiatry* **61**(10): 1171–1178.

Thompson, A. (2001). Personal communication.

Thomson, R. F. (1985). *The Brain: An Introduction to Neuroscience*. New York, W. H. Freeman.

Toulopoulou, T., F. Mapua-Filbey, *et al.* (2006). Cognitive performance in presumed obligate carriers for psychosis. *British Journal of Psychiatry* **187**: 284–285.

Treffert, D. A. (2000). *Extraordinary People: Understanding Savant Syndrome*. Lincoln NE, iUniverse.com.

Treffert, D. A. (2001). Savant syndrome: "Special faculties" extraordinaire. *Psychiatry Times*: 20–21.

Treffert, D. A. (2006). Savant syndrome. *The Official Autism 101 Manual: Autism Today*. K. L. Simmons. Alberta, Canada, Autism Today: 8–22.

Treffert, D. A. and D. D. Christensen (2005). Inside the mind of a savant. *Scientific American* **293**(6), December: 88–91.

Tréhin, P. (2006a). Different cognitive processes in art and creativity: The case of autistic savants in prehistoric art. PowerPoint presentation, LSE, London, 13 November.

Tréhin, G. (2006b). *Urville*. London, Jessica Kingsley Publishers.

Trevarthen, C., K. Aitken, *et al.* (1998). *Children with Autism 2nd Edition: Diagnosis and Interventions to Meet Their Needs*. London and Philadelphia, Jessica Kingsley Publishers.

Trivers, R. (1974). Parent-offspring conflict. *American Zoologist* **14**: 249–264.

Trivers, R. (1981). Sociobiology and politics. *Sociobiology and Human Politics*. E. White. Lexington, MA, Lexington Books: 1–43.

Trivers, R. L. (1997). Genetic basis of intrapsychic conflict. *Uniting Psychology and Biology: Integrative Perspective on Human Development*. N. Segal, G. Weisfel, *et al.* Washington, DC, American Psychological Association: 1–19.

Troisi, A. (2008). Psychiatric disorders and the social brain: Distinguishing mentalizing and empathizing. *Behavioral and Brain Sciences* **31**(3): 279–280.

Tulving, E. (1985). Memory and consciousness. *Canadian Psychologist* **26**: 1–12.

Uht, A. K. (2008). Personal communication.

Vaillant, G. E. (1962). John Haslam on early infantile autism. *American Journal of Psychiatry* **119**: 376.

van Goozen, S. H. M., P. Cohen-Ketennis, *et al.* (1995). Activating effects of androgens on cognitive performance: Causal evidence in a group of female-to-male transsexuals. *Neuropsychologica* **32**: 1153–1157.

Vanston, C. M. and N. V. Watson (2005). Selective and persistent effect of foetal sex on cognition in pregnant women. *Neuroreport* **16**(7): 779–782.

Veltman, M. W., R. J. Thompson, *et al.* (2004). Prader-Willi syndrome—a study comparing deletion and uniparental disomy cases with reference to autism spectrum disorders. *European Child & Adolescent Psychiatry* **13**(1): 42–50.

Vermeulen, P. (2001). *Autistic Thinking—This is the Title*. London and Philadelphia, Jessica Kingsley Publishers.

Viertiö, S., A. Laitinen, *et al.* (2007). Visual impairment in persons with psychotic disorder. *Social Psychiatry and Psychiatric Epidemiology* **42**: 902–908.

Vladusich, T. (2008). Towards a computational neuroscience of autism-psychosis spectrum disorders. *Behavioral and Brain Sciences* **31**(3): 282–283.

Volkmar, F., A. Klin, *et al.* (1998). Nosological and genetic aspects of Asperger's syndrome. *Journal of Autism & Developmental Disorders* **28**: 457–463.

Voracek, M. (2008). Digit ratio (2D:4D) as a marker for mental disorders: Low (masculinized) 2D:4D in autism-spectrum disorders, high (feminized) 2D:4D in schizophrenic-spectrum disorders. *Behavioral and Brain Sciences* **31**(3): 283–284.

Vyse, S. A. (1997). *Believing in Magic: The Psychology of Superstition*. New York, Oxford University Press.

Walter, H., A. Ciaramidaro, *et al.* (2009). Dysfunction of the social brain in schizophrenia is modulated by intention type: An fMRI study. *Social Cognitive and Affective Neuroscience* (Advance Access) published March 14, 2009: doi:10.1093/scan/nsn047.

Ward, P. W. (1993). *Birth Weight and Economic Growth*. Chicago, IL and London, University of Chicago Press.

Webster, J. P., P. H. L. Lamberton, *et al.* (2006). Parasites as causative agents of human affective disorders? The impact of anti-psychotic, mood-stabilizer and anti-parasite medication on *Toxoplasma gondii*'s ability to alter host behaviour. *Proceedings of the Royal Society of London B* **273**: 1023–1030.

Weiner, S. K. (2003). First person account: Living with the delusions and effects of schizophrenia. *Schizophrenia Bulletin* **29**: 877–879.

Whalen, P. J., J. Kagan, *et al.* (2004). Human amygdala responsivity to masked fearful eye whites. *Science* **306**: 2061.

Whittington, J., A. Holland, *et al.* (2004). Cognitive abilities and genotype in a population-based sample of people with Prader-Willi syndrome. *Journal of Intellectual Disability Research* **48**(2): 172–187.

Whittington, J. and T. Holland (2004). *Prader-Willi Syndrome: Development and Manifestations*. Cambridge, Cambridge University Press.

Whittington, J. E., A. J. Holland, *et al.* (2001). Population prevalence and estimated birth incidence and mortality rate for people with Prader-Willi syndrome in one UK Health Region. *Journal of Medical Genetics* **38**: 792–798.

Wicks, S. (2005). Social adversity in childhood and the risk of developing psychosis: A national cohort study. *American Journal of Psychiatry* **162**(9): 1652–1657.

Williams, D. (1994). *Somebody Somewhere*. London, Jessica Kingsley Publishers.

Williams, G. (1985). A defense of reductionism in evolutionary biology. *Oxford Surveys in Evolutionary Biology*. R. Dawkins and M. Ridley. Oxford, Oxford University Press: 1–27.

Williams, G. C. (1996). *Plan and Purpose in Nature*. London, Weidenfeld & Nicolson.

Williams, T. J., M. E. Pepitone, *et al.* (2000). Finger-length ratios and sexual orientation. *Nature* **404**: 455–456.

Wimmer, H. and J. Perner (1983). Beliefs about beliefs: Representation and constraining function of wrong beliefs in young children's understanding of deception. *Cognition* **13**: 103–128.

Wing, L. (1988). The autistic continuum. *Aspects of Autism: Biological Research*. L. Wing. London, Gaskell/Royal College of Psychiatrists.

Wing, L. (1991). The relationship between Asperger's syndrome and Kanner's autism. *Autism and Asperger Syndrome*. U. Frith. Cambridge, Cambridge University Press: 93–121.

Woogh, C. (2001). Is schizophrenia on the decline in Canada? *Canadian Journal of Psychiatry* **46**: 61–67.

Xu, J., M. T. Pato, *et al.* (2001). Evidence for linkage disequilibrium between the alpha 7 nicotinic receptor gene (CHRNA7) locus and schizophrenia in Azorean families. *American Journal of Medical Genetics* **105**(8): 669–674.

Yolken, R. H. and E. F. Torrey (2008). Are some cases of psychosis caused by microbial agents? A review of the evidence. *Molecular Psychiatry* **13**: 470–479.

Zaitchik, D. (1990). When representations conflict with reality: The preschooler's problem with false beliefs and "false" photographs. *Cognition* **35**: 41–68.

Zatorre, R. (2005). Music, the food of neuroscience? *Nature* **434**: 312–315.

Zwaigenbaum, L., S. Bryson, *et al.* (2005). Behavioral manifestations of autism in the first year of life. *International Journal of Developmental Neuroscience* **23**: 143–152.

Index